VISUAL QUICKSTART GUIDE

HANDSPRING VISOR

Jeff Carlson

Peachpit Press

Visual QuickStart Guide
Handspring Visor
Jeff Carlson

Peachpit Press

1249 Eighth Street
Berkeley, CA 94710
510/524-2178
800/283-9444
510/524-2221 (fax)
Find us on the World Wide Web at: http://www.peachpit.com
To report errors, send a note to errata@peachpit.com.
Peachpit Press is a division of Pearson Education

Editor: Nancy Davis
Production Coordinator: Connie Jeung-Mills
Copyeditor: Liane Thomas
Compositor: Jeff Carlson
Indexer: Caroline Parks
Cover Design: The Visual Group

ISBN 0-201-74579-8

9 8 7 6 5 4 3 2 1

Printed and bound in the United States of America

Dedication

As I work on more books, I realize how many people are involved in getting them out the door—and that's not including the technical pros who take a book from concept to paper. I'd like to dedicate this book to my parents: Larry and Janet, and Susan and Ron. They're the ones who have long understood that encouragement fuels the beginning of every idea.

Special Thanks to:

Nancy Davis, for getting this book project started in the first place, for remaining flexible and cheerful, and for simply chatting about the weather in New York when my brain needed a much-needed break.

Jennifer McMullen at Switzer Communications (Handspring's public relations firm), who is just as great in person as via email and telephone—even though she may have postponed her Disneyland trip so we wouldn't accidentally bump into each other.

Steve Bistricky, also at Switzer Communications, for following up quickly on my requests and giving me more information than I thought I'd need (and ended up needing anyway).

Ed Colligan, **Allen Bush**, and **Mitch Huitema**, of Handspring, Inc., for providing me with early Visor information.

Liane Thomas, for being a kindred spirit and succinctly nailing the way we both tend to work (despite our best efforts): "think, think, think, plan, plan, think, oh yeah...write!"

Jeff Tolbert for helping to lay out the book, and for listening to me babble about handhelds on frequent trips to the store.

Caroline Parks for shouldering my work schedule in order to get the index done well and on time.

My colleagues at the Green Lake compound for their advice and experience. More important, for recognizing that look in my eye that says, "I'm totally focused now: go away," and not being offended (or at least not letting me know they were offended).

Nancy Aldrich-Ruenzel, **Connie Jeung-Mills**, **Gary-Paul Prince**, and even some non-hyphenated folks like **Kate Reber**, **Marjorie Baer**, **Kim Lombardi**, **Mimi Heft**, **Paula Baker**, and **Jimbo Norrena** at Peachpit Press. They continue to navigate me through the book process and answer all of my questions.

Kim Carlson, who selflessly fielded bad handwriting and my worries, and gave up far too many evenings because this guy she married remains driven to write books.

TABLE OF CONTENTS

TABLE OF CONTENTS

INTRODUCTION

The Handspring Visor

I bought my first handheld, a PalmPilot Personal, in 1997 for a number of reasons. Of course, the gadget factor was pretty high. Plus, the PalmPilot was getting raves for its ability to store volumes of formerly paper-based contact and scheduling information in a device slightly larger than a deck of cards. You could download third-party software directly from the Web, then synchronize those programs and your data with your PC at the single push of a button. The PalmPilot was a huge success.

In the midst of that success, the core team that invented the PalmPilot had their eyes on something more than just more modified Palms. So they left their parent company, 3Com, and founded Handspring, Inc. Their new device, the Visor, was much like a PalmPilot, and used the same Palm operating system. But the Visor included the Springboard expansion port, recasting the handheld from a glorified address book to a multifaceted organizer that supported extras like MP3 music players, digital cameras, and even a cellular phone. That modularity, plus multicolored translucent product designs, gave the Visor personality.

The combination of expandability, attitude, and organizational power makes the Visor more than just a replacement for paper calendars and address books.

Yes, it's a cool gadget. Yes, you can accessorize it to your heart's content with styli, cases, and custom flipcovers. Yes, it piques people's curiosity and makes complete strangers walk up and ask, "What's that?" But it's also an efficient, well-thought-out organizational tool that performs its tasks exceptionally well. It's not a self-contained computer in a smaller container, but an extension of the information that millions of people rely on every day.

Handspring Visor: Visual QuickStart Guide

This book is meant to be a compact, functional extension of the Visor. Not just a how-to approach to using an electronic tool, this Visual QuickStart Guide is a primer on how to effectively get control of your schedule, contacts, and all the data that used to occupy reams of papers and Post-it notes.

My aim for this book is to show you what's possible with the Visor, from its basic features to tips and tricks for using it smarter and faster. At times I'll personally recommend a product or a technique because it's what I've found useful. As a result, and to keep this book from becoming ten times larger than the device it covers, I don't list every product on the market—I want you to have fun exploring what's available (see Appendix C for some good starting points).

People who swear by their handhelds also tend to integrate them into their lives, moving beyond business meetings to birthdays, home finances, electronic books, and the occasional game of solitaire. It continues to be an invaluable part of my everyday life.

I'd love to know how your Visor helps (or hinders) your life. Feel free to email me with feedback at jeff@necoffee.com.

Part 1
Using the Visor

The Handheld Portal to Your Information

You've probably read articles about them, or seen them in advertisements. More likely, you know someone who has one, and his or her enthusiasm was infectious. That's how I was introduced to Visors and Palm organizers, and now it's hard to find me without one.

Chapter 1, **Visor Basics**, introduces you to the Handspring Visor, discussing the different models and their hardware controls, battery usage, and available accessories.

Chapter 2, **The Palm OS**, covers the handheld's most undervalued feature: the powerful, yet minimalist, operating system. We'll explore system-wide preferences, memory management, and learn how to write Palm's celebrated—and simple—Graffiti alphabet.

Chapter 3, **HotSync**, examines the feature for synchronizing information from your handheld with the desktop software, including infrared synchronization and using other programs to tie your data into your Personal Information Manager (PIM) software.

Chapters 4–6 (**Date Book**, **Address Book**, and **To Do List & Memo Pad**) deal with the four main built-in programs, showing you why a tiny screen can be so much better than crumpled pages of scribbled appointments and Post-it notes tucked into a bulging "personal organizer."

Chapter 7, **Calculator & Expense**, delves into the number-crunching applications provided by Palm and Handspring.

Chapter 8, **System Extensions**, opens the door to third-party system extensions that will make you wonder how you ever operated a Visor without them.

VISOR BASICS

The Visor's ancestry can be traced to the Pilot, the original creation of inventor (and, later, Handspring co-founder) Jeff Hawkins. It began as a block of wood that Hawkins carried around the hallways of Palm Computing. It was the essence of the term hardware—no buttons, no batteries, no screen (certainly no backlight, though a fluorescent highlighter might have worked), no software.

It was also simple. The device in Hawkins's mind didn't take a modern PC and cram its guts into a smaller case, or try to woo consumers with its multimedia capabilities. Instead, the handheld machine focused on performing a handful of essential tasks well, in tandem with the computers and data that people were currently using.

As an evolutionary surprise, today's Palm devices can do much more than their founder's intent: wireless Internet access, color photos, global positioning, and more. And yet, despite the wide array of software and hardware add-ons you can get for them, today's handhelds remain true to Hawkins's original vision: simple to use and simple in scope (though not limited, as you'll discover). It's also become simply essential for millions of owners.

The Visor Family

In 1998, the creators of the Pilot—Hawkins, Donna Dubinsky, and Ed Culligan—left Palm to form Handspring, Inc. (http://www.handspring.com/). Although some people expected the trio to remake the wheel with their new startup, they focused on revising their original intentions for the PalmPilot: Handspring licensed the Palm OS from Palm and developed a low-cost device called the Visor.

The Visor family includes the same built-in applications found on the Palm models, but with a few twists: DateBook+ offers more views and options than the built-in Date Book program; the Calculator features an advanced mode; and a new application, City Time, gives you a visual display of what time it is around the world.

More significantly, Handspring's handhelds include the Springboard expansion slot, where you can insert modules that add functionality ranging from more memory and games to modems, global positioning system devices, and even MP3 audio players. Another interesting addition: a small hole at the bottom-left of the case houses a microphone, although by default it's not activated; innovative Springboard module developers can hook into the microphone to add sound input into their applications.

Visor

The Visor is the low-cost entry to Handspring's lineup. It includes 2 MB of memory, a high-contrast monochrome screen, and is powered by two AAA batteries. For those looking for just a simple organizer, the Visor is also offered in a less expensive Visor Solo package, which does not include the Hot-Sync cradle. The Visor is only available in the graphite color.

Figure 1.1 Handspring's Visor Deluxe features translucent plastics and a different case styling than its Palm counterparts.

Figure 1.2 The Visor Platinum adds a 50 percent speed increase to the Visor lineup.

Figure 1.3 It's hard to appreciate here, but the Visor Prism's vibrant color screen displays more than 65,000 colors. (Sadly, we were unable to bundle a set of colored pencils with the book, but feel free to color the image yourself.)

Figure 1.4 Sleek and beautiful, the Visor Edge feels more like a futuristic data pad than a big box of cards.

Visor Deluxe

Handspring's most popular device is the Visor Deluxe (**Figure 1.1**). Its distinguishing characteristic is the case, which is available in graphite or four translucent colors (orange, green, blue, and ice). It includes 8 MB of memory, a monochrome screen, and runs on AAA batteries.

Visor Platinum

Although the Visor Deluxe was selling well, Handspring introduced the Visor Platinum when it was time to refresh their product lineup (**Figure 1.2**). Like the Deluxe, the Platinum includes 8 MB of memory, a monochrome screen, and runs on batteries. However, the Platinum sports a faster 33 MHz processor, which makes it 50 percent faster than a Visor Deluxe. The case comes in silver or graphite colors.

Visor Prism

The luxury model of the Visor family is the Visor Prism (**Figure 1.3**). It has 8 MB of memory, a rechargeable internal battery... and color! More than 65,000 colors, to be precise, in a stunning color screen. The case is only available in cobalt blue.

Visor Edge

If the Prism is Handspring's luxury sedan, then the Visor Edge is the sports car that speeds around town showing off (**Figure 1.4**). Available in metallic silver, blue, or red, the Edge includes 8 MB of memory, an internal rechargeable battery, and a monochrome screen. In addition, the power button has an LED that can flash for silent alarms. The Edge also has a metallic flip-cover lid that conveniently snaps into place when opened. Despite its thinness, the Edge can also accommodate Springboard modules using a clip-on adapter (though it adds bulk to the svelte profile).

THE VISOR FAMILY

Visor Overview

No matter which Visor you use, they all share the following characteristics.

Screen

The Visor's screen accounts for most of the device. The liquid-crystal display (LCD) is normally black and white only, and measures 160 pixels by 160 pixels. (Actually, the screen can display four levels of gray, which some developers have taken advantage of; gray-scale wasn't officially supported by Palm until Palm OS 3.5.) The Visor Prism's active-matrix color screen can display 65,536 colors. Most important, every screen is touch sensitive, which is why you can interact with it using a stylus.

Power button/backlight

The button at the lower left or lower right (depending on model) turns the Visor on and off (**Figure 1.5**). The Visor will automatically power down after two minutes (you can change the time delay; see Chapter 2).

Holding the power button down for two seconds activates the screen's backlight, which illuminates the screen by lighting the active (black) pixels. In very dark situations, this tends to be more readable, though in moderate lighting it can sometimes be difficult to read the screen.

Since the Prism's screen is always backlit, holding the power button activates the screen brightness control (**Figure 1.6**).

✔ Tip

- The Prism's default brightness setting is about 75 percent of maximum. Although you may be tempted to crank it to the highest level, you'll get more battery life out of a lower setting.

Power/ backlight button

Figure 1.5 The power button doubles as the backlight control (or contrast control on the Prism).

Figure 1.6 The Visor Prism's power button activates the software-based screen brightness setting.

Applications/Home *Graffiti writing area* *Calculator*
    Menu   *Find*

Figure 1.7 Use the silkscreened area to input text using Graffiti, plus launch certain functions.

Power/backlight   *Scroll buttons*
    Date *Address*   *To Do* *Memo*
    Book *Book*   *List*   *Pad*

Figure 1.8 The plastic application buttons take you directly to the built-in programs. The scroll buttons are often a better substitute for tapping the scroll arrows found in many applications.

Stylus

The stylus is your main method of interacting with the Visor, though just about anything that isn't sharper than a No. 2 pencil can work (that includes fingers and toes too!). The stylus is made of a metal barrel that comes with a plastic tip and end pieces that screw at each end. The Visor Edge has an all metal stylus that bulges toward the bottom, which I find to be more comfortable. It snaps onto the side of the Edge, versus sliding into a silo on the other Visor models.

✔ Tip

■ Unscrew the top and bottom sections of the standard Visor stylus to find a couple of surprises: the top includes a small Phillips screwdriver; the bottom sports a pin that pushes the Visor's reset button.

Silkscreen Graffiti area

This is where you input text using Graffiti, the Visor's method of handwriting (see Chapter 2). It's usually referred to as the "silkscreened" area, because the Graffiti input area and the buttons on either side of it are printed on a layer of glass by a silkscreening process. The Applications (also known as Home) and Calculator buttons are located here, as well as the triggers for accessing menus and using the Palm OS's Find feature (**Figure 1.7**).

Application buttons

The plastic buttons on the case immediately activate the Date Book, Address Book, To Do List, and Memo Pad (**Figure 1.8**). I rarely launch these programs any other way.

Scroll buttons

These up and down buttons are a handy way to scroll through text and other information. The Edge has just one rocker switch, versus two separate scroll buttons.

Infrared port

Every Visor includes an infrared port that enables you to "beam" information from one device to another (**Figure 1.9**). See Chapter 2 for more information about beaming applications, and program-specific chapters (such as Chapter 4, *Date Book*) for more on beaming individual records and categories.

Contrast control

Adjust the screen's contrast using the button tucked into the lower-left corner of the silkscreened area next to the menu button (**Figure 1.10**).

✔ Tips

- Pressing one of the application buttons when your Visor is powered down will turn it on and launch that program.

- You can launch any program—not just the built-in ones—by pressing one of the application buttons. To remap their functions, go to the Buttons section of the Preferences application (see Chapter 2).

- To put the contrast button to better use, install Contrast Button App Hack (http://www.synsolutions.com/). You can program the button to launch any program. See Chapter 8 for more information on Palm OS extensions, or "hacks."

Infrared port

Figure 1.9 The infrared port can be used to beam information between Palm organizers, and for synchronizing with an IR-equipped PC.

Contrast button

Figure 1.10 The Visor's contrast control hides here.

Stylus
(in slot)

Infrared port

Springboard
slot (filled by
placeholder)

Reset hole

Battery bay
(open)

Serial port

Figure 1.11 The back of a Visor looks bland, but it's riddled with features.

HotSync cradle

Figure 1.12 To transfer data between the Visor and your PC, use the accompanying HotSync cradle: slide the Visor into place and press the HotSync button in front to synchronize the information.

Reset button

There will probably come a time when something has happened that renders your Visor unusable (it will stop responding to your input). To get back to business, locate the tiny reset hole in the back of the unit (**Figure 1.11**). Use the reset pin located in the stylus, or straighten part of a paperclip, and insert it into the hole to reset the Palm OS (known as a *soft reset*—it won't erase your data).

HotSync cradle

The ability to synchronize information between the handheld and a desktop computer is one of the reasons for its success. Every Visor comes with an angled HotSync cradle (**Figure 1.12**) and synchronization software for your PC. Place the device into the cradle so that the connector at its base slides into the cradle's serial port. To begin synchronizing, press the HotSync button on the front of the cradle.

The cradle that comes with the Visor is USB-based, but you also have the option of purchasing a serial cradle if you order from Handspring (it should also be available from most retailers).

If you use a Macintosh that doesn't have USB, you'll need to purchase the Macintosh Serial Adapter. See the Palm Computing online store (http://store.palm.com/) for more information.

✔ Tip

- The cradle is also where the internal lithium ion battery in the Prism and Edge is recharged.

VISOR OVERVIEW

Springboard Expansion

The great irony about the Visor's Springboard module slot is that it comes from a team who for years stressed the importance of keeping handhelds simple. Hawkins didn't intend it to be a catch-all device for anything you could hold in your hand, but rather an organizer that served as an extension of the data you already used on your PC. However, from the time they created the PalmPilot to the time they founded Handspring, the Palm OS market had exploded and users were asking for more than just basic functionality.

Their answer was Springboard (**Figures 1.13** and **1.14**). You can keep the basic functionality of a Palm OS handheld if you choose, or you can open it up to modules as varied as adding extra memory to a cellular phone. You don't even have to install any software for a Springboard module to work. When you snap a module into place, its software appears in the Applications screen like it had always been there (though module-based programs have a bullet preceding their names). When you remove the module, the software disappears as well. If you've ever suffered through the installation process of adding new hardware or software to your computer, you're going to love Springboard.

Throughout the book, I'll be pointing out some notable Springboard modules as they pertain to the subject at hand.

✔ Tip

- Don't remove a Springboard module while one of its programs is active.

Figure 1.13 The Visor's Springboard expansion slot accommodates memory, games, or hardware such as modems, wireless receivers, or MP3 music players.

Figure 1.14 The Visor Edge uses a clip-on adapter to accommodate Springboard modules.

SPRINGBOARD EXPANSION

Battery Use

Visors run either on two AAA batteries or on a built-in rechargeable lithium ion battery, and last anywhere between four and six weeks (except for the Prism, which averages 2 weeks). Feel free to read that sentence again, especially if you're a laptop computer (or Windows CE device) owner who's used to measuring battery life in *hours*. The Visor battery use is minimal (the CPU is asleep most of the time, even when powered on), so even if you use it often, you can still expect about three weeks of life from one set.

Visor, Visor Deluxe, and Visor Platinum: AAA batteries

The Visor is powered by typical store-bought AAA batteries. A new set of two batteries will give you 3 volts of power. When they approach 2 volts, the Visor will begin to warn you that it's time to install a fresh pair. Although some people go ahead and swap out the old batteries after the first warning, you can probably get several more days of moderate use before switching. Since I hate being nagged about such things, I usually go ahead and replace the batteries after the first or second warning.

Visor Edge and Visor Prism: rechargeable lithium ion battery

The exceptions to the crowd are the Edge and Prism: the Edge is simply too thin to accommodate even tiny AAA batteries, and the Prism needs a better method of providing power to its energy-hungry color screen. Instead, both devices have built-in lithium ion batteries that recharge whenever they're in their HotSync cradles; a green light in the Edge's power button indicates it's charging.

BATTERY USE

✔ Tips

- It only takes a few minutes each day to charge the battery in the Edge or Prism. Under normal use, the charge applied during a HotSync operation should be sufficient to top off the gauge (**Figure 1.15**). The fact that the batteries won't fall out or get knocked loose accidentally make the Edge and Prism the most solid handhelds I've used.

- If you've just opened your brand new Edge or Prism, stop! Be sure you charge the unit for three hours before first use to ensure that the battery is fully charged. Not following this simple step can cause the battery to hold less of a charge over the long run.

- Some Springboard modules use power from the Visor, so keeping them in the Springboard slot may deplete your batteries faster. Other modules, like the Visor-Phone, include their own power sources that must be charged separately.

Battery level indicator

Figure 1.15 The battery level is shown at the top of the Applications screen.

BATTERY USE

Remove the battery door, then replace the batteries, first one, then the other.

Figure 1.16 Batteries are included with your new Visor. When it's time to replace the AAA batteries, you have about 60 seconds to swap them out before your data is lost.

Recommended battery types

Handspring recommends using Alkaline batteries, which have a steady rate of discharge (as opposed to nickel-cadmium, or NiCad, batteries, which drop off suddenly when they're spent; you may not have enough juice to HotSync your data before installing new batteries). Many users also report longer battery life using the newer Duracell Ultras and Energizer Advanced Formula batteries.

If you want to use rechargeable batteries, go with rechargeable alkalines like Rayovac Renewal. Just be sure to recharge them at around 50 percent capacity—don't wait until they're dead—to get the best use out of them.

To change batteries:

1. HotSync your data. There are provisions built into the Visor to prevent data loss during a battery swap, but the best is to have a backup of your data. See Chapter 3 for more on synchronizing data.

2. Shut off your Visor, turn it over, and remove the battery door (**Figure 1.16**).

3. Pull out the old batteries and replace with the new ones. Handspring recommends swapping them one at a time (i.e., bad battery out, good battery in, repeat). You have about 60 seconds from the point when you remove the batteries to when you install fresh ones to avoid data loss.

4. Replace the battery door, and turn the Visor back on.

✔ Tip

■ If you're using different battery types (Alkaline/NiCad/Rechargeable Alkaline/NiMH), write the following in a text field (such as the Memo Pad) to toggle between more accurate battery gauges: "ﻝ . �7" (shortcut, period, 7).

BATTERY USE

Screen Care

Your screen is the gateway to your data, so take care of it. You shouldn't have to do much besides wipe it with a clean cloth every once in a while, but there are several solutions for keeping the glass clear of scratches and giving the silkscreened Graffiti area a better "writing" feel beneath the stylus.

Screen protectors

Several companies offer clear plastic or vinyl strips that fit over your Visor's screen. I've used WriteRights, by Concept Kitchen (http://www.conceptkitchen.com/), which keep the screen clear of scratches and provides for a better writing texture. Applying them successfully is an art in itself, but the end result works well for me.

Every Visor except the Edge includes a plastic screen cover that snaps onto the front of the device and helps protect the screen when you're not using it. Due to the way it snaps onto the case, you can reverse it so the cover is connected to the back. The Edge's flip-up lid is a better solution (although it covers the connection slot where the Springboard adapter goes), and provides a bit of shade against direct sunlight.

✔ Tips

- Perhaps the most popular low-tech solution is to put strips of tape (Scotch 811, in the blue box, is the preferred variety) over the Graffiti area, which gets the most stylus use. Other people have used Post-it notes, tape flags, and transparency film.

- If a damp cloth is outmatched by the grime on your screen, Concept Kitchen also offers PDA Screen Clean, a set of cloths and wet/dry formulas.

Figure 1.17 Replacement styli range from simple substitutes to pen/stylus combinations to traditional pens with PDA nibs. The LandWare Floating•Point stylus is shown here.

Figure 1.18 Handheld case manufacturers have taken advantage of this new niche market—you can buy a style of case customized for your needs.

Accessorizing

A characteristic of a successful product is how well you can accessorize it, so it's not surprising to find a cottage industry that caters to handheld accessories. These range from stylish styli to screen protectors to clothing specially designed with PDA-ready pockets.

Styli

As you might expect, you can buy replacement styli, ranging from brass styli that fit into the stylus slots to hybrid pens such as the Cross Digital Writer (http://www.cross.com/). The Landware Floating•Point stylus, for example, has a special nib that replicates the feel of writing on paper (http://www.landware.com/) (**Figure 1.17**). See PDA Panache (http://www.pdapanache.com/) for more variations.

Cases

There are numerous case variations on the market, such as RhinoSkin's Cockpit (http://www.handheld-cases.com/), a titanium hard case with a melting point of 1,666 degrees Celsius! Handspring's Visor case (**Figure 1.18**) comes in all sorts of colors and materials, or you can even design your own. There are also varieties of belt-loop cases, zippered pouches, and shoulder-strap carriers. For a few good resources on cases, check out Fredlet's Pilot Page (http://www.fredlet.com/palm/) or the Gadgeteer (http://www.the-gadgeteer.com/).

Other accessories

Depending on your needs, a variety of other helpful goodies can be ordered. Examples include extra HotSync cradles, travel kits and chargers, and extra HotSync cables.

Keyboards

The Visor's pen has proved mightier than the chiclet keyboards on many other PDAs, but there are times when a real physical keyboard can come in handy. Anyone who's tried to work on a regular-sized laptop computer in an airplane's coach seat knows that space is at a premium.

Over the past couple of years, a handful of external keyboards have appeared. Although perhaps overkill for everyday handheld usage, they're great for typing long memos, emails, and especially taking notes during a meeting. Of the keyboards available, two models stand out.

Targus Stowaway Keyboard

Of all the handheld peripherals I've carried around lately, this is the one that knocks people out. Designed by Think Outside (http://www.thinkoutside.com/) and sold by Targus (http://www.targus.com/), the Stowaway is a full-size keyboard that folds into a compact rectangle not much larger than a Visor (**Figure 1.19**). In addition to being small and light, it has special keys that launch applications and access Palm OS features like command shortcuts.

GoType! Pro

LandWare (http://www.landware.com/) struck gold with the GoType! Pro keyboard, an all-in-one clamshell design with a slot to plug in a Visor (**Figure 1.20**). It features special Palm OS-specific keys to access applications, commands, and shortcuts. The GoType! Pro also has a built-in USB port for performing a HotSync operation with your computer.

Figure 1.19 The Targus Stowaway Keyboard is a full-size keyboard that folds up to a size slightly larger than a Visor, and weighs only about 8 ounces (Palm V model shown here).

Figure 1.20 LandWare's GoType! Pro keyboard includes a USB connector to HotSync directly from the keyboard.

Figure 1.21 Palm Desktop for Windows replicates most of the Palm OS's functionality, but puts most of the information on the same screen.

Palm Desktop

Most of this book concerns the Palm OS and the Visors that use it, but there's also another very important component to the Visor: the desktop software. A Palm OS handheld is primarily intended to be an extension of your personal data, so the desktop software acts as the core.

It's not essential that you use Palm Desktop; in fact, you can purchase a Visor Solo, which doesn't include a HotSync cradle (though you do get the desktop software in the box anyway, just no immediate way to synchronize the Visor). You also have the option of using other PIM programs like Microsoft Outlook or Lotus Notes. But Palm Desktop is the one that most closely resembles what you find on the palmtop.

Palm Desktop makes it easy to access your data when you're working on your computer, printing information, installing software on the handheld, or just need to enter a lot of data without cramping your fingers writing Graffiti. At the very least, Palm Desktop provides the framework for keeping backup copies of the data on your handheld.

Throughout the book, I'll cover specific features of each module in their respective chapters (such as Chapter 4, *Date Book*).

Palm Desktop for Windows

Most of the functionality found on the Palm translates directly to the Windows version of Palm Desktop (**Figure 1.21**). On the desktop, however, you get the advantage of a computer's larger screen size, so you can see more information at a glance than on a handheld.

Palm Desktop is also the place to access archived data (which you've deleted from the Visor but want to store on the PC).

Waiting on Palm Desktop 4.0

As this book went to press, Palm had recently released Palm Desktop 4.0. However, Handspring's developers were still evaluating the new version and working on compatibility with the Visor line. When it's released, though, its functionality will resemble what you see in this book, albeit with a new interface.

✔ Tip

- If you're just itching to run the new version, you can—though at your own risk (I haven't yet heard of any problems, however). First, make sure you have backups of your user data, then install Palm Desktop 4.0 (available from http://www.palm.com/). Next, run Handspring's Palm Desktop installer and perform a custom install so that only the HotSync software is installed.

Palm Desktop for Macintosh

The first incarnation of the Macintosh Palm Desktop only synchronized the built-in applications, with no way for developers to write additional conduits (software bridges between the Palm OS and the desktop). For a few years, Pilot Desktop 1.0 remained the only choice for Palm-owning Macintosh users. Eager to reestablish contact with its Mac user base, Palm made an interesting choice when updating the desktop software: it bought Claris Organizer from Apple. Rather than build something new from scratch, they built upon Organizer.

The result is a vastly different desktop PIM from both Pilot Desktop 1.0 and the Windows counterpart (**Figure 1.22**). Although it shares basic functionality with Palm Desktop for Windows, there are notable differences: some features, such as support for a second address field (so you can store home and work addresses, for example), exist only on the desktop, not in the Palm OS (**Figure 1.23**); you can assign sub-categories to records; and, of course, the interface is quite a bit different.

The new software isn't without its shortcomings, however. For example, private records on the desktop cannot be hidden, though they will retain their Private setting under the Palm OS.

However, as of this writing Palm is working on a version of Mac Palm Desktop that handles private records, runs natively under Mac OS X, and other goodies the developers aren't ready to divulge.

✔ Tip

■ If you don't have at least version 2.6.3 of Mac Palm Desktop, get it. It solves a host of crashing problems dealing with the Instant Palm Desktop extension.

Figure 1.22 The Palm Desktop for Macintosh includes the features of Claris Organizer, upon which it was based.

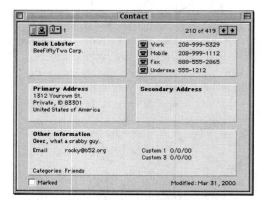

Figure 1.23 You can store more data, although not all of it will transfer to the handheld.

THE PALM OS

Much is said and written about the Visor's portability, the Springboard expansion slot, and the ease of synchronizing data with a desktop PC. When the attention is turned to the software running inside it, though, the focus usually shifts to how many events can be stored, or how quickly one can look up an address.

I would argue that the Palm Operating System (Palm OS) is actually the strongest, and most overlooked, of the Visor's features. Like a well-scored movie soundtrack, which adds to the atmosphere of a film without drawing attention to itself, the Palm OS provides a lot of power while remaining essentially invisible to most owners. If you're used to the shaded buttons and colors of Windows, the Palm OS probably looks sparse and boring (and if you're a Macintosh user, you may think you've returned to the early days of System 6!). As a result, using a Palm device for the first time is surprisingly easy.

Yet it isn't just ease of use that makes the Palm OS notable. Beneath the uncluttered interface lies an operating system that's been designed with an emphasis on efficiency and usability. After using the Palm OS for only a few hours, you'll realize that your stylus is only tapping its surface.

Navigating the Palm OS

There are three basic methods of interacting within the Palm OS, all of which depend on the stylus (or a similar writing instrument). Since the screen is touch-sensitive, there's no need for a "proxy" device such as a mouse.

Tap

Most of the elements you encounter require a tap with the end of the stylus. Tapping a record selects it by either opening up a new window or placing a cursor within the text. You also use taps to manipulate the following interface elements (**Figure 2.1**):

◆ **Icons.** In the Applications screen, tapping a program's icon or name launches it. Smaller custom icons, such as the alarm clock and note, are also used.

◆ **Buttons.** Similar to the buttons found under Windows and the Mac OS, these rounded-corner boxes are used to activate commands or confirm actions.

◆ **Menus.** When you tap a title bar or the silkscreened Menu icon, drop-down menus become visible at the top of the screen. Tap to select menu items.

◆ **Scroll arrows.** When data spills beyond the size of the screen, tap the up/down scroll arrows to move the active information up and down. You'll also encounter left/right scroll arrows, like the Date Book arrows that move between weeks (see Chapter 4).

◆ **Popup menus.** Whenever you see a small triangle pointing down next to a word, it indicates that more options are available via a popup menu.

◆ **Checkboxes.** Tap on a checkbox to mark or unmark it, toggling the action that is assigned to it (such as the Private indicator in most records' detail screens).

Scroll arrows

Button

Popup menu

Checkbox Dotted-rectangle field

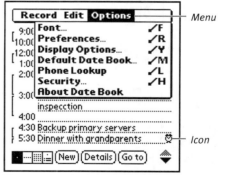

Menu

Icon

Figure 2.1 Tapping just about any interface element in the Palm OS evokes a response.

NAVIGATING THE PALM OS

Tap and
hold
original
item...

... to drag it
to a new
location.

Figure 2.2 The Memo Pad provides one example of dragging a list item to a new location.

| Memo 13 of 13 | Unfiled |

Videos to Rent
Comedy
How to get Ahead in Advertising
Zorro, tGB
Back to the Future
Drama
My Dinner with Andre
Hear My Song
King of the Hill
Cold Fusion

(Done) (Details)

Figure 2.3 Tap to set your cursor, then drag through letters to highlight them.

◆ **Dotted-rectangle fields.** These fields display the information that has been selected for them, but also indicate that tapping the field allows you to change it.

Drag

In a few cases, you will want to drag an item using the stylus. The most common examples include (but are not limited to):

◆ **Scroll bars.** If you have more than 11 memos displayed in the Memo Pad, a vertical scroll bar appears at the right side of the screen. You could tap the arrows at the top or bottom of a scroll bar, but a quicker way to view the full list is to tap and hold on the dark solid portion of the scroll bar, then drag it vertically.

◆ **Custom ordered memos.** In the Memo Pad and some applications, you can "grab" an item and drag it to a new position within a list (**Figure 2.2**). A thick dotted line indicates where the item will be placed when it is "dropped" (i.e., when you lift the stylus from the screen).

◆ **Highlighting text.** To select a series of letters or words, tap to place your cursor, then drag to select the text (**Figure 2.3**).

◆ **Weekly Date Book entries.** In the Date Book's week view, you can select events and reschedule them by dragging to a new date and time. (See Chapter 4.)

Write

Using the silkscreened Graffiti area, you can use the stylus as a pen and write letters that appear within text fields. See "Graffiti," later in this chapter.

✔ Tip

■ Under Palm OS 3.5 and later, double-tap to select a word; triple-tap to select a line.

NAVIGATING THE PALM OS

Accessing Menus

Although hidden to conserve valuable screen space, drop-down menus similar to those found in Windows and the Mac OS are available for most applications. Access menus to take advantage of commands not displayed on the current screen, and to edit text using Cut, Copy, Paste, and Undo commands.

To access menus in applications:

1. Tap the Menu icon located in the lower-left corner of the silkscreened area of the screen. You'll see a row of words appear at the top of the screen such as Record, Edit, or Options.

2. Tap a word to see a drop-down menu of related commands (**Figure 2.4**). You don't have to maintain contact with the stylus; these menus are "sticky" and will stay visible until you tap the stylus on a command or elsewhere on the screen.

3. Tap the desired menu item to perform its action.

✔ Tips

- Palm OS 3.5 finally adds the ability to tap a program's title bar (the solid black area in the upper-left corner) to access its menus. You may never tap the Menu icon again!

- If you're not running Palm OS 3.5, you can get the same functionality by installing the HackMaster extension MenuHack (http://www.daggerware.com/mischack.htm). (For more about similar system enhancements, see Chapter 8.)

To make menus visible...

... tap this icon first.

Figure 2.4 It may not make much sense to jump from bottom to top to access menus, but it's nice that menus are normally hidden to save space.

ACCESSING MENUS

Figure 2.5 Tap the "circle-i" icon in the upper-right corner of dialog boxes to access help and other information.

Figure 2.6 It's worth checking out a new program's Tips screens—often you'll find real tips, not just online help.

Onscreen Help and Tips

Nestled within the tight memory confines of the Palm OS exists a handy location for accessing onscreen help and application tips. Most dialog boxes (windows that are identified by a thick outside line and a black title bar at the top) include a "circle-i" information icon in the upper-right corner (**Figure 2.5**). Tapping this small icon displays a screen titled Tips, which often provides instruction or pointers for using an application's features (**Figure 2.6**). It's often worth poking around the dialog boxes of a new program to see if there are any "hidden" features that may be revealed on the Tips screen.

Using the Onscreen Keyboard

The Palm OS includes two methods for entering information: Graffiti, the style of lettering you use to write individual letters (see the next section), and a virtual keyboard for tapping letters on the screen. The keyboard can be accessed only when your cursor is in a text field. Activating it brings up a new window containing the text field (or as much as can be displayed in the smaller space), with the keyboard located below (**Figure 2.7**).

Three separate keyboards are available: the abc keyboard, which is laid out in Qwerty format (like most computer and typewriter keyboards); the 123 keyboard, which gives you access to numbers and common symbol characters; and the Int'l ("international") keyboard, which creates common letters with diacritical marks (such as é) as well as characters like ß, ¿, and æ. Switch between layouts by tapping the corresponding button beneath the keyboard.

To activate the keyboard:

There are four ways of accessing the keyboard: tap either the abc or 123 dots in the lower corners of the Graffiti area; drag the stylus vertically across the screen from bottom to top; select Keyboard from the Edit menu (when available); or write ╱-K in the Graffiti area. Tap Done when finished.

✔ Tips

- If you like the onscreen keyboard but find the Qwerty layout difficult, install Fitaly (http://www.twsolutions.com/), which arranges letters based on frequent usage.

- If you don't mind Qwerty, but don't like tapping the small letter squares, install DotNote (or ".Note") (http://www. utilware.com/) to display larger keys.

Figure 2.7 If you'd prefer to tap on letters instead of write them, bring up one of the onscreen Keyboard layouts. This is often the best way to access symbol and international characters.

ThE—OUICↄ BROWN—ΓOX JUMPEↁ OVЄR—ThЄ LɅZЫ—ↁOG

Figure 2.8 At first glance, Graffiti looks like an alien scrawl, but pretty soon you'll find yourself writing like this on everything—not just your Visor.

Figure 2.9 Create Graffiti letters on the left side of the Graffiti area; write numbers on the right.

Graffiti

One of the only things that makes potential Visor buyers hesitate before purchasing is the prospect of hand-writing letters on the screen. Some are concerned that they'll have to learn a new "language." Others are gun-shy after hearing about the difficulties with handwriting recognition that plagued other handhelds (notably Apple's discontinued Newton MessagePad). In the Palm OS, you use the stylus to write the Graffiti alphabet, which translates those written gestures into proper text characters (**Figure 2.8**).

Call me a Graffiti evangelist, but I'm here to reassure you that: (a) Graffiti is simpler than you think (you'll pick up the basics in the first few hours, I promise); and (b) because it doesn't technically do any handwriting recognition, your chances of writing something like "The quack bruin fax junked over the hazy fog" are fairly minimal (unless that's what you meant in the first place).

The Graffiti area

One of the key differences between traditional handwriting recognition and Graffiti is that you don't write directly on the active portion of the screen using Graffiti. Instead, you form letters in the silkscreened Graffiti area, where they are interpreted and displayed wherever your cursor happens to be.

The Graffiti area is split into two sections: write letters on the left side, numbers on the right (**Figure 2.9**). This is an important distinction, because some characters, such as B and 3, can be written using identical strokes.

GRAFFITI

Writing Graffiti

Here's the big secret about Graffiti: nearly every character can be written with only one stroke of the stylus. (The exception is X, which requires two strokes—but you can also use an alternate version of X that's still just one stroke.) The identity of the character is determined both by the shape of the stroke, and by the combination of the stroke's origin point and direction. As an example, let's write the word "Tack" (**Figure 2.10**).

To write basic Graffiti characters:

1. First, you need to be in an application where you can write text. Press the Memo Pad button on the front of the Visor, then tap New to create a new memo. Put the stylus at the left side of the Graffiti area.

2. Write the Graffiti stroke for T (⌐), starting at the dot. Make sure you write the complete stroke without lifting the stylus until the end (**Table 2.1**). You should see a capital T in the memo above.

3. Using the same side of the Graffiti area, write the stroke for A (∧), again starting at the dot. Repeat the process for C (C), and—my favorite letter to write—K (∢).

4. Admire your (sharp) handiwork.

Writing numbers is exactly the same, only you write strokes in the right side of the Graffiti area (**Table 2.2**).

✔ Tip

■ You probably noticed that the first letter was automatically capitalized, and subsequent letters were in lowercase. When you begin a new field, or write an end-of-sentence punctuation such as a period or exclamation point, the Palm OS assumes that you want a capital letter.

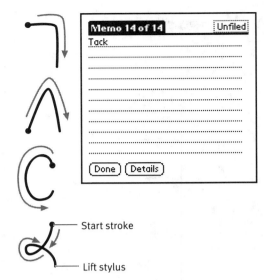

Figure 2.10 Each character can be written using one stroke of the stylus in the Graffiti area. Start at the dot (but don't try to draw the dot), and lift the stylus at the end of the stroke.

Table 2.1

The Graffiti alphabet			
LETTER	GRAFFITI	LETTER	GRAFFITI
A	∧	N	N
B	B	O	O
C	C	P	P
D	D	Q	O
E	Ɛ	R	R
F	Γ	S	S
G	G	T	⌐
H	h	U	U
I	I	V	V
J	J	W	W
K	∢	X	X
L	L	Y	y
M	M	Z	Z

Table 2.2

Graffiti numbers and special strokes

SYMBOL	GRAFFITI	SYMBOL	GRAFFITI
1	|	8	8 8
2	2	9	9
3	3	0	O O
4	L	backspace	→
5	5 b	return	/
6	6	shift	|
7	7	space	—

Table 2.3

Graffiti punctuation (with alternates)

SYMBOL	GRAFFITI	SYMBOL	GRAFFITI
.	• •	+	• ∝
,	• ⁄	=	• Z
'	• ˈ	|	• ↓
?	• ? ˥	<	• ⊂
!	• |	>	• ⊃
-	• —	\	• \
(	• C	{	• ε
)	• ⊃	}	• 3
/	• ⁄	[	• ε
$	• S	]	• 3
@	• O	~	• N ~
#	• ⋃ h	`	• \
%	• ⋈	;	• ⁄
^	• ∧	:	• ↓
&	• 8	"	• N
*	• ∝	tab	• Γ
—	• —		

In Graffiti, there are no separate strokes for upper- and lowercase letters. Instead, as when typing on a computer keyboard, you need to specify when to enable Caps Shift.

To write uppercase letters:

1. Write the Caps Shift stroke (|) in either side of the Graffiti area (**Table 2.1**). An up arrow symbol (⬆) will appear in the lower-right corner of the screen to indicate that Caps Shift is enabled.

2. Write a normal Graffiti letter. You'll see the uppercase version appear in the text field. The up arrow will disappear.

3. If you're going to write a series of uppercase letters, you can enable Caps Lock by writing two Caps Shift strokes. The up arrow is replaced by an underlined up arrow (⬆).

To write punctuation:

1. Tap once on either side of the Graffiti area to enable Punctuation Shift. You'll see a large dot in the lower-right corner.

2. Write the stroke for the punctuation mark you want (**Table 2.3**).

✔ Tip

- If you change your mind and want to switch back to normal writing before committing to a capital letter or punctuation character, write a Back Space stroke (→), which effectively "deletes" the Shift or Punctuation Shift stroke you just made.

WRITING GRAFFITI

To write symbols and extended characters:

1. Enable the Symbol Shift mode by drawing a diagonal line in either side of the Graffiti area, starting at the top-left corner and finishing at the lower right. You'll see a similar line (\) in the lower-right corner of the screen.

2. Write the stroke for the symbol you want (**Table 2.4**).

To write accented characters:

1. It takes two strokes to create accented characters. First, draw the letter you want to apply the accent to, such as E ($\mathcal{E}$).

2. Write the corresponding accent stroke. The character changes to the new accented letter (**Table 2.5**).

Navigating using Graffiti

You can move your cursor within a field or to an adjacent field without erasing the letters you've already written using Graffiti navigation strokes (**Table 2.6**).

Command strokes

There's a better way than menu items to access commands. Rather than use three taps to access a menu item (tap the Menu icon, tap the menu name, tap the menu item), it's much easier and faster to write a command stroke. Draw a diagonal line from the bottom-left to the upper-right of either side of the Graffiti area (**Table 2.6**). You'll see the word Command:, or the Command Bar (see next section), appear at the bottom of the screen. Write the stroke that activates the menu item you want (such as ╱-C for Copy).

Table 2.4

Graffiti symbols/extended characters

SYMBOL	GRAFFITI	SYMBOL	GRAFFITI
•	＼ ·	X	＼ ╱
TM	＼ m	÷	＼ ꝏ
®	＼ R	=	＼ Z
©	＼ C	¢	＼ C
'	＼ ⌐	¥	＼ ɣ
'	＼ ⌐	£	＼ L
"	＼ N	¿	＼ L
"	＼ И	¡	＼ I
§	＼ S	ß	＼ B
·	＼ O	µ	＼ m
+	＼ ∝	ƒ	＼ S
−	＼ ―	ø	＼ O

Table 2.5

Graffiti accent characters

SYMBOL	GRAFFITI	SYMBOL	GRAFFITI
à	∧ ＼	è	Ɛ ＼
á	∧ ╱	é	Ɛ ╱
â	∧ ∧	ê	Ɛ ∧
ä	∧ ꝏ	ü	U ꝏ
å	∧ O	ç	C
ñ	N N	æ	Ɛ

Table 2.6

Graffiti navigation strokes

COMMAND	GRAFFITI	COMMAND	GRAFFITI
cursor right	━	next field	↓
cursor left	━	shortcut	ʒ
previous field	↑	command	╱

Command bar

Figure 2.11 In Applications, the command bar provides access to common features, like the Info or Delete screens.

Figure 2.12 With nothing selected, the command bar offers few choices.

Figure 2.13 With a record selected, the command bar displays icons for commands which work in that context.

The Command Bar

Palm OS 3.5 takes the concept of command strokes one step further with the command bar (**Figure 2.11**). When you write a command stroke, the command bar displays icons for actions that are usable depending on the current context.

For example, with no records selected in the To Do List, the only icon to appear is the Security icon (**Figure 2.12**). However, with a task selected, the Beam Item, Paste, and Delete Item options appear (**Figure 2.13**).

If you don't act within three seconds, the command bar disappears until invoked again.

To access the command bar:

1. Draw a diagonal line from the bottom-left to the top-right corner of either Graffiti area (╱).

2. Tap an icon on the command bar to perform an action. You can tap and hold on the icons to see their description; when you lift the stylus, the action is executed.

✔ Tips

- The command bar is an addition to the Palm OS's command-stroke function; if a command isn't represented by an icon, you can still invoke it by writing the command shortcut letters found in the application's menus.

- If you've tapped an icon but decide not to invoke its action, drag the stylus away from the icon before lifting it from the screen's surface.

THE COMMAND BAR

Graffiti Improvement Tips

Simple tips for improving Graffiti recognition

- **Write large.** Feel free to use the full Graffiti area to write your letters—that way, more touch-sensitive sensors are registering your strokes.

- **Write at a natural speed.** If you write too slowly, you can confuse the sensors and generate errors.

- **Don't write on a slant.** Try to keep vertical strokes vertical, and horizontal strokes horizontal.

Alternate characters

If you're finding that the downstroke on the B is creating a D and vice-versa, or if you just want to write faster, there are a number of built-in alternate strokes that work just as well (or sometimes better) than the standard Graffiti set (**Table 2.7**).

TealEcho

Install TealEcho (http://www.tealpoint.com/) to see Graffiti characters as you write them. Having that visual feedback helps improve Graffiti skills by showing you exactly why your scribbles may be incomprehensible. See Chapter 8 for more about TealEcho.

TealScript

If you'd rather go in and tinker with each individual Graffiti character, install TealScript (http://www.tealpoint.com/). By marking the Enable Globally checkbox on the main screen, you can replace Palm's Graffiti alphabet (though you're not deleting the original) with the infinitely configurable TealScript. You're still using Graffiti, but you can set up a TealScript profile that reacts better to the way you write (**Figure 2.14**).

Table 2.7

Normal and alternate characters				
LETTER	GRAFFITI	LETTER	GRAFFITI	
A	∧	T	⌐	
B	ß B ꜯ	U	U	
C	C <	V	V V	
D	Ꭰ Ꭾ ℓ	W	ω	
E	Ɛ ≤ ℓ	X	X ∞	
F	⌐ Γ	Y	ɣ ɣ r	
G	G 6	Z	Z	
H	h	1	I	
I	I	2	2 ≈	
J	J ⌐	3	3	
K	⋖	4	∟ C <	
L	L ∠	5	5 ᄂ S	
M	ɱ m	6	6	
N	N ∿ ~	7	7 ⊃	
O	O ○	8	8 ✗ ℓ	
P	ρ P Γ	9	9	
Q	Ȣ U	0	O ○	
R	ꓘ R ꓤ	æ	ℇ	
S	S ⌇ ᔕ			

Figure 2.14 TealScript builds profiles based on your Graffiti usage.

The Visor's Welcoming Committee

The Visor includes a program called Welcome that automatically runs when starting the device for the first time, or after the memory has been completely wiped (such as from a hard reset or battery failure) (**Figure 2.15**).

It initially sets up the date, time, and localization options, then calibrates the digitizer, which maps pen taps with the correct pixels on screen (**Figure 2.16**). You then have the option to follow a short tutorial on writing Graffiti characters (**Figure 2.17**).

Once you've run Welcome, however, there's little reason to go back to it unless you want to refresh yourself using its brief tutorials; all of the settings (and more) can be accessed from the Prefs application.

✔ Tips

■ If you want to easily change your basic settings (such as when you travel to a different time zone), the Welcome application can be a quicker method than accessing the Prefs program.

■ The Graffiti tutorial in Welcome replaces Giraffe, a favorite game of early Palm owners that taught Graffiti by forcing you to write letters falling from the top of the screen before they hit the bottom.

   If you miss the old animal, don't worry: you'll find the file "Giraffe.prc" in the Add-on folder that was created during the Palm Desktop installation.

Figure 2.15 You probably found Welcome when first powering on.

Figure 2.16 Welcome establishes the date and time settings from the start.

Figure 2.17 Welcome offers a formal area to practice writing Graffiti.

THE VISOR'S WELCOMING COMMITTEE

Setting General Preferences

The Prefs application looks mundane at first, but closer inspection reveals that the rest of the OS hinges upon the settings you choose here. To access the preferences, tap the popup menu in the upper-right corner (**Figure 2.18**).

To set General preferences:

1. Choose General from the Preferences popup menu.

2. Set the current time and date by tapping on the dotted boxes beside Set Time and Set Date.

3. As a battery-saving feature, a Palm device will shut itself off after a period of inactivity (two minutes by default). Tap the Auto-off after popup menu to choose either a one-, two-, or three-minute delay.

4. Specify the volume settings for the three default sound levels as High, Medium, Low, or None (**Figure 2.19**).

5. Specify whether people can beam records to you using the Beam Receive popup menu.

6. If you own a Visor with a rechargeable battery, like the Visor Edge or Prism, check the Stay on in Cradle box to prevent the device from powering off when it's docked in the HotSync cradle. This is a good way to use your organizer as an expensive desk clock.

Figure 2.18 All of the Preferences settings can be accessed via the popup menu in the upper-right corner.

Figure 2.19 Set several volume levels, as well as choose if you want to receive beamed materials. The Visor Edge and Visor Prism feature rechargeable batteries, so you can choose to keep them turned on while in their recharging cradles.

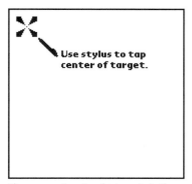

Figure 2.20 Tapping the targets in the Digitizer ensures that your touch-sensitive screen is accurately registering the location of the taps.

✔ Tips

- Be careful about changing the time to reflect new time zones on your Visor and on your laptop when traveling. Since the time and date stamps are referred to when you perform a HotSync, having your Visor and your PC living in separate zones can cause your data to be overwritten incorrectly.

- Leaving the Beam Receive option on can drain your battery at a higher rate. However, returning to the Prefs application each time you wish to receive something can be a pain. Instead, write the ShortCut ℛ .| (shortcut stroke, period, I) in any text field, which turns on Beam Receive for a single instance.

Setting the Digitizer Preference

When you first turn on a new Palm handheld, or if you're forced to perform a hard reset, the Welcome application includes the Digitizer screen.

To calibrate the Digitizer:

Tap the center points of the X shapes that appear (**Figure 2.20**). This process ensures that the pixels you tap on the screen correspond with the pixels that the Palm OS thinks you're tapping.

✔ Tip

- Due to temperature variations, repeated use, and the general passing of time, the digitizer can gradually slide off track. If your pen taps don't seem to be working the way they used to, choose Digitizer from the popup menu and recalibrate.

Customizing Buttons

Although the plastic application buttons on the case and the silkscreened icons near the Graffiti area are handy for directly launching the built-in applications, there are times when you might want to specify different programs, such as Super Names (http://www.standalone.com) instead of the Address Book application (**Figure 2.21**).

To customize buttons:

1. Choose Buttons from the Preferences popup menu.

2. Select the button you wish to replace, and tap the popup menu to the right of its icon.

3. Choose an application from the popup list. To return to the Palm OS factory settings, tap the Default button.

✔ Tips

- You can configure not only the plastic buttons and the silkscreened icons, but also the one-stroke pen drag. In the Buttons screen, tap Pen..., then tap the popup menu in the center (**Figure 2.22**). You can choose to turn on the backlight, activate the onscreen keyboard (this is the default), display Graffiti help, turn off and lock the device, or (using Palm devices with infrared capability) beam data. Setting this feature to turn on the backlight is better than pressing the power button for two seconds.

- Install Swipe (http://www.doublebang.com/) to get six more one-stroke commands, using different areas of the screen (**Figure 2.23**).

Figure 2.21 Launch other programs from the physical application buttons.

Figure 2.22 Specify an action for the bottom-to-top screen stroke shortcut.

Figure 2.23 Swipe gives you six more options for customizing strokes.

Figure 2.24 The Formats screen offers preconfigured settings for 24 countries.

Figure 2.25 The Owner screen can be filled with whatever text you like, though most people enter contact information.

Changing Formats

If you dream of traveling abroad, select Formats from the Preferences popup menu and tap the Preset to popup menu to select the country in which you'd like to reside. Otherwise, it's probably a better idea to choose your current location.

To change time, date, week, and number formats:

1. The formats have already been configured for each country, but you can adjust them individually by tapping each setting's popup menu (**Figure 2.24**).

2. Switch to another application or Preferences menu item to apply the settings.

Editing the Owner Screen

Since you'll likely become attached to your Visor, you should go ahead and put your name in it (thereby resolving any potential playground ownership disputes by asserting that yes, your name *is* on it!).

To set up the Owner screen:

1. Select Owner from the Preferences popup menu.

2. Write your contact information (or other text) on the lines provided. If you should misplace your Visor someday, the honorable person finding it can learn where to ship it back (**Figure 2.25**).

✔ Tip

■ After configuring your preferences, return to the Owner screen before switching to another program. This should speed up access the next time you open the Preferences application, as some sections—especially ShortCuts—take longer to load.

Using ShortCuts

Graffiti is an efficient way to input data, but you'll soon get tired of entering commonly used words and phrases letter by letter. Instead, set up ShortCuts that substitute full texts when you enter an abbreviation.

To create and edit ShortCuts:

1. Select ShortCuts from the Preferences popup menu (**Figure 2.26**).

2. Tap New to create a ShortCut, or Edit to change an existing one. The Palm OS includes seven built-in ShortCuts.

3. In the ShortCut Entry window, write the abbreviation under ShortCut Name. The shorter the abbreviation, the fewer the letters you'll have to write to activate it, but you're not limited to just two or three (**Figure 2.27**).

4. Write the full text that will replace the abbreviation when you activate the ShortCut. Tap OK when you're done.

To use a ShortCut:

1. In any text field, write the ShortCut Graffiti character (ℛ); you will see it appear in your text.

2. Write the abbreviation for the word or phrase you're going to use. The abbreviation and ShortCut character will be erased and replaced by the full text.

Figure 2.26 All but one of the predefined ShortCuts are named with two-letter abbreviations, but you're not bound to that limit.

Figure 2.27 ShortCuts make entering frequently used texts much easier.

Figure 2.28 Preconfigure a variety of methods of moving data to and from your Visor.

Figure 2.29 Editing a connection type controls how the OS interacts with devices such as modems.

Figure 2.30 Changing the speed or editing the initialization screen can sometimes improve a poor connection.

Setting Connection Preferences

If Palm OS devices are truly "connected organizers," as Palm says, then they need to connect with a variety of devices. Under Palm OS 3.3 and later, the Connection preferences handle peripherals like modems as well as serial and infrared connections.

To create or edit a configuration:

1. Select Connection from the Preferences popup menu (**Figure 2.28**).

2. Tap a configuration to highlight it, then tap the New or Edit button.

3. From the Connection Method popup menu, choose the type of connection that fits your purpose: Serial to PC, Serial to Modem, IrCOMM to PC, or IrCOMM to Modem. IrCOMM refers to the Palm OS's built-in libraries necessary for infrared communication (**Figure 2.29**).

4. If connecting to a modem, choose Touch-Tone™ or Rotary from the Dialing popup menu, and specify the loudness from the Volume popup menu. These options aren't available if connecting to a PC.

5. Tap the Details button (**Figure 2.30**).

6. Select a data speed from the Speed popup menu. If you're running into HotSync problems under a serial connection, reducing the data speed may help.

7. If you're using a modem, the Country and Init String options will be available. Choose your country and enter a modem initialization string if you need one.

8. Set the flow control on the Flow Ctl popup menu. Flow control regulates the rate of incoming information. Leaving this set to Automatic should be fine in most cases.

Setting Modem Preferences

Palm OS 3.1 uses a set of Modem preferences rather than the Connection settings found in Palm OS 3.3 and later. If this is the case on your handheld, select Modem from the Preferences popup menu to configure an attached modem (**Figure 2.31**).

To set Modem preferences:

1. Choose a modem model from the Modem popup menu, along with the modem's baud rate (measured in bits per second, or bps) on the Speed popup menu.

2. Tap the Speaker popup menu to change the modem's volume when it dials.

3. Set the modem's flow control on the Flow Ctl popup menu. Flow control regulates the rate of incoming information. In general, leaving this set to Automatic should be fine in most cases.

4. If you require a specialized initialization string (a set of text commands that get sent to the modem when activated), write them in the String field. Refer to your modem's manual for information on how to use initialization strings. The modem settings available under the Modem popup include the strings required for each type and brand of modem.

5. Depending on the type of phone line you're using, tap on the TouchTone™ or Rotary buttons.

✔ Tip

- Most Springboard modems fill in the Modem or Connection information the first time they're connected to the Visor, so you may never need to enter these settings. However, it's good to know how to tweak the settings if necessary.

Figure 2.31 If you have a modem connected to your Visor, you can change its settings in this dialog box.

Figure 2.32 The Network preferences screen allows you to connect directly to an Internet service provider. Palm OS 3.3 and higher include the Connection popup menu.

Figure 2.33 Secret code? Not if you know how to read modem commands. Use the Network Log to troubleshoot your connections.

Setting Network Preferences

Attaching a modem to your Visor enables you to connect directly to an Internet Service Provider (ISP) (**Figure 2.32**).

To set up Network preferences:

1. Select Network from the Preferences popup menu.

2. Choose the name of your ISP under the Service popup menu. If yours is not listed, select New from the Service menu, or write ╱-N.

3. Write the name you use to connect in the User Name field.

4. Tap the dotted box next to Password to write your login password. If you leave this blank, you will be prompted for your password each time you connect.

5. If you're running Palm OS 3.3 or later, choose a connection mode from the Connection popup menu.

✔ Tip

■ The Palm OS keeps a log of network connections; select View Log from the Options menu (**Figure 2.33**).

To configure Network phone settings:

1. Tap the dotted box next to Phone to configure dialing options (**Figure 2.34**). In addition to the phone number required to dial, you can specify that a calling card be used, that a prefix be dialed (for example, dialing 9 to reach an outside line), or that call-waiting be disabled (if your phone package includes this; the signal tone generated by call-waiting services often breaks existing Net connections). Tap OK.

2. Tap the Details... button to continue with the setup (**Figure 2.35**). Depending on the service you use to connect to the Internet, choose PPP, SLIP, or CSLIP from the Connection type popup menu.

3. Use Idle timeout to specify when the network connection should be disconnected if there is no activity. The default Power Off setting ensures that an active connection continues until the unit shuts off—even if you switch between applications.

4. Use Query DNS (Domain Name System), to instruct your Internet application (such as an email client or Web browser) to ask your ISP's server to resolve domain names (addresses) on the Internet. If you uncheck this box, you will need to enter your primary and secondary DNS server addresses.

5. Check IP Address: Automatic to grab a random IP (Internet Protocol) address from your ISP, which identifies your machine on the Internet. If you have a fixed IP address, uncheck the box and enter it into the blanks that will appear below.

6. Finally, tap the Script... button to create a customized login script to facilitate connecting to your ISP's server. If you don't require one, leave the first line so that it reads "End."

Figure 2.34 Tapping the Phone field in the Network preferences screen displays several dialing options.

Figure 2.35 Choose the type of Internet connection, along with the action to take if the connection is idle.

Figure 2.36 Each program has its own icon, listed alphabetically on the Applications screen.

Figure 2.37 You can also view applications in a list format, and group them into categories.

Launching Applications

Now that you have all of your preferences set up, you can finally start using applications. (You've probably been using applications from the beginning, but I felt it was important to cover the preferences early.)

Unlike nearly all personal computers, a Visor has no hard drive or floppy disk to store its data—everything is held in RAM (random access memory), including third-party applications and their data (the built-in applications and the core Palm OS files are stored in separate read-only memory, or ROM). As a result, you technically never have to open or quit programs. All the applications are running concurrently, paused at the state where you last left them. Although I may refer to "launching" or "opening" applications throughout this book, Palm OS is actually only switching between them. (But "launching" sounds more exciting.)

To open an application:

1. Bring up the Applications screen by tapping the silkscreened Applications icon.

2. Tap a program's name or icon to launch it (**Figures 2.36** and **2.37**).

✔ Tips

■ If you have more programs than will fit onto a single screen, write the first letter of the program you want in the Graffiti area to make it visible.

■ Repeatedly tapping Applications switches between application categories (see "Categorizing Applications" later in this chapter).

Installing Applications

Many Visor owners get by just fine using the built-in applications. However, one of the platform's strengths is that there are thousands of third-party programs and utilities available to install. In most cases, you can download the software from the Web on your desktop computer, then install it onto your Visor.

To install applications using the Palm Install Tool (Windows):

1. Launch the Palm Install Tool either from the Windows Start menu, or by clicking the Install button from within Palm Desktop.

2. Click Add... to select the programs to install. Palm OS applications end with the extension .prc (no matter whether you use a PC or a Mac). You can also drag the program files from the Windows desktop to the Palm Install Tool window to add them to the list (**Figure 2.38**).

3. When you've added the programs you want to install, click Done.

4. Perform a HotSync to transfer the programs into the handheld's memory.

To install applications using the HotSync Manager (Macintosh):

1. Launch the HotSync Manager.

2. From the HotSync menu, choose Install, or press Command-I.

3. Click the Add to list button to locate the .prc file you want to add. You can also drag the files to the installation window from the Finder to add them to the list (**Figure 2.39**), or even just drag them to the Finder's HotSync Manager icon.

4. Perform a HotSync operation.

Figure 2.38 Under Windows, click the Add... button to prepare programs to be installed. Alternately, you can drag the files to the Palm Install Tool window.

Figure 2.39 The Macintosh installer looks different than its Windows cousin, but works much the same. Clicking the Application info button displays attributes of the selected file, such as creation date and version number.

Figure 2.40 My Little Buddy creates a floating toolbar that gives you access to application files, Palm Web sites, the Palm Desktop, and more.

Figure 2.41 DirectInstall shows up in the Windows Explorer contextual menu, flagging a file to be installed at the next HotSync.

Dropping a file onto Palm Buddy's desktop window installs it immediately.

Figure 2.42 Palm Buddy eliminates the need to install applications via HotSync on the Macintosh. Just drag and drop your .prc file onto Palm Buddy's window to immediately install it.

Other Installation Options

Although the Palm Install Tool is the main method of adding files to your handheld, other third-party programs feature streamlined methods of doing the job.

My Little Buddy (Windows)

On the Windows side, I've found My Little Buddy (http://www.precise-solutions. cix.co.uk/pilot.htm) to be an important fixture on my desktop. My Little Buddy is a floating toolbar that lets you quickly open Palm Desktop and the HotSync Manager, install batches of files, store Web URLs for easy access, and more (**Figure 2.40**).

DirectInstall (Windows)

Another nifty Windows installation helper is the near-invisible DirectInstall (http://www. rob.cybercomm.nl). Simply right-click a Palm data file or application, then select a Palm user from the Install on handheld popup menu (**Figure 2.41**). The file will be transferred at the next HotSync operation.

Palm Buddy (Macintosh)

One of my favorite Mac programs is Palm Buddy (http://perso.wanadoo.fr/fpillet/), which doesn't synchronize files but rather makes installing and backing them up a breeze (**Figure 2.42**). Palm Buddy maintains a live connection to the handheld, so you don't have to HotSync to install files: simply drag and drop any .prc file onto Palm Buddy's window. Be aware, though, that leaving Palm Buddy and the Visor actively connected will drain your batteries much quicker.

However, as of this writing, the program doesn't support USB, and therefore doesn't support the Visor. But it's worth mentioning, since hopefully by the time you read this Palm Buddy will be updated.

Categorizing Applications

Grouping all of your applications onto the same screen isn't always helpful. That's why the Palm OS lets you set up categories to help organize your programs.

To switch between views:

1. In Applications, choose Preferences... from the Options menu, or write ╱-R.

2. Choose either Icon or List from the View By popup menu.

To categorize applications:

1. In Applications, choose Category... from the App menu, or write ╱-Y.

2. You'll see a list of all installed applications. Tap a category name from the popup menu to the right of a program.

3. If you don't see the category you want, select Edit Categories... from the popup list to create a new category or edit an existing one (**Figure 2.43**).

To remember the last category:

1. All categories are shown if you switch to the Applications screen from another program. To keep the same category visible, choose Preferences... from the Options menu, or write ╱-R (**Figure 2.44**).

2. Mark the Remember Last Category box.

✔ Tip

■ Tapping the Applications button repeatedly scrolls through the categories, but you won't see everything: Unfiled programs don't appear. So, to take advantage of this switching view, be sure to file your unfiled programs.

Figure 2.43 Tap the popup menus at right to specify a program's category. New applications are set to Unfiled.

Figure 2.44 Viewing applications by category lets you organize them according to your preference. Tapping Remember Last Category prevents all applications from being viewed the next time you tap the Applications icon.

Figure 2.45 View your memory usage from within Applications by choosing Info... from the App menu.

Figure 2.46 The Visor's built-in applications cannot be deleted, so they don't appear in the list of files.

Memory Management

Palm data is teeny compared to data on a typical PC, but you can still get carried away and load your memory to maximum capacity.

To view the amount of free memory:

1. From the Applications screen, choose Info... from the App menu, or write ∕-I. Under Palm OS 3.5, you can tap the Info icon (**❶**) on the command bar.

2. The Size button displays memory usage in kilobytes (**Figure 2.45**); tap the Records button to view how many records are stored in each application; tap the Version button to see each program's version number. Tap Done when finished.

Deleting Applications

At some point you'll install a program that doesn't hold your attention, or maybe you'll just need to free up some memory to add more applications. Deleting the ones you don't want is a painless process.

To delete applications:

1. From within Applications, choose Delete from the App menu, or write ∕-D. Under Palm OS 3.5, you can also tap the Delete icon (🗑) on the command bar.

2. Choose the application you wish to remove, then tap the Delete button and confirm your choice (**Figure 2.46**).

✔ Tips

- You cannot delete the Palm OS's built-in applications; they are stored in ROM.

- When you delete an application, any data files associated with it are deleted as well.

- To quickly jump down to the program you want to delete, write the first letter of its name in the Graffiti area.

Storing Files on Springboard Modules

Some Springboard modules, such as Innogear's InnoPak/2V (http://www.innogear.com/), include memory for storing files, much like adding an extra hard disk to a computer. Although the Palm OS doesn't include a utility for transferring files, many modules include a simple utility like File Mover.

To transfer files to a Springboard module:

1. Launch File Mover (or similar). Tap the buttons at the upper-right corner to display the contents of the Visor or the Springboard module (**Figure 2.47**).

2. Check the applications or data files that you wish to transfer to the module.

3. Tap either the Copy button or the Move button; Move deletes the original from the Visor (unless it is copy-protected, like the built-in Palm OS applications). Or, tap the Delete... button to remove the marked files.

✔ Tips

- In File Mover, select All from the selection popup menu above the file list to see which files belong to which applications (**Figure 2.48**).

- Use the Sort options to not only sort the files, but display more information about them such as their file types.

- Don't remove the module when you're in the File Mover application, or when transferring files (I've learned the hard way).

- When a Springboard module with available memory is installed, the Info screen can display file information on the Visor or the module (**Figure 2.49**).

Figure 2.47 FileMover copies and moves files between the Visor and the Springboard module.

Figure 2.48 Listing All files displays applications and the files that belong to them.

Figure 2.49 See how much memory is available on the current Springboard module.

Replacing the Applications Application

The Applications screen does its job moderately well, but people with more than a handful of programs soon grew weary of scrolling. It wasn't long before an enterprising programmer built a way out of the old Applications box.

The result was Eric Kenslow's LaunchPad, one of those programs that make you want to say, "Why didn't they think of that sooner?" Currently, there are multiple variations of LaunchPad including Synergy Solutions' Launch 'Em (http://www.synsolutions.com/), and Bozidar Benc's Launcher III (http://www.benc.hr/).

Instead of one long scrolling field, these launchers provide a configurable tabbed interface, visual and numeric battery level display, and time and date display (**Figure 2.50**). They also hook into many features of the Palm OS such as Show/Hide Records, backlighting, Lock & Turn Off, and dragging programs to a trash icon to delete them.

Perhaps the best improvement is the ability to categorize applications by simply dragging their icons to a tab. Forget the endless popup menus in Applications' Category screen.

Figure 2.50 A familiar tabbed interface greets users of Launch 'Em, a replacement application launcher based on Eric Kenslow's LaunchPad utility.

✔ Tips

- Select the Always use option in the Preferences screen to make the launcher your default application screen. However, be sure to uncheck this option if you need to delete or update the launcher, or risk hitting an error requiring a soft reset.

- You still need to use the Applications program to view free memory and, depending on which launcher you use, delete files. You can either tap the Applications program icon (not the silkscreened icon) to go there, or you can select Apps/Memory (or equivalent) from the Pilot or Apps menu (again, depending on your choice of launching programs), which will take you to Applications.

Figure 2.51 Launch 'Em provides many more options for working with, and viewing, your applications.

- Launch 'Em includes an extra feature that allows you to hide individual tabs, so you can keep some programs and their data under at least one level of security (**Figure 2.51**).

Chapter 2

The Security Application

You're probably carrying around your most important information in a device no bigger than your hand. Although you're no doubt careful with your organizer, there's a half-decent chance that it may get swiped, or even left on top of your car as you're rushing off to work. The Palm OS's built-in security features provide a first line of defense in case your Visor is picked up by the wrong person.

The Security application controls whether or not records marked private—no matter which program they reside in—are either shown or hidden (**Figure 2.52**). Palm OS 3.5 enhances Security by adding a third option that masks private records. It also provides a means for changing the global security setting within individual programs, saving a trip to the Security application itself (**Figure 2.53**).

To set up a password:

1. Tap the dotted Password box, which should read Unassigned if this is your first time using Security.

2. Enter a password, then tap OK.

3. Reenter your password to verify it.

To change or delete a password:

1. Tap the dotted Password box, which should read Assigned.

2. Enter your current password.

3. Write a new password to change it; tap the Delete button if you want to not have an assigned password at all.

4. If you changed your password, reenter it to verify it.

Figure 2.52 Security controls whether records marked as Private throughout the Palm OS are shown or hidden (Palm OS 3.1 shown here).

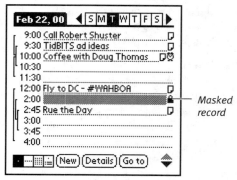

Masked record

Figure 2.53 Palm OS 3.5 adds the capability to mask private records instead of just hiding them.

THE SECURITY APPLICATION

48

Figure 2.54 If you want to see your data again, write your password in the blank provided.

Figure 2.55 If you've forgotten your password, your private records will be deleted until the next HotSync.

✔ Tip

■ You don't have to set up a password if you don't want to. Setting Security to hide or mask records without specifying a password still makes private records unreadable. You won't be asked to provide a password if you switch to Show Records.

To use the Lock & Turn Off feature:

1. In the Security application, tap the Lock & Turn Off... button. You will be prompted to verify your choice.

2. The next time you turn on your handheld, enter your password to access your data (**Figure 2.54**).

To access a forgotten password:

1. If you've forgotten your password, you can remove it, but at a price. Tap the Forgotten Password... button in the Security application; under Palm OS 3.5, tap the Password field, then tap the Lost Password button in the Password screen.

2. If you wish to proceed, tap Yes (**Figure 2.55**). The state of the Password field will revert to Unassigned.

✔ Tips

■ Even if you've marked your sensitive records as Private, that'll do you no good if you forget to hide them again. SafeHack (http://www.waterworld.com.hk/) automatically reverts the Private Records setting to Hide or Mask at shutdown.

■ Don't use easy passwords: birthdates, addresses, family members' names, and especially pet names. The best passwords are a combination of letters, numbers, and symbols. Unfortunately, the Palm OS fails to recognize the difference between upper- and lowercase letters.

Beaming Applications

All Visors possess the ability to send data between similar devices equipped with infrared hardware. In addition to sending records (such as addresses), you can transfer full applications.

To beam applications:

1. From the Applications screen, choose Beam... from the App menu, or write ╱-B. Under Palm OS 3.5, you can also tap the Beam icon (☎) from the command bar.

2. Select an application from the list that appears (**Figure 2.56**). Programs marked with a padlock symbol beside them cannot be beamed.

3. Aim your infrared port at the recipient's handheld and tap the Beam button.

To receive beamed applications:

1. Go to the Preferences application and make sure that Beam Receive is set to On in the General preferences screen.

2. Aim your infrared port at the sender's handheld and wait for them to initiate the transfer.

3. When the application has been beamed, choose to accept or deny the program.

Figure 2.56 Rather than transfer programs to a friend via your PC, beam them from the Applications screen.

BEAMING APPLICATIONS

Figure 2.57 Beam Box can beam just about anything, provided the recipient also has Beam Box installed (which you can beam to them if they don't!).

✔ Tips

- Palm asserts that infrared transfers can be achieved from a maximum distance of one meter (39.37 inches).

- Write the ShortCut ℛ.I (shortcut stroke, period, I) in any text field, which turns on Beam Receive in the General preferences for a single instance.

- Beaming records and applications is helpful, but out of the box you can't beam data (such as a BrainForest outline) or HackMaster hacks (see Chapter 8). Beam Box (http://www.inkverse.com/) allows you to beam nearly anything on your Visor, as long as the recipient also has Beam Box installed (**Figure 2.57**).

- If you don't have much free memory on your Visor, you may run into trouble trying to beam applications or records to another handheld. When you beam something, the Palm OS needs enough free memory to store a temporary copy of what you're beaming. So if you're trying to beam a large application and getting an out of memory error, you'll need to delete some files before you can send it. The good news is that if the recipient's handheld has plenty of free space on it, you can temporarily beam smaller files to her, delete them from your device, then get them back after you've transferred the larger file.

BEAMING APPLICATIONS

HotSync

The underlying approach to functionality in the Palm OS is almost more philosophical than practical: the handheld is not a computer in itself, but an extension of one's computing environment. It recognizes that people aren't going to abandon PCs in favor of PDAs, but rather use both tools to accomplish the greater task of organizing and managing one's information. For it is this goal, grasshopper, that leads to greater productivity, plus the justification to purchase yet another cool electronic gadget.

The key that unlocks this data convergence is the HotSync feature, the ability to synchronize data between the Visor and the PC—not just copy it from one box to the other. This is an important distinction, because it means both platforms will always have the most current information at your disposal.

HotSync Overview

Performing a HotSync operation is essentially a one-step procedure: push a button and it happens. You can do this when connected directly to your PC, or over a modem or network. However, knowing about what's going on in the background will help you deal with potential problems in the future.

How HotSync works

In normal copy operations, such as when you copy a file from a floppy disk to your hard drive, the PC's operating system checks to see if a similarly named file exists in the location you're copying to. If a match is found, it checks the modification dates of each file to determine which is newer, then throws up a dialog box requesting confirmation to continue (under some operating systems, this feature can be disabled). If the user clicks OK, the old file is overwritten. The problem here exists when both files have been separately modified; if so, the older data is wiped out (**Figure 3.1**).

In contrast, the Palm OS (by way of the HotSync Manager on the desktop) compares every record within a file like the Address Book database. If you make a change to different records on the handheld and the desktop, the changes appear on both platforms following a HotSync. If you make separate changes to the same record on each platform, both versions are retained, and you are notified of the duplication (**Figure 3.2**).

Standard file date comparison

Entire file copied   *New records deleted*

Figure 3.1 Most files on your PC are "synchronized" by comparing their modification dates and overwriting the older file—big trouble if both files have changed.

HotSync synchronization

New records added   *Each record compared*

Figure 3.2 HotSync synchronization compares each record within Palm database files, ensuring that you have up-to-date information on your Visor and on your PC.

Figure 3.3 Your data is stored on your PC's hard drive, in the user folder matching your Palm user name.

Table 3.1

User folder contents (Windows)	
FOLDER	**CONTENTS**
address	Address Book data
Backup	Nearly everything except data for the built-in applications. This includes program files, related database files, Doc text files, some preferences files, etc.
datebook	Date Book data
expense	Expense application data
Install	Program files to be installed at the next HotSync. See the Tip on this page for important information about this folder.
Mail	Email data
memopad	Memo Pad data
todo	To Do List data

Table 3.2

User folder contents (Macintosh)	
FOLDER	**CONTENTS**
user name	No funky truncation of the user name on the Mac—in my case, the folder is titled "Jeff Carlson." The file within, which is also the full user name, contains all of the built-in databases' data, plus the following:
Conduit Settings	Preferences for each conduit
Archived Files	Records deleted from the device, but stored on the desktop computer
Files to Install	Files to be transferred at the next HotSync
Backups	Everything else

Where HotSync stores your data

A HotSync operation copies data from the handheld to the PC and vice-versa, which means that information has to live on your hard drive—but where?

When you install the Palm Desktop software, enter your name (or whatever name you wish to use) at the Create User Account screen. This name becomes the name of the Visor.

You'll find a new folder on your hard drive named "Palm" or "Handspring" (unless you specified a different location and folder name during setup). Within that folder is a folder that closely matches your User Name; on my PC, for example, the files are located in the folder "CarlsoJ" (**Figure 3.3**), though on my Mac it comes up as "Jeff Carlson." The information in **Table 3.1** and **Table 3.2** detail the folder structure on each platform.

✔ Tips

■ When you run the Palm Install Tool, the programs you choose are stored in the Install folder within your user folder. However, under Windows you can't just toss .prc files there and expect them to be transferred at the next HotSync. The HotSync Manager needs to be told that the Install folder is "active" before it will copy the files located within. Running the Install program once toggles this setting—so, after you install one program using the Palm Install Tool, switch to the Windows desktop to copy new program files to the folder in bulk.

■ The Backup(s) folder stores all programs you've installed on your Visor—even ones you've deleted from the handheld. So, if the folder size seems impossibly large, don't be alarmed.

■ It's a good—no, great—idea to regularly make backups of your user folder.

Configuring HotSync Manager

The HotSync Manager isn't often seen, but it does quite a bit of work behind the scenes to ensure that your data is transferring properly. Its primary task is to monitor the port reserved for the HotSync cradle so it can act when the handheld signals a sync operation.

To access the HotSync Manager under Windows:

From within Palm Desktop, choose Setup... from the HotSync menu. You can also click the HotSync icon on the Taskbar, then select Setup... from the popup menu (**Figure 3.4**).

To access the HotSync Manager under Mac OS:

Launch HotSync Manager from the Palm folder on your hard disk, or choose Setup... from the HotSync® (*active user name*) sub-menu of the Instant Palm Desktop menu (next to the Applications menu in the upper-right corner of your screen; **Figure 3.5**).

To enable HotSync port monitoring:

Make sure the cable attached to your HotSync cradle is connected to one of your PC's USB or serial ports.

Access the HotSync Manager as described above and go to the Setup... screen. Under Windows, you have three options for enabling port monitoring (**Figure 3.6**):

- **Always available.** Activates HotSync Manager when you start your computer.

- **Available only when Palm Desktop is running.** Automatically enables and disables port monitoring when you use Palm Desktop.

Figure 3.4 The HotSync icon on the Windows Taskbar offers a quick way to configure HotSync settings.

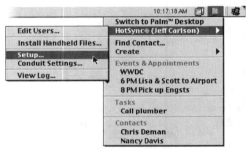

Figure 3.5 The Mac Palm Desktop software includes the Instant Palm Desktop menu, where you can access HotSync Manager commands.

Figure 3.6 Choose when HotSync Manager will be active to avoid port conflicts with other devices.

CONFIGURING HOTSYNC MANAGER

Figure 3.7 Enable HotSync port monitoring from the HotSync Controls tab on the Macintosh.

Figure 3.8 Schedule your HotSync operations at a more convenient hour with AutoSync.

◆ **Manual.** Starts up port monitoring at your discretion, freeing up the port for other uses when you're not using HotSync.

Under the Mac OS, you can leave HotSync running all the time by selecting Enable HotSync software at system startup under HotSync Options, or you can choose the Enabled or Disabled radio buttons at the top of the screen (**Figure 3.7**).

✔ Tips

■ Do you find yourself forgetting to Hot-Sync during the course of your busy day? Let the Visor do the work for you: Auto-Sync (http://www.rgps.com/AutoSync. html) can automatically HotSync your handheld according to one or two schedules. Be sure to have your computer running and the Visor in its cradle, then let it go to work (**Figure 3.8**).

■ There never seem to be enough ports on a computer. Older PowerBooks, for example, have only one port that shares duties with printers, external modems, and LocalTalk network connections. If you don't want to switch cables each time you need to print or perform a HotSync, consider buying an inexpensive hub that connects multiple devices.

■ If you use a Macintosh with a serial port (as opposed to newer machines with USB), make sure that AppleTalk is disabled before attempting to perform a HotSync: in the Chooser, select the AppleTalk Inactive radio button. Apple-Talk can hog the serial port and not allow other applications, like HotSync Manager, to use it. The same is often true of fax software.

Setting up Conduits

Each of the built-in applications, as well as the Palm OS and the program installer, has its own conduit, a software translator that specifies how records should be compared and copied between platforms. In addition, many third-party applications, such as AvantoGo and HourzPro, include their own conduits for manipulating their specific data.

To configure conduits:

1. Choose Custom... from the HotSync menu in Windows. In the Mac OS, launch the HotSync Manager and choose Conduit Settings from the HotSync menu, or press Command-H.

2. Highlight the conduit you wish to edit, then click the Change... (Windows) or Conduit Settings (Mac) button. Double-clicking a conduit also lets you modify its settings (**Figure 3.9**).

3. Choose an action for that conduit (**Figure 3.10** and **Table 3.3**). Click the Set as default checkbox (Windows) or the Make Default button (Mac) to make the new setting permanent each time you do a HotSync. Click OK.

Under Windows, clicking the Default button in the Custom dialog box restores the conduit settings to the last default state.

✔ Tip

■ Many people use PIMs such as Microsoft Outlook and Symantec's ACT! instead of Palm Desktop. In addition to the Outlook conduits included with the Visor software, a variety of third-party applications, like Desktop to Go (http://www.dataviz.com/) and PocketMirror (http://www.chapura.com/), replace the built-in conduits with ones that synchronize data with your favorite desktop PIM.

Figure 3.9 Conduits control the way each program's data is handled during a HotSync.

Figure 3.10 Multiple HotSync actions let you override the default synchronization settings.

Table 3.3

HotSync conduit actions

SETTING	ACTION
Synchronize the files	All records are compared individually; newer records overwrite older records.
Desktop overwrites handheld	Individual records are not compared; entire desktop file replaces handheld file.
Handheld overwrites desktop	Individual records are not compared; entire handheld file replaces desktop file.
Do nothing	Records are skipped; no action is taken.

The Two Faces of HotSync

Palm OS 3.1 and earlier assumed two approaches to HotSyncing data: Local Sync, which used the device's serial port to interface with a HotSync cradle or cable, and Modem Sync, for synchronizing over a modem connection (**Figure 3.11**). Tapping one of the two buttons would initiate that type of HotSync. (Pressing the physical button on the HotSync cradle would automatically trigger the correct connection.)

Palm OS 3.3 acknowledged that there are more ways to HotSync data, so Palm added Connections, an option in the Preferences application that lets you create different configurations based on the connection type (see Chapter 2 for more on the Connections screen). Now, Visors running Palm OS 3.3 or later still have the option to select between Local and Modem synchronization, but a connection popup menu beneath the single HotSync button lets you specify which type of local or modem connection to use (**Figure 3.12**). This also affords the flexibility of specifying your own devices, like wireless modems. To edit connection configurations from within HotSync, choose Connection Setup... from the Options menu, or write ∕-S.

Given the inevitable march of progress, why is this important? Visors store the operating system in standard read-only memory (ROM); since Visors can't be flash-upgraded (meaning an update that replaces a writeable version of the ROM), these devices can't be upgraded from earlier versions—you need to purchase a more recent model to get the new HotSync version. This doesn't mean they're crippled in any way, so don't think you need to ditch your Visor anytime soon. There are just two slightly different approaches to accomplishing the same task.

Figure 3.11 HotSync under Palm OS 3.1 assumes there are only two ways to synchronize your data.

Connection popup menu

Figure 3.12 Palm OS 3.3 and later includes a popup menu to specify different connection types.

Local HotSync

Most of your HotSync actions fall into the category of Local HotSync, in which the handheld and PC are connected directly by either a serial cable or cradle, or via infrared.

To set up a Local HotSync:

1. Choose Setup... from the HotSync menu. On the Macintosh, you can also press Command-K.

2. Click the Local tab (Windows, **Figure 3.13**) or the Serial Port Settings tab (Mac).

3. From the Serial Port popup menu, specify the COM port to which your HotSync cable or cradle is connected.

4. Specify the speed of the connection from the Speed popup menu. Click OK, or close the window.

5. From the Windows Taskbar popup menu, specify that Local HotSync monitoring should be activated by clicking the name; a checkmark appears. On the Macintosh, this information is available in the Serial Port Settings window.

✔ Tip

■ If you're having trouble maintaining a connection, reduce the speed setting in the Setup dialog box.

To perform a Local HotSync:

1. Place your Visor in the cradle.

2. Push the HotSync button on the front, or press the button in the HotSync application on the Visor. A short series of tones indicates that a connection is made.

3. A window appears on the desktop indicating the HotSync progression. A similar screen also appears on the handheld (**Figure 3.14**). Another set of tones indicates when the synchronization is done.

Figure 3.13 Use the Local tab to specify which port your HotSync cradle is connected to.

Figure 3.14 Pressing the HotSync button on the cradle activates the HotSync; the progression is visible on both the handheld and the PC.

Figure 3.15 If your laptop or desktop PC is equipped with an infrared port, you can set your preferences to recognize the handheld and perform a HotSync.

Figure 3.16 Use the HotSync application on the Palm to initiate an infrared HotSync operation.

Infrared HotSync

Knowing a good opportunity when it zaps them in the head, the engineers at Palm and Handspring incorporated infrared HotSync capabilities into the Palm OS. The system's IR communication is built upon the IrCOMM protocol. If you're using a Macintosh Power-Book G3 Series or later, or a PC laptop running Windows 98 or later, IrCOMM support should be built in.

To set up infrared HotSync (Mac):

1. Open the HotSync Manager, and switch to the Serial Port Settings tab.

2. Choose Infrared from the Port popup menu under Local Setup.

To set up infrared HotSync (Win):

1. Open the Infrared Monitor from the Settings folder and click the Options tab.

2. Check the box labeled Enable infrared communication on, and choose the COM port (usually COM4 or COM5) used by the infrared port (**Figure 3.15**).

3. In the HotSync Manager, choose the COM port as the Local source.

To perform an infrared HotSync:

1. Launch the HotSync application on the Visor, and make sure that IR to a PC/Handheld is selected from the Connection popup menu.

2. Tap the large HotSync button to begin (**Figure 3.16**).

✔ Tip

- Visors running Palm OS versions earlier than 3.5 need the SerIrCommLib.prc file from Palm (http://www.palm.com/support/downloads/irenhanc.html), or the third-party program IRLink (http://www.iscomplete.com/).

Modem HotSync

Make sure you have disabled any programs on your PC (such as fax software) that may cause installation headaches.

To set up a Modem HotSync on your computer:

1. Choose Setup... from the HotSync menu to bring up the Setup dialog box. On the Mac, you can also press Command-K.

2. Click the Modem tab (Windows, **Figure 3.17**) or the Serial Port Settings tab (Mac).

3. From the Serial Port popup menu, specify the COM or serial port to which your modem is connected.

4. Specify the speed of the connection from the Speed popup menu. Click OK, or close the window.

5. From the Taskbar popup menu, specify that Modem HotSync monitoring should be activated by clicking the name; a checkmark appears. On the Macintosh, this information is available in the Serial Port Settings tab—click the Modem Setup or Both Setups radio button (**Figure 3.18**).

To set up a Modem HotSync on your Palm device:

1. Launch the HotSync application.

2. Choose Conduit Setup... from the Options menu, or write ╱-D.

3. Choose which conduits should be run by marking the checkboxes to the left of each program's name (**Figure 3.19**). Tap OK.

4. If you haven't set up your Modem preferences, go to the Prefs application and select Connection (or Modem) from the popup menu in the upper-right corner (see Chapter 2).

Figure 3.17 As with a Local HotSync, specify your modem's COM port and speed, as well as the model.

Figure 3.18 The Modem Setup information on the Macintosh shares the same screen as the Local Setup.

Figure 3.19 To save some connection time, mark only the conduits you want to have synchronized.

Figure 3.20 With everything configured, simply tap the HotSync button.

Figure 3.21 Modem Sync looks slightly different in Palm OS versions prior to 3.3, but accomplishes the same task. Tap the Modem Sync button.

To perform a Modem HotSync:

1. Go to the main HotSync screen. If you're running Palm OS 3.3 or later, tap the Modem button.

2. Tap the dotted Enter Phone # box (under the Modem Sync icon; or, under the Connection popup menu in Palm OS 3.3 or later) to specify a phone number.

3. Attach a modem (connected to a phone line, of course) to your handheld (see Chapter 10).

4. If you're using a modem with a HotSync button on the case, push it to initiate the HotSync (skip the next step). If not, launch the HotSync application on the handheld.

5. Tap the main HotSync button (**Figure 3.20**), or the Modem Sync icon in Visors running Palm OS 3.1 (**Figure 3.21**). You should hear the startup tones.

6. When the HotSync is complete, you'll hear the tones signaling the end, and the connection will terminate.

LANSync/Network HotSync

Network HotSync extends your range and flexibility by providing a method to synchronize your data from any computer on your PC network—whether it's using someone else's HotSync cradle down the hall or several states away. (Network HotSync isn't available for Macintosh computers.) If your network has dial-in remote access, you can also connect using a compatible modem.

To set up Network HotSync:

1. Launch the HotSync application.

2. Depending on which mode you're in, pressing the HotSync icon (or the Local Sync or Modem Sync icon for Visors running Palm OS 3.1) will attempt to connect directly to the PC attached to the current HotSync cradle, or to your PC out on the network. If you're dialing-in to a modem that acts as the gateway for a network, choose Modem Sync Prefs... from the Options menu, or write ✓-O. Tap either the Network or Direct to modem button to specify the Modem Sync action (**Figure 3.22**).

   If you're connected directly to the network, choose LANSync Prefs... from the Options menu, or write ✓-L. Choose between LANSync and Local HotSync (**Figure 3.23**).

3. Choose Primary PC Setup... from the Options menu, or write ✓-P. In most cases, you shouldn't have to change this information, since it's downloaded from your PC when you perform a HotSync.

4. On your PC, bring up the HotSync settings by choosing Setup... from either the HotSync menu within Palm Desktop or from the popup menu on the Taskbar.

Figure 3.22 The Modem Sync Preferences dialog box lets you choose between a direct dial-up connection or a dial-up network connection.

Figure 3.23 By choosing LANSync or Local HotSync, you dictate the action of the main screen's Local Sync icon.

Figure 3.24 The Network tab in the HotSync Setup screen sets up your PC for LAN synchronization.

Figure 3.25 Dial up your network by tapping the Modem button, then the HotSync button.

5. Tap the Network tab, then place a checkmark next to the users who will have access to your machine (**Figure 3.24**).

6. If you need to adjust the TCP/IP configuration, click the TCP/IP Settings... button. Otherwise, click OK.

To perform a Network HotSync:

◆ If the computer you're connecting from is on the same local area network (LAN) or wide area network (WAN), and you've set the LANSync preferences to LANSync, tap the Local button, then tap the HotSync icon to connect. Under Palm OS 3.1, tap the Local Sync button.

◆ If you need to dial in via modem to connect to your network, and you've set the Modem Sync preferences to Network, tap the Modem button, then tap the single HotSync button. Under Palm OS 3.1, tap the Modem Sync icon to dial the number and establish a connection (**Figure 3.25**). Once connected, the HotSync operation should proceed normally.

LANSYNC/NETWORK HOTSYNC

Viewing the HotSync Log

The details of each of the last ten HotSyncs are stored in a text file on your computer. Although the information usually isn't important, the HotSync Log is the first place to turn to if you're having HotSync problems (fortunately, most error messages are written in understandable English; **Figure 3.26**).

To view the HotSync Log:

◆ **Windows:** Choose View Log... from the HotSync menu within Palm Desktop, or from the HotSync popup menu located on the Taskbar (**Figure 3.27**).

◆ **Mac OS:** Choose Log... from the HotSync menu within the HotSync Manager.

◆ **Palm OS:** Tap the Log button on the main HotSync screen. However, don't get angry with me for suggesting it, since the Palm HotSync Log gives only the most basic of information (like the scintillating "OK Date Book").

◆ Alternately, open the log file itself with a word processor or text editor. You'll find the log in your user folder.

✔ Tip

■ To record a detailed log on the Macintosh (instead of the minimal log that's stored on the handheld), mark the Show more detail in HotSync log checkbox at the bottom of the HotSync Controls screen.

```
HotSync started 09/03/01 02:12:12
  - Installed file:
C:\Palm\CarlsoJ\Install\giraffe.prc
OK Install
OK Mail
OK Date Book
OK Address Book
OK To Do List
OK Memo Pad
OK Expense
ZoskSync Conduit 2.3.3 Begin:
  ZoskSync: No reports were transferred
from the handheld.
OK ZoskSync Conduit End
OK System
```

Figure 3.26 A typical HotSync Log looks like this, with plain-English comments to indicate the steps taken.

Figure 3.27 The HotSync Log can be viewed from within Palm Desktop (Windows and Mac versions shown here), or you can use a word processor or text editor to read the file from your hard drive.

Figure 3.28 In the event of a hard reset, your first HotSync should be set so that the desktop information overwrites the handheld's data.

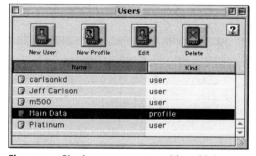

Figure 3.29 Sharing one computer with multiple Visors entails creating a new user account for each person. The Macintosh screen is shown here.

Multiple HotSync Options

The majority of owners use their handhelds on an individual basis: one Visor, one PC. However, there are some cases where you may want to synchronize one device with multiple machines, or several organizers on the same machine.

Since HotSync *synchronizes* your data, not overwrites it, the information on each machine should remain updated without any special work on your part. Simply HotSync as you normally would; the desktop software keeps track of multiple users.

However, if you should happen to lose your handheld's data (for example, due to a hard reset), customize your first HotSync as described here.

To set up a first HotSync on an empty Visor:

1. On your PC, choose Custom... from the HotSync popup menu on the Taskbar, or from the HotSync menu in the Palm Desktop application.

2. Specify Desktop overwrites handheld for all of the conduits (**Figure 3.28**). Press OK.

3. Perform a HotSync. Your data on the Visor should be in the state it was before it was lost.

4. Before you HotSync again, change the conduit settings back to Synchronize.

To set up a new user:

1. In Palm Desktop, select Edit Users from the User submenu of the HotSync menu (Mac), or select Users from the Tools menu (Windows).

2. Click the New (Windows) or New User (Mac) button (**Figure 3.29**) and type a name. Click OK.

MULTIPLE HOTSYNC OPTIONS

File Link

Frequently updating memos or addresses is made simple for Windows users. Using the File Link feature, you can create a Windows file that is in plain text (.txt), comma separated (.csv), or Palm archive format that gets transferred to the handheld according to scheduled intervals (**Figure 3.30**).

To create a File Link:

1. Prepare the file you wish to link. For example, let's say everyone who accesses my PC needs each week's movie box office listing. Save it as either straight text, comma-separated, or as a Memo Pad archive (see later in this chapter for details). If you're saving a list of addresses (say, the month's new clients), save the file as either comma-separated or as an Address Book archive.

2. Choose File Link... from the HotSync menu in Palm Desktop, or the HotSync popup menu on the Taskbar.

3. Select a user name, make sure the Create a new link radio button is activated, and click the Next button.

4. Choose either Memo Pad or Address Book from the Application name popup menu.

5. If you know the path to your file, type it into the File path field. Otherwise, click the Browse... button to locate it.

6. Linked file data is stored in its own category to avoid conflicts with your other data. Enter a name in the Category name field (**Figure 3.31**), and click Next.

7. A dialog box confirming your link settings appears. By default, the file will be queued for HotSync whenever it changes. If this is okay, click the Done button.

Figure 3.30 Set up a File Link that points to a file filled with important information that changes often.

Figure 3.31 Choose the application, file path, and specify a category name to set up a File Link.

Figure 3.32 You can set the frequency at which the linked file is transferred to the handheld.

Figure 3.33 If you want to put your File Link into hibernation for a while, choose to keep the category and records, or just the category, for later.

To schedule a File Link update:

1. If you want to specify other options (such as daily, weekly, or monthly updates), click the Update Frequency... button on the Confirm your Link Settings dialog.

2. Specify the interval for how often the category should be updated (**Figure 3.32**).

   If you know the file isn't going to change for a while, mark the checkbox next to Disable the link temporarily but maintain the settings.

3. Click OK to exit the Update Frequency dialog box, then click the Done button.

To remove a File Link:

1. Choose File Link... from the HotSync menu in Palm Desktop, or the HotSync popup menu on the Taskbar.

2. Choose a user name, and select the option marked Modify or remove an existing link. Click the Next button.

3. Highlight the link you wish to delete and click the Remove... button. The Remove Link dialog box appears.

4. Choose how you'd like to handle your existing linked data (**Figure 3.33**).

5. Click OK.

✔ Tip

■ Although it may look like something's gone wrong, don't be surprised if, after you've set up a link, the category you set up appears to be empty. The linked data won't get copied to Palm Desktop until you perform a HotSync.

■ Unfortunately, File Link is not available on the Macintosh.

FILE LINK

Working with Archived Records

When you delete a record from the handheld or the Palm Desktop, you're given the option to save it on your PC by marking the Archive deleted program item(s) at next HotSync checkbox (**Figure 3.34**). This is a great feature if you've accidentally deleted something, or you need to free up some memory on your handheld, but don't want to lose the information permanently. But where does it go? And how do you get it back?

Each of the built-in applications creates an archive file (such as an Address Book archive (.aba) or Date Book archive (.dba)) for each category that contains deleted records. Those files are stored in each application's folder, although recent deleted items won't show up until you perform a HotSync (**Figure 3.35**).

To restore archived records:

1. In Palm Desktop, go to the Palm application module you want to restore records from (such as the Memo Pad). Choose Open Archive... from the File menu.

2. In the Open Archive dialog box, highlight the archive file named after the category you're looking for (such as "Personal.mpa"), and click the Open button.

   Your deleted records are now visible in the main window. You'll see the name of the file, followed by "(Archive)" in the window's title bar; there's also a scroll icon at the lower-right (**Figure 3.36**).

3. Highlight the records you want to restore, and choose Copy from the Edit menu (or press Control/Command-C).

4. Switch back to your active Palm records by choosing Open Current from the File menu.

Figure 3.34 You may have seen this dialog dozens of times...but do you know where the data actually goes? If you mark the checkbox, you can retrieve deleted records from your PC's hard drive at any time.

Figure 3.35 Archives are named according to the deleted records' categories.

Figure 3.36 Opening an archive file is straightforward, but the records are displayed in the main window, which can be confusing if you're not paying attention. Look to the title bar and the icon in the lower-right to signal that an archive is currently active.

Figure 3.37 You don't have to limit yourself to using archives for resurrecting deleted data. Export selected records, or your entire set of addresses, to-do items, and memos into archive format.

Figure 3.38 Records can be imported from tab-delimited files, in addition to Palm's archive formats.

5. Choose Paste from the Edit menu, or press Control/Command-V to paste the restored records.

6. Perform a HotSync to restore the data to your Visor.

You can also use the archive format to create customized archives, rather than just files containing deleted records. This can be useful if you need to email a batch of addresses to another Visor owner, for example.

To export archive files in Palm Desktop:

1. Go to the Palm application module you wish to export. If you want to export only certain records, highlight them.

2. Choose Export... from the File menu. In the Export To File dialog box, choose Currently selected records if you're not exporting the entire contents of the application. Give the file a unique file name, then click the Export button (**Figure 3.37**).

Note that if you have private records hidden, you will need to choose Show private records from the View menu before exporting them.

To import archive files in Palm Desktop:

1. Go to the Palm application module you wish to import.

2. Choose Import... from the File menu. In the Import dialog box, highlight a file and click Open.

✔ Tips

- You can also import records in text-only and comma-delimited file formats (**Figure 3.38**).

- To change the category for many records at once: export them, switch to the new category, then import them back in.

WORKING WITH ARCHIVED RECORDS

Creating HotSync Profiles

Profiles allow you to set up a group of master records that can be transferred to new Palm devices. For example, you can set up a profile containing your company's important meetings to be copied to each person's Visor. However, the profile erases any existing data, so you can only copy a profile to a brand new or empty device.

To create a HotSync profile:

1. Windows: In Palm Desktop, select Users... from the Tools menu.

   Macintosh: In Palm Desktop, go to the HotSync menu and select Edit Users from the User submenu.

2. Windows: In the Users dialog box that appears, click the Profiles... button to view a list of profiles. Click the New... button (**Figure 3.39**).

   Macintosh: Profiles are marked in the Users window with a different icon (**Figure 3.40**). Click New Profile.

3. Windows: Highlight the name of your new profile and click OK.

   Macintosh: After your profile is created, click the close box in the upper left corner, or press Command-W.

4. Stock your profile with the information that you want to appear on every Palm device you copy it to. Enter the data by hand, or switch between the profile and a user account to copy and paste records.

✔ Tip

■ To preserve your existing categories when copying records to the profile, first set up the category names in your new profile. Then, in your user account, view by category and copy the records you want. Switch to the profile, view the similarly named category, and paste the records.

Figure 3.39 In the Profiles screen, you can toggle between the Users and the Profiles lists.

Figure 3.40 On the Mac, profiles are displayed using a separate icon. Click the Edit button to rename them.

Figure 3.41 TrueSync synchronizes your handheld data with both Palm Desktop (or the PIM of your choice) and Yahoo's Web-based calendar.

The Really Expensive Calculator

It may seem odd to use the Web to track your schedule, since that's what your Visor is for (which doesn't need Internet access). Isn't this a step backward?

Rather, it's more like having the option to step to the side when needed. When I was traveling in Britain recently, the only electronic gadget I took with me was my handheld. Like any good geek, I'd stored trip notes, emergency phone numbers, and a host of other important information on my convenient organizer. Unfortunately, while sitting at the train station in Chepstowe, I replaced the batteries, fumbled the job, and lost my data! Normally, this would be no big deal, but my laptop was thousands of miles away.

If I had put my data online, I could have connected the handheld to a PC at an Internet café later in Windermere (I was smart enough to carry a HotSync cable, apparently), then transferred my data back to the handheld. Instead, I carried around a very swanky calculator for two weeks.

Synchronizing with Web-Based Organizers

A handheld organizer is intended to be an extension of your personal data, but just how extended do you want to be? Several Web services have appeared in recent years that let you store your calendar and contacts online. The idea is that you can check your schedule from any place with a Web connection: a client's office, Kinko's, an Internet café, or even some other far-flung destination.

Most of the services available now are free, and can store your addresses, to do items, and memos as well as calendar items. I'm using Yahoo!'s service (http://calendar.yahoo.com/) as an example; others include MyPalm (http://www.palm.net/) and IntelliSync (http://www.intellisync.com/). As Web calendars have become more sophisticated, more features are now available, such as making a public version available to friends or the general public, online chat forums, and the like. Be sure to read the terms of agreement when you sign up to ensure that the company will safeguard the integrity of your data.

To set up a Yahoo! Web calendar:

1. If you don't already have a personal account set up, go to http://calendar.yahoo.com/ to set one up. It takes only a few minutes to get started.

2. Make sure you have a backup of your Palm data for safekeeping, then download and install the TrueSync software (currently only for Windows).

3. HotSync the device (**Figure 3.41**).

To update the Web calendar:

1. Use the forms provided on the Web page to create or edit appointments, addresses, and other information (**Figure 3.42**).

2. With the TrueSync software running (an icon appears in the Windows Taskbar), HotSync your device. Both sets of data will be the same when the synchronization is finished (**Figure 3.43**).

✔ Tip

■ The MyPalm synchronization software currently doesn't recognize user names with spaces, so it may report that your data is not available to sync. One option is to wipe your Visor, give it a new name, and start over; however, I have several programs that use registration codes based on my user name. Palm has posted something of a workaround while their engineers are working on the problem. Go to http://www.palm.net/Corporate/support.jsp and do a search for incident number 010328-0125.

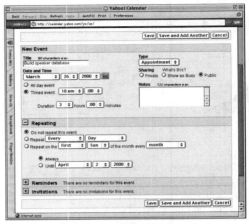

Figure 3.42 The advantage of a Web-based calendar is that you can add appointments from any computer connected to the Web.

Figure 3.43 After HotSync, the handheld and Web versions contain the same appointments.

DATE BOOK

My mother called me at college one night to see how things were going. After updating her on my classes, friends, and the usual local intrigue, I inquired what was new with her. "Not much," she replied. "We just finished my birthday cake."

Oops. So, my brain isn't hardwired for dates and holidays—that doesn't mean I have to forever miss important events and appointments. Although Mom was good-humored about my chronological ineptitude, it made me realize that I needed more than just the rusting calendar in my head.

Now several years later, I use the Visor's Date Book to store meetings, social occasions, and holidays, confident that they're quickly available at hand. Better yet, Visors also include Date Book+, which makes up for many of the original program's shortcomings. (However, even though Date Book+ is the default calendar on most Visors, I'll begin by covering the shared features of Date Book.)

Plus, unlike the calendar that hangs in my kitchen, Date Book can remind me of events before they happen, not after. My mom should be proud.

Setting Preferences and Display Options

The 160 by 160 pixel screen on Visors can display 25,600 pixels, which sounds like a lot until you consider that the minimum PC screen resolution today is 640 by 480 pixels (or a total of 307,200 pixels). It's easy to see why every effort has been made to keep the Visor's small screen uncluttered yet understandable. Date Book displays time in daily, weekly, and monthly views. The Agenda view, introduced in Palm OS 3.5, displays a day's events with tasks from the To Do List (**Figure 4.1**).

Changing some of the display options allows you to specify how dense or sparse your calendar will appear.

To set Date Book preferences:

1. Choose Preferences... from the Options menu.

2. If you've ever wished you could set your own hours, here's your chance. Select the Start Time and End Time by tapping the arrows to the right of the time boxes (**Figure 4.2**).

3. The Preferences dialog box also contains settings for Date Book's alarm. Checking Alarm Preset specifies that each new event includes an alarm, which will go off according to the number of minutes you specify.

4. You can also specify which sound the alarm will use, how often it plays when the alarm goes off, and at what interval it will play until you dismiss it.

5. Tap OK to return to the Date Book views.

Figure 4.1 The Date Book displays your time in (from top) daily, weekly, and monthly views. The Agenda view (bottom), introduced in Palm OS 3.5, shows tasks as well.

Figure 4.2 Most people choose regular business hours, but for some of us that means all day long, as shown here. Checking the Alarm Preset box adds an alarm to each new event you create.

Figure 4.3 Date Book's Day view makes the best of its limited screen real estate, displaying elements such as time bars and icons while hiding unused time lines.

Figure 4.4 You can control the degree of clutter in the day and month views. I prefer to see everything.

Figure 4.5 Choose from three fonts to display the Day view records (this example uses the largest font).

Day View

Whenever you access the Date Book, either by tapping its icon from the Applications screen or by pressing the physical Date Book button at the lower-left of your Visor, you are presented with the Day view. From the other Date Book views, you can also tap the first box (containing one dot) in the lower-left corner of the screen. This is where you enter and edit events, and generally manage your schedule (**Figure 4.3**).

Day view features

- ◆ Events of the day appear on the dotted lines beside their allotted times, which adjust to conform to your schedule (so, a meeting ending at 9:45, for example, is marked as such, instead of displaying somewhere before 10:00). If there isn't enough space on the screen to view all your events, the Date Book removes any unused lines. To disable this feature, de-select Compress Day View in the Display Options dialog box (**Figure 4.4**).

- ◆ If you select Show Time Bars in the Display Options dialog box, the black brackets at left will indicate an event's time span—a handy way to see if you've scheduled overlapping events.

- ◆ Tap the days of the week buttons at the top of the screen to switch days. Tapping the arrows on either side of the buttons moves you forward or backward in weekly increments.

- ◆ The icons at right signify that an event contains a note (⬚), an alarm (⬚), or that it is a repeating event (⬚).

- ◆ You can also specify which font is used to display event text (**Figure 4.5**). Select Font from the Options menu (or write ╱-F) and choose from three styles.

✔ Tips

- The Day view provides a fine overview of the day, but doesn't tell you what time it is now. Tap the date tab in the upper-left corner to briefly display the current time (**Figure 4.6**). This works in each Date Book view except for the Agenda view, which shows the time by default.

  However, tapping the title bar under Palm OS 3.5 brings up the program's menus, so although the time appears, it's quickly obscured by the menu. Instead, tap and hold to view the time, then move your stylus off the tab (without lifting the stylus) to return to normal without engaging the menu.

- For those times when manipulating the stylus is inconvenient, or just to save time, press the Date Book button on the case to switch between views.

- In school, I knew a kid who (for whatever irrational reason) always hated those blue horizontal lines on the notebook paper we had to use. If he has a Visor now, I'm sure he'll be happy to learn that he can get rid of the Day view's dotted lines. Set the Start Time and End Time to the same hour, and only the existing events will be displayed (**Figure 4.7**).

- On color devices such as the Visor Prism, red time bars indicate time conflicts between appointments (**Figure 4.8**).

Figure 4.6 What time is it? Tap the tab in the upper-left corner to view the current time.

Figure 4.7 Setting the Start Time and End Time to the same hour displays only the lines that contain events.

Conflict in red

Figure 4.8 A subtle but helpful touch on color devices is the red time bar indicating conflicting appointments.

DAY VIEW

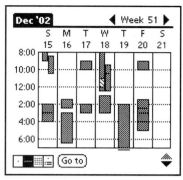

Figure 4.9 The Week view isn't necessarily a weak view: time blocks show how busy your week is, with overlapping events shown as thin bars.

Figure 4.10 Deciphering the identity of a time block is easy—tapping one brings up its description at the top.

Week View

Viewing an entire day's schedule is helpful, but I often want to know what's coming up during the week without having to switch between multiple day views. To get an idea of my schedule's density, I display the Week view by tapping the second box (containing a line of four dots) in the lower-left corner.

Week view features

◆ Events in the Week view are represented by gray bars that span vertically across the displayed hours. If the appointments overlap, the bars become narrower and sit side-by-side on the week's grid. If you have several items happening at once, subsequent events are displayed with a diagonal pattern (**Figure 4.9**).

◆ To see what a particular bar indicates, tap it once to bring up a floating window at the top of the screen containing the description you entered in the Day view, and its specific time span (**Figure 4.10**).

◆ Tapping the arrows in the upper-right corner of the screen move you forward or backward one week, indicating the week's number in the year. Pressing the up or down button on the device case also shifts between weeks.

◆ Tapping the weekday abbreviation at the top of the screen switches to the Day view for that day. The current day is in bold.

◆ Unlike the Day view, the week grid does not compress to fit all events onto one screen. Items appearing before or after the visible 11-hour period are indicated by a solid horizontal line appearing above or below the day's column. A dot at the top indicates an untimed event. You can scroll to these events by tapping the arrows in the lower-right corner.

WEEK VIEW

Month View

So, you're the type of person who likes to see the big picture? The Month view is your viewfinder, although at first glance you may think you've stumbled upon Morse code: who added all those dots? Tap the third box in the lower-left corner (containing a grid of 16 dots) to switch to the Month view.

Month view features

◆ This screen displays the entire month in a typical calendar format, with the days of the week running along the top of each column. Today's date, if you're viewing the current month, shows up as white text within a black square (**Figure 4.11**).

◆ To move forward and backward among months, tap the arrows at the top-right corner of the screen, or press the up and down buttons on the handheld case.

◆ Event blocks are indicated by black bars on the day in which they occur. Due to a lack of space, events are noted by the period of the day they occur: morning, midday, and evening. Similar to the Week view, this gives you an idea of the density of your schedule (**Figure 4.12**). Note that the day's month view will only display one bar for that part of the day, even if you have multiple appointments.

◆ If you have selected the Show Daily Repeating Evts box in the Display Options window, repeating events show up as a line of dots running along the bottom of the days they occupy. This option, the equivalent to "banners" in most desktop calendar programs, is off by default.

◆ If you have selected Show Untimed Events in the Display Options dialog box, these items are shown as little plus-signs at the bottom left of the day's square.

Figure 4.11 Your entire schedule is displayed using a minimum of space.

Today's date   Noon bar   Morning bar

Repeating event   Untimed event   Afternoon/evening bar

Figure 4.12 Realizing the limitations of their screen, Palm's designers opted for a "less is more" approach to the Date Book's Month view.

Figure 4.13 View the day's events and to do items in the Agenda view.

Agenda View

Recognizing that what you do is often tied to when you do it, Palm's programmers added a fourth view to Date Book under Palm OS 3.5. The Agenda view is similar to the Day view, but also contains the day's tasks from the To Do List in the lower half of the screen (**Figure 4.13**). Tap the fourth box in the lower-left corner to bring up the Agenda view.

Agenda view features

◆ Tap an appointment to switch to the Day view, where it will be actively selected. Similarly, tapping a task switches to that record in the To Do List.

◆ Tap the horizontal scroll arrows at the top of the screen to move forward or backward one day.

◆ The to do items are displayed just as they appear in the To Do List. To see data such as the due date or category name, enable those options in the To Do List.

◆ View different To Do List categories by selecting them from the category popup menu above the to do items.

✔ Tip

■ If you have the Agenda view displayed, then switch to another application, the Agenda will appear when you come back to the Date Book. Normally, the Date Book returns to the Day view when you switch back to it. To keep the Agenda view, make sure it's active before you exit Date Book.

Date Book Navigation: Jumping Through Time

I've become so dependent upon my hand-held for scheduling that if an event isn't in Date Book, then it isn't happening. (This approach has prevented several event conflicts!) As a result, I find myself frequently looking ahead to specific dates, a process the Palm designers have streamlined pretty well.

To jump to specific dates:

1. From any Date Book view, tap the Go to button. The Go to Date dialog box is context sensitive based on your previous view. So, the Day view gives you the option to jump to a specific day, the Week view jumps to weeks, and the Month view jumps to months (**Figure 4.14**).

2. Select a year using the arrows at the top of the page.

3. Select a month and a date or week (if you came from the month view, selecting the month will take you there immediately).

   If you've been time-traveling and want to get back to the present, tap the Today, This Week, or This Month button.

✔ Tip

■ A faster method of jumping to today's date is to press the Date Book button on the handheld's case—the first press will return you to today's Day view from anywhere in the Date Book (except the Agenda view under Palm OS 3.5).

Figure 4.14 Tapping the Go to button brings up the day (top), week (middle), and month (bottom) navigation screens, depending on your previous view.

Figure 4.15 Splitting the time into two vertical bars may appear odd at first, but this approach puts the controls in a smooth path for your stylus.

Figure 4.16 After exiting the Set Time window, go ahead and name your event.

Entering and Deleting Date Book Events

I'm sure Mrs. Wilson, my second-grade teacher, would pale at the sight of my hand-writing. All that cursive training, wasted! Date Book allows me to enter legible events quickly, using a variety of methods—and delete them just as easily without the mess of strikethroughs and scribbles.

To enter an event using the New button:

1. In the Day view, tap the New button to bring up the Set Time dialog box. You can also choose New Event from the Record menu, or write ╱-N in Graffiti.

2. Specify a starting time. If you tap the Start Time box, the day's beginning time (from Date Book's Preferences) is entered by default. The time in the End Time box automatically sets to one hour after the Start Time. Tap on an hour and minute (the first and second vertical columns) to change the Start Time (**Figure 4.15**). The All Day button (Palm OS 3.5 and higher) enters the time span you set up in the preferences.

   You can also elect to create an untimed event by tapping OK before specifying Start and End Times, or by tapping the No Time button if those fields are already filled. Birthdays, anniversaries, and other holidays work best as untimed events.

3. Change the End Time, if desired, and tap OK.

4. Write a descriptive title (**Figure 4.16**).

✔ Tip

- A slightly faster way to enter an event is to tap directly on one of the times running down the left side of the display.

To enter an event by naming it on the appropriate line:

1. The quickest method for creating a new record is to tap the line belonging to the time you wish to use. Date Book creates a one-hour event and positions the text cursor on the line for you to name the record; no dialog boxes or OK buttons are involved (**Figure 4.17**).

2. Tap on a null area of the screen to enter your new event. To modify the event's time, tap either the time itself or the Details button.

To enter events in the Week view:

1. In the Week view, tap on a day and time for your new event—a black rectangle appears (**Figure 4.18**).

2. When you remove the stylus from the screen, Date Book changes to the Day view and automatically enters an untitled record at the time you specified.

✔ Tips

- If you're feeling like a hunter-gatherer while poking at all of these buttons and locations, consider using a more expressive method to enter Date Book events. In the Day view, begin writing your event's Start Time using Graffiti's number-entry area (the right portion). A new record will be created at that time.

- A similar approach is to just start writing the title of a new appointment in Graffiti. An untimed event appears; use the Details button or tap the time to schedule it.

- Also, if you're tired of pecking at the vertical hour and minute columns in the Set Time dialog box, you can write Graffiti numerals that will show up in the Start Time box (and also in the End Time box after selecting it).

Figure 4.17 Tap directly on the time you wish to create an event for, and bypass the Set Time dialog box.

Figure 4.18 In the Week view, tap the time for a new event (indicated by the box with a dark border).

Figure 4.19a Set up your "pencil-in" notation by creating a ShortCut in the Palm OS Preferences application.

Figure 4.19b Write the Graffiti characters you set up as a ShortCut, then enter the event's title.

Figure 4.19c Your event is now easily recognizable as a temporary date/time. After confirming the specifics, remove the "pencil-in" notation.

"Pencil-in" Events

One capability I miss from paper-based organizers is being able to "pencil-in" an event, which you can then confirm later. In the Date Book, temporary and confirmed appointments show up the same. What I'd really like to see is the ability to write an event in gray, but until that day comes, here's a simple workaround using the Palm OS's ShortCut feature (**Figures 4.19a**, **4.19b**, and **4.19c**).

To add a "pencil-in" event:

1. From the Applications screen, launch the Prefs utility and select ShortCuts from the popup menu in the upper-right corner.

2. Tap New and name your ShortCut something like "pn".

3. Figure out how you'd like penciled items to display—I've always liked the curly brackets, so I enter both characters under ShortCut Text.

4. Tap OK and return to Date Book.

5. When you want to create a penciled-in event, preface its title with the shortcut you just created. In my case, the brackets appear and I either tap to put my cursor between them, or use the Graffiti cursor-left stroke (➝).

6. When the event is confirmed, remember to remove the "pencil-in" notation.

✔ Tip

■ I hoped that Palm OS 3.5's color support would let me create events in gray, but that's not yet the case. However, DateBk4 (http://www.pimlicosoftware.com/) can: create an event, tap the Details button, then tap the Font field to set the color. You can also set up a template to create new penciled-in events. (See later in this chapter for more on DateBk4.)

"PENCIL-IN" EVENTS

Editing and Deleting Existing Events

Once created, events aren't set in stone. The ways to change their attributes are as varied as creating new appointments.

To change an event's time and/or date (the long way):

1. In the Day view, tap a record to select it, then tap the Details button.

2. In the Event Details window, tap the Time field or the Date field (**Figure 4.20**).

3. Adjust the time in the Set Time window, and the date in the Set Date window.

To change an event's time (the short way):

1. In the Day view, tap on the time to the left of the event you wish to edit.

2. Adjust the time in the Set Time window.

To change an event's time and/or date (the shortest way):

1. In the Week view, tap and hold the event you wish to edit (**Figure 4.21**).

2. Drag the event to its new time and/or date (within the same week).

To delete an event:

1. In the Day view, tap the event to select it and then tap the Details button.

2. In the Event Details window, tap Delete..., choose Delete Event... from the Record menu, or write ╱-D .

3. If you want the record to be saved on your PC the next time you perform a HotSync, be sure to mark the Save archive copy on PC option; uncheck the box to banish it forever (**Figure 4.22**).

Figure 4.20 You can easily change the date and time of any event by accessing the Event Details window.

Figure 4.21 The quickest way to change an event's time and date is to tap and drag it in the Week view.

Drag to new time

Figure 4.22 If you don't want an event taking up valuable memory in your handheld, you can keep a copy of it on your PC's hard drive.

EDITING AND DELETING EXISTING EVENTS

Figure 4.23 Traffic likely to be bad? Specify a longer time period for the alarm to go off before an event.

Figure 4.24 The alarm's Reminder screen appears before an event, accompanied by a cheerful chime (Palm OS 3.5 shown here).

Figure 4.25 Date Book gives you several options for alarms, including repeating reminders and seven different sounds.

Setting Alarms

Any Visor user will tell you that the volume of the built-in alarm is less than alarming. However, even a soft alarm is better than no alarm at all.

To set an alarm:

1. After you've created an event, tap Details and mark the Alarm checkbox.

2. Choose the amount of time before the event that the alarm should go off. Minutes is the default, but you can also select Hours or Days (**Figure 4.23**).

3. Tap OK to dismiss the Reminder screen when the alarm activates (**Figure 4.24**). Under Palm OS 3.5, tap the Snooze button to give yourself a few extra minutes before the alarm goes off again.

To change alarm options:

1. Go to the Date Book Preferences dialog box (choose Preferences... from the Options menu, or write ╱-R).

2. Choose your favorite Alarm Sound.

3. Choose the "snooze" options: Remind Me specifies how often the alarm will go off before you dismiss it. Play Every sets the time between reminders (**Figure 4.25**).

✔ Tips

■   The Visor's speaker is located at the back of the device, so the sound is often absorbed by owners' cases. Place your Visor face down on a nearby surface to better project the sound.

■   Other hardware options exist for alarms. The Springboard TaleLight (http:// members.aol.com/gmayhak/tcl/) flashes asa silent alarm. The InnoPak/2V (http:// www.innogear.com/) module acts as a vibrating alarm.

Creating Repeating Events

Scheduling meetings, appointments, and reminders is a great use for Date Book, but one of the primary reasons I wanted an electronic organizer was to keep track of those recurring events that I never seem to remember: birthdays, holidays, weekly meetings, and the like. Date Book's repeating events feature allows me to do just that.

To create a repeating event:

1. Select an event and tap the Details button.

2. Next to the word Repeat, tap None. This brings up the Change Repeat dialog box.

3. Specify if the event is a daily, weekly, monthly, or yearly event by tapping one of the boxes at the top of the screen.

4. Write the numerical frequency of the event in the Every field.

5. If the event stops repeating on a certain date, select Choose Date... from the End on popup menu; otherwise, leave it set to No End Date (**Figure 4.26**).

6. Depending on your selection in step 3, you can specify additional event criteria.

   Weekly events can be set to repeat on certain days by tapping in the appropriate Repeat on boxes.

   Monthly events can be repeated by day ("The 1st Wednesday of every month"), or by date ("The 5th of every month") (**Figure 4.27**).

   Yearly events, by default, are set to repeat according to the date of the first event.

7. Tap OK to exit the dialog; you'll see the repeating event icon appear to the right of your record in the Day view, and a dotted line in the Month view if Show Untimed Events is selected in Display Options (**Figure 4.28**).

Figure 4.26 Why manually add the same events over and over? Repeating events allow you to specify multiple days of the week, among other options.

Figure 4.27 Date Book is smart enough to base the repeated event depending on the date that's selected.

Day view

Repeating event icon

Month view

Figure 4.28 Repeated events are shown with an icon in the Day view, and a dotted line in the Month view.

Figure 4.29 If you change an existing repeating event, you're asked how you prefer to implement the changes.

Figure 4.30 Yearly occasions that fall on a particular day of the week can be set up as monthly, not yearly, repeating events, such as Thanksgiving.

To change a repeating event:

1. Tap any occurrence (you don't have to edit the first record you create) to select it, then tap the Details button.

2. Make any changes you like, including time, date, or attached notes, then tap OK.

3. Choose whether you wish to apply the change to the Current record, All instances of the event, or if you'd rather Cancel (**Figure 4.29**).

   Palm OS 3.5 adds a fourth option: Future leaves past occurrences intact and deletes only the current and future repetitions.

   If you only change the title of the event, the change is automatically applied to all occurrences without displaying the Repeating Event dialog box.

✔ Tips

- What about those events, like Thanksgiving, that occur yearly but are based on a particular day of the week? Since the yearly repeat option only specifies the event's date, you have to out-think Date Book. Set up a monthly repeat that occurs every 12 months, and choose Repeat by Day (**Figure 4.30**).

- One of my biggest scheduling problems is not being aware of an event, such as a birthday, until the day is upon me. One workaround is to set alarms to go off several days before the event. Another solution is to install Birthdate (http://www.birthdate.com/), a shareware utility that collects birthdates from other areas of the Palm OS (such as the Address Book) and optionally notifies you when they are coming up.

CREATING REPEATING EVENTS

Attaching and Deleting Notes

Initially, I thought the ability to attach notes was a superfluous add-on, best used when you wanted to record snide (er, I mean "constructive") comments during a meeting.

Since then, I've seen the light. Not only are they good for jotting random thoughts in context, but they have become indispensable for storing information that I know I will need at a particular time.

To attach a note to an event:

1. Tap an event to select it.

2. Tap the Details button, then tap Note. Alternately, choose Attach Note... from the Record menu, or write /-A.

3. Compose your note using Graffiti or the onscreen keyboard (**Figure 4.31a** and **4.31b**).

4. When you are finished, tap Done.

✔ Tip

■ To edit the attached note later, follow the steps above to access the note. If you want a quicker method, however, go to the Day view and tap the note icon (🗐) to the right of the event's name.

Navigating a note

◆ If your note occupies more than one screen, use the scroll bar on the right side of the screen to move within the text.

◆ Choose Go to Top of Page from the Options menu to jump quickly to the beginning (this and the next command apply only to Palm OS 3.1).

◆ Choose Go to Bottom of Page from the Options menu to jump quickly to the end (**Figure 4.32**).

Figure 4.31a Tap the Note button in the Event Details window to attach more text to an event.

Figure 4.31b A new note presents you with a slightly limited version of the Memo Pad application.

Figure 4.32 For longer texts (up to 4,025 characters), use the quick-navigation commands located under the Options menu (Palm OS 3.1).

Figure 4.33 Move through a long note quickly by "select-scrolling" the stylus through the text.

Figure 4.34 When you no longer need a note, delete it—keep in mind that you don't have the option to archive it to your PC, as you do with memos.

✔ Tip

■ A quicker option, though harder to navigate, is to "select-scroll" through long notes (**Figure 4.33**). Position your cursor somewhere in the middle of the text, and, without lifting the stylus from the screen, drag down the screen. The text will be highlighted, and soon you'll find yourself at the bottom of the note (or whichever point you chose to lift the stylus).

To delete a note:

1. In the Day view, choose Delete Note... from the Record menu, or write ╱-O.

   Or, if you're on the note editing screen, tap the Delete... button. The Delete Note dialog box appears.

2. Click Yes or No to confirm if you really want to delete the note (**Figure 4.34**).

Performing a Phone Lookup

Luckily for those of us who value good data, the built-in applications don't live independently of each other. One of the handier features employed in the Palm OS is the ability to perform phone number lookups from the Address Book.

To perform a phone lookup:

1. If you know the name of the person you're scheduling an event with (such as "Coffee with Pedro Finn"), write his or her name into a field in the Day view.

   If you don't know the person's name, just leave that part blank (i.e., "Coffee with ").

2. Choose Phone Lookup from the Options menu, or write ╱-L.

3. If a name in your Address Book matches the name you wrote, the phone number will be added to your event's description. If not, or if you didn't specify a name, scroll through the list of names and highlight the one you want (**Figure 4.35**).

4. Tap Add to include the phone number in the Date Book record (**Figure 4.36**).

✔ Tip

■ The Palm OS searches for last name when performing a lookup, so you can write a person's last name and, if theirs is the only instance of that name, the phone number will appear without making a trip to the Address Book screen.

Figure 4.35 Finally, contact information that's convenient to contact. Performing a phone lookup lists the names in your Address Book with phone numbers.

Figure 4.36 The looked-up number automatically gets added to the time line you had created.

Figure 4.37a Tap the Private checkbox to keep an event safe from curious onlookers.

Figure 4.37b If you don't have Show/ Hide Private Records selected in the Security application, you are reminded that the event is not yet hidden.

Figure 4.38 Under Palm OS 3.5, changing the security setting alters it in every application.

Marking Events Private

I have a tendency to show my handheld to anyone who asks, but I don't always want them to see everything in my schedule. (Okay, so maybe I don't have very much information that needs to be kept secret, but it's good to know I can when I need to.)

When you mark Date Book events as Private, their appearance depends on the state of the Show/Hide Private Records option in the Palm OS's Security application (Palm OS 3.5 lists this as the Current Privacy setting). If you've specified an alarm for a hidden private record, a Reminder screen will still appear when scheduled.

To mark events Private:

1. Select an event and tap the Details button.

2. In the Event Details dialog box, mark the Private checkbox (**Figure 4.37a**). If the Show/Hide Private Records setting is switched to Show, you will receive a warning dialog about how to hide private records after you tap OK (**Figure 4.3b**).

To change the security setting under Palm OS 3.5:

1. Choose Security... from the Options menu, write ╱-H, or tap the lock icon from the command bar. The Change Security dialog box appears.

2. From the Current Privacy popup menu, choose Show Records, Mask Records, or Hide Records (**Figure 4.38**). This changes the security setting in all applications on your Visor.

Beaming Events

In the movies, conspirators are always synchronizing their watches to make sure everyone's on the same schedule. In the real world, I use the Palm OS to beam appointments to colleagues and family members, and thereby avoid having anyone say, "Why didn't you tell me there's a meeting today?"

To beam an event:

1. Tap an event to select it.

2. Choose Beam... from the Record menu, write ✓-B, or tap the Beam Event icon (📡) from the command bar (**Figure 4.39**). If the recipient's Beam Receive preference is set to On and the IR ports are aimed at each other, the record will be transferred (**Figure 4.40**).

To receive a beamed event:

1. Make sure your Beam Receive preference is set to On. Aim your IR port at the other person's Palm device.

2. After you've received the beamed record, you will be asked if you wish to add it to the Date Book. Tap Yes or No.

✔ Tip

■ The Visor's Date Book+ application (see later in this chapter) has a bug that prevents it from receiving beamed events if Date Book+ is the active application. The record will be received, but not recorded. To get around this, be sure to switch to another program before receiving a beamed event.

Figure 4.39 Palm devices equipped with infrared capabilities can beam records to one another easily.

Figure 4.40 Be sure your Palm device is pointed at the recipient, and within seconds the record is transferred.

Figure 4.41 Some people choose to leave their past behind them—select Purge... to wipe away old events.

Figure 4.42 I know people who have saved every event for as long as they've been able. Others wipe the old information and store it on their PCs.

Purging Old Events

Although the Palm OS has been written to accommodate very small file sizes, there comes a point at which the volume of past events begins to eat into your available memory. Will you have to shoulder the weight of the past forever? Luckily, you don't have to.

Date Book gives you the option to permanently delete older records from your device, while still maintaining an archive of the past on your PC.

To purge old events:

1. From the Day view, choose Purge... from the Record menu, or write ╱-E in the Graffiti area (**Figure 4.41**). The Purge dialog box appears.

2. Choose the time frame of records that will be purged by selecting an item on the Delete events older than: popup menu. You can select 1 Week, 2 Weeks, 3 Weeks, or 1 Month (**Figure 4.42**).

3. If you want to maintain a copy of the purged records on your PC, be sure the checkbox next to Save archive copy on PC is marked; otherwise, uncheck the box. Tap OK.

Handspring's Date Book+

In many ways, the Visor is just a Palm device in a different package. It runs the Palm OS, which includes all of the built-in applications found on any handheld manufactured by Palm, Inc. However, closer inspection reveals a number of details that set the Visor apart. One of these is Date Book+, an application that lives on top of the standard Date Book and gives it the features that Date Book should have included long ago.

Date Book+ adds three new views, plus an assortment of features like floating events (i.e., scheduled to-do items), a daily journal, the ability to view tasks and appointments on the same screen (like the Date Book's Agenda view), plus other tweaks and improvements (**Figure 4.43**).

To activate Date Book+:

1. If it's not already active by default, launch Date Book and select Default Date Book… from the Options menu, or write ╱-M in the Graffiti area. The Set Default dialog box appears.

2. Tap the Date Book+ button, then tap OK (**Figure 4.44**).

✔ Tips

■ Date Book and Date Book+ exist as two separate applications on the Visor, even though they share the same database. You can manually launch one or the other from the Applications screen without disrupting the Default Date Book setting.

■ The first time you set Date Book+ as the default from within the application, the Palm OS button setting (in Preferences) is changed to launch Date Book+ when you press the Date Book button on the Visor's case. If you change the button preference to load the normal Date Book, that choice will override the application's setting.

Figure 4.43 Date Book+ looks like the original Date Book, but includes more views, activated at lower left. Also note the appearance of to do items from the To Do List at the top of the screen.

Figure 4.44 You can choose between the standard and enhanced Date Book versions, but really, you won't want to go back to the old calendar, trust me.

Figure 4.45 The awkwardly named Week View with Text view offers a better idea of your schedule than the standard Week view.

Figure 4.46 View two weeks on the same screen, though it's not as readable.

Figure 4.47 The Year view is handy for getting a sense of how crowded your schedule is.

Date Book+ Week View with Text View

The standard Week view can be helpful, but its assortment of dots and dashes is often too cryptic. The Week View with Text view displays as many event and to do titles as can fit (**Figure 4.45**). Tap the third button from the left to access this view.

Features of the Week View with Text view

◆ Tap any day area to switch to the Day view.

◆ Tap the numbered box at the top of the screen to switch between viewing one week or two weeks (**Figure 4.46**).

◆ If you have a mix of morning and after-noon appointments, tap the arrow button next to the Go button to display those portions of the day.

Date Book+ Year View

The Year view offers an even bigger picture of your schedule, but at the expense of pulling out any details at a glance (**Figure 4.47**). Tap the fifth button in the lower-left corner to bring up the Year view.

Features of the Year view

◆ Tap a box on the calendar to view that day's date and the first appointment scheduled.

◆ The scroll arrows at the top of the screen advance or go back one year per tap; the scroll arrows at the lower-right corner move one day at a time (which can be easier than trying to accurately peck a date box). Pressing the device's scroll buttons accomplishes the same task.

Date Book+ List View

Seeing my schedule in a number of different calendar layouts is good, but sometimes I just want a list of what's coming up. Sure enough, the List view does exactly that. Tap the rightmost box at the lower-left corner of the screen (**Figure 4.48**).

Features of the List view

◆ Tap an event to display its start and end times in the title bar.

◆ Double-tap an event to bring it up in the Day view.

◆ If you've used the Go button to view a different day, tap the List view button to return to the current day.

◆ Tap the up arrow at the top-right corner of the screen to specify which increment (day, week, month) to move up the list, or pick a date in the past (**Figure 4.49**). The down arrow advances a full screen.

◆ Tap the Prefs button to specify which records appear in the list.

✔ Tip

■ From the List Preferences screen, you can filter the list by entering text on the Find field under Filter by Text. Only events containing that text will be listed.

Figure 4.48 Date Book doesn't need to get fancy displaying calendars when a list will do just as well.

Figure 4.49 Tap the up arrow in the List view to choose a range of time to jump back through.

Figure 4.50 Choose the options you wish to use in Date Book+.

Figure 4.51 Setting a different day to begin the week changes the calendar layout throughout Date Book+.

Date Book+ Preferences

With more features come more preferences, and Date Book+ is loaded with options. These settings define global behavior (**Figure 4.50**).

Important Date Book+ Preferences

◆ By default, new events appear with a one hour duration. In Date Book+, specify any time span from zero to 23 hours and 55 minutes by tapping the Event Duration field and setting the amount.

◆ Use the Initial View preference to set the view displayed when you enter the application. The Day view is the default.

◆ Pressing the Date Book button on the Visor's case shuttles you through the different Date Book+ views. Deselect views you don't scroll through by tapping them in the Button Views preference.

◆ Gone are the days of the standardized workweek. If you want your weeks to begin on a certain day, like Tuesday, choose it from the Week Start popup menu. Every calendar view is affected (**Figure 4.51**).

Entering Date Book+ Events

Since Date Book+ can display more than just appointments, it adds an easy method of entering new records. Yes, you can choose their commands from the Record menu or write their Graffiti strokes (as explained soon), but there's a much easier way.

To enter a new Date Book+ event (the easy way):

1. With no records selected, tap the New button; a popup menu appears, listing the types of records available (**Figure 4.52**).

2. Choose Floating Event, To Do, Daily Journal, Template, or Appointment. A new untimed record appears (or in the case of the journal, a new note screen appears with a time stamp).

3. Fill in the record's title and other pertinent information as you normally would.

To duplicate a Date Book+ event:

1. Select an existing record in the Day view.

2. Choose Duplicate Item from the Record menu, or write ╱-Y.

3. Change the new item's settings in the Details screen, then tap OK to return to the Day view.

✔ Tips

- Unfortunately, there's no way to beam events to other Palm devices in Date Book+. To beam records, switch to the normal Date Book application.

- There's also an issue with receiving beamed appointments while Date Book+ is the current application. Switch to another program to receive beamed events.

Figure 4.52 The easy way to create new records in Date Book+ is to select from the menu that appears when you tap the New button.

Figure 4.53 Floating events are really just scheduled to-do items.

Daily Journal

11:15 pm: Heard a funny joke today: what did one fish say to the other fish when they swam into a wall? 11:18 pm: Oops, forgot the end. Darn.

(Done) (Delete...) (Restore...)

Figure 4.54 A timestamp is automatically added to the bottom of the day's journal record.

Figure 4.55 The Daily Journal is really just an untimed record with an attached note, but it's a quick method of jotting down ideas and snippets of information.

Date Book+ Floating Events

There are times when I need to make sure I do something at a certain time. Floating events can be scheduled like any event, but carry over until the next day if they're not marked completed.

To work with floating events:

1. Create a new floating event from the New popup menu, or by choosing New Floating Event from the Record menu, or by writing ╱-B. Assign it a title and time. It will be identified by a circle to the left or right of the name, depending on whether it's scheduled or not (**Figure 4.53**).

2. Tap the circle to indicate that the task is completed, or tap Details and select the Done option under Type. If left alone, it will display the following day.

Date Book+ Journal Entries

For an easy method of keeping track of thoughts and ideas, use the Daily Journal.

To create a journal entry:

1. Choose Daily Journal from the New button's popup menu, or New Journal Entry from the Record menu, or write ╱-J. A new note screen appears with the current time entered (**Figure 4.54**).

2. Insert pithy thought, wry observation, erudite comment, or overheard joke.

3. Tap Done to return to the Day view. Journal records appear as untimed records at the top of the screen (**Figure 4.55**).

4. If, at the end of your scribblings, you decide to delete what you've written (or if you wrote over a previous record), tap the Restore... button to revert back to the state at which you first entered the journal.

Date Book+ Templates

The template feature in Date Book+ exemplifies yet another aspect of the Palm philosophy of saving time and avoiding repetition. When you make a template from an existing record, it retains all of the event's settings like alarm, privacy, and attached note.

To create a template:

1. Create a record that you want to use as a template.

2. Select the record and choose Create Template from the Record menu, or write ∕-V (**Figure 4.56**).

To use a template:

1. Tap the New button and choose Template from the popup menu.

2. Select a template from the Appointment Templates screen, then tap OK to place the event (**Figure 4.57**).

To edit a template:

1. Tap the New button and choose Template from the popup menu.

2. Select a template and tap the Details or Edit button to change its properties.

3. Tap OK to return to the Day view.

Restoring Archived Events

If you leave the Save archive copy on PC checkbox marked when you delete records, there's a way to get them back.

To restore archived events:

Select UnDelete from Archive from the Record menu. The records appear in reverse order based on when they were deleted. Repeat the command until you've restored the record you want.

Figure 4.56 Templates store all the data about a selected event.

Figure 4.57 Set up templates for frequently used events to avoid having to enter the same info time and again.

DateBk4: The Supercharged Date Book

The Palm OS's built-in applications haven't changed much over the past few years, in accordance with Palm's mandate to keep its handhelds simple and useful. As long as appointments are scheduled, tasks recorded, and phone numbers easily looked up, most users don't require more than the basics. But we don't all qualify as "most users." For the most full featured calendar application on the Palm OS, look to Pimlico Software's DateBk4 (http://www.pimlicosoftware.com/).

DateBk4 essentially adds all the features that you've wanted (or didn't know you've wanted) in Date Book. Like Date Book+, DateBk4 sports six calendar views, displays to-do items as well as events, and features a daily journal, floating events, and templates. (It's no coincidence: Handspring commissioned the developer of DateBk4 to create a "light" version of his program that would ship on every Visor.) In addition, DateBk4 adds categories, icons, time zone support, color, and the ability to set font styles for any record, not just the entire application (**Figure 4.58**).

Figure 4.58 DateBk4 adds more features to the built-in Date Book database than any three programs combined.

But that's not all. You can split the Day view screen and choose the contents for the new window pane. To do items are usually listed, but you can also view your Address Book records, or memos, and then filter the lists based on any text you specify. Visor Prism owners have good reason to install DateBk4: unlike the built-in applications, this program enables you to color-code categories or individual records, making it easier to quickly differentiate between events (**Figure 4.59**). And if that's not enough, you can also link records between the built-in applications (though you have to view them within DateBk4).

Figure 4.59 This is the reason to buy a color Visor Prism: events can be categorized and displayed in different colors for easy recognition—a capability missing from the initial color implementation from Palm.

What's the dark side to this miracle application? The only serious criticism is its size: around 460K, which is huge by Palm OS standards. For users who don't have that much free space available, Pimlico also offers the previous version, DateBk3, which weighs in at 247K. Of all the applications I've installed on my Palm devices, DateBk4 (and DateBk3 before that) remains a permanent fixture.

DateBk4 costs $24.95 (all of which goes to the developer's organization, Gorilla Haven, a non-profit preserve that provides a secure temporary holding facility for gorillas awaiting permanent zoo housing, and helps ensure the welfare and genetic diversity of the species).

Palm Desktop Special Features

For the most part, you'll find that working within Palm Desktop's Date Book is similar to using the Palm OS Date Book: click New... to create new events, Edit... to change them, and view them using either the Day, Week, or Month views. However, the desktop software also includes several features that make it easier to create and modify appointment times, and add events based on phone lookups. And because it operates on your PC, you can also print your calendar.

To edit events in the Day view:

1. Select the day you need in the calendar to the right.

2. Click on the time that you'd like to schedule your event. You can click either the time numerals in the left column, or click an empty area in the right column.

3. Type your event's description, then press Enter.

4. To add an alarm or a note, right-click on the event to bring up a contextual menu. You can also delete the record here, as well as access the main Edit dialog box.

5. If you need to quickly move the event to another date, drag it to the calendar in the pane at right. It retains the same time.

To edit events in the Week view:

1. Click on an empty time slot, or click the time numerals, to create a new event.

2. As in the Day view, drag events to new times and dates using the event handle, or reschedule lengths using the duration handle (**Figures 4.60, 4.61,** and **4.62**).

3. Right-click on any event to bring up the editing contextual menu.

Figure 4.60 Click and drag an appointment's bottom handle to change its time span; click and drag the right-side event handle to reschedule its time or date.

Figure 4.61 Events are more configurable in the desktop Day view than in the Palm OS Day view.

Figure 4.62 Untimed events appear in the upper field marked by a diamond. The field expands to accommodate the number of untimed events.

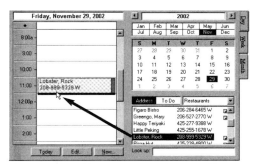

Figure 4.63 Quickly create an appointment with a phone lookup by dragging a name from the Address pane at lower right to the time of the event.

Figure 4.64 Choose how you want your schedule printed. Clicking on the tiny calendar icons gives you a popup calendar to specify the date ranges.

To perform a phone lookup in Palm Desktop:

1. Switch to the Day view, and select the date on which you wish to create an event.

2. Click Address in the lower-right pane to display your Address Book entries.

3. Locate the contact either by scrolling through the names, or typing in the Look up field.

4. Drag the contact's name to the time of the appointment (**Figure 4.63**).

✔ Tip

■ You can also drag a To Do item from the lower-right pane onto your day to schedule a task. Although the records aren't linked (changing the date on one won't affect the other), this capability is good for setting aside blocks of time to complete your tasks.

To print your appointments:

1. In any Date Book view, select Print... from the File menu, or press Control-P. The Print Options dialog box appears.

2. Choose a print option: Today's appointments, a list of Dates, or a time span in Months format (**Figure 4.64**).

3. If printing in month format, you can use the small calendar icons to specify which days you want to print.

Macintosh Palm Desktop Special Features

Most cross-platform applications share the same interface and features, but that's not the case with the Macintosh Palm Desktop software. Because it's built on top of Claris Organizer (see Chapter 1), you'll find many features that don't exist in the Windows version of Palm Desktop.

Navigating Palm Desktop for Macintosh

One of the first things you'll notice is the presence of a toolbar at the upper-left corner of the screen (**Figure 4.65**). Clicking on the buttons offers a quick alternative to common actions, such as:

◆ **Create Appointment** (or press Command-Option-A). This opens the Appointment dialog box, allowing you to enter the schedule information without finding the time and date on the calendar first (useful when you're entering several events at different times). Click Add Another to stay in the dialog box and enter multiple events instead of switching back to the calendar view (**Figure 4.66**).

◆ **Create Event Banner** (or press Command-Option-B). Event banners are equivalent to untimed events in the Palm OS. See the next page for details.

◆ **Go To Date** (or press Command-R). This jumps to a specific date (**Figure 4.67**).

◆ **Go To Today** (or press Command-T). Jump to the current date. Carpe diem, etc.

◆ **View Calendar** (or press Command-Option-C). If you're viewing to do items or contacts, clicking this button takes you to the last calendar view you were using.

Create Appointment · Go To Date · View Calendar

Create Event Banner · Go to Today

Figure 4.65 Palm Desktop for Macintosh features a floating toolbar with buttons to work within the Date Book module.

Figure 4.66 Click the Add Another button to create a new event without exiting the dialog box.

Figure 4.67 Go To Date switches your current calendar view to the date you specify. This small window is also handy when you're viewing the Day or Week views, giving you a monthly calendar without switching to the Month view.

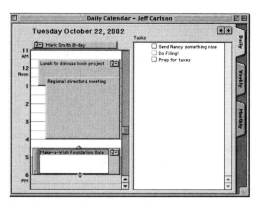

Figure 4.68 Click and drag within the Day or Week views to create a new event.

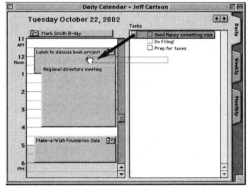

Figure 4.69 Attach to-do items in the Tasks pane to events in the Day and Week views by dragging-and-dropping them. Existing links can be viewed by clicking the folder icon that is created after linking.

Figure 4.70 Create repeating events by setting up event banners, which can be assigned categories and sub-categories.

To create and edit events:

◆ Double-click in one of the calendar views to bring up the Appointment dialog box.

◆ Click and drag on the event's time. Unlike the Windows version of Palm Desktop, the Mac software allows you to create an event with one click that spans its full duration (**Figure 4.68**).

◆ Choose Appointment... from the Create menu, or press Command-Option-A.

To edit an existing event, double-click it in any calendar view, or single-click it and select Edit Appointment... from the Edit menu.

You can also attach related records to other records (such as to-do items attached to events, or contacts attached to events—the Mac equivalent of phone lookups).

To attach records to events:

◆ If both records are visible, drag and drop one to the other. A link is created in both records (**Figure 4.69**).

◆ Click the folder icon ([📁▾]) and choose Attach To from the popup menu.

Repeating events are known as banners in Palm Desktop for Macintosh.

To create a repeating event:

1. Choose Event Banner... from the Create menu, or press Command-Option-E. The Event Banner dialog box appears.

2. Set the starting date in the Date field (or use the popup calendar to the right).

3. Specify the event's length in the Duration field (**Figure 4.70**).

4. Click the Repeat Annually checkbox to make the banner show up again next year (though it then becomes just a one-day event, like a birthday or holiday).

Attaching Notes in Mac Palm Desktop

The one truly bizarre thing about the Macintosh Palm Desktop software is the roundabout manner of attaching notes to records. Although you can attach records to events (see previous page), that's not the same as adding a note to a record (as discussed at the beginning of this chapter). Fortunately, there is a way to attach notes to events so they show up properly on the handheld device.

To attach notes in Mac Palm Desktop:

1. Attached notes are considered memos just as if you had written them into the Memo Pad. So, create a new memo (which is called "note" in Mac Palm Desktop, making things a bit more confusing), and write your text.

2. In the Title field, type "Handheld Note: Date Book" exactly (**Figure 4.71**).

3. Locate the calendar entry to which you want to add your note. Drag the note's gripper (the icon in the upper-left corner of the message window) to the calendar entry (**Figure 4.72**).

✔ Tips

■ There's a faster way of making attachments that will appear on the handheld. With a blank note visible, write "Handheld Note: Date Book" in the Title field as you did above. Now, choose New Template... from the Create menu, and enter a name; if you want, choose a Command-key number from the ⌘ popup menu. From now on, choose one of the templates from the Create menu or press the Command-key to display a new formatted note window (**Figure 4.73**).

Figure 4.71 To create an attached note, you must first create the note separately (unlike in the Palm OS).

Figure 4.72 Drag the note's gripper icon to an event to attach the note.

Figure 4.73 Create notes easily with templates.

Figure 4.74 Though helpful, turn off the Show alarm dialogs option to avoid interruptions on your Mac.

Drag tasks to the calendar

Figure 4.75 Quickly schedule tasks by dragging them from the Tasks pane to the calendar.

■ In the Palm OS Date Book, performing an address lookup puts a person's name and phone number in the title of an event. On the Mac, however, dragging a contact to an event only creates a link between the two on the desktop. Instead, you'll have to manually cut and paste the person's phone information for it to appear in the title.

■ In the calendar's Daily view, double-click the date to bring up the Go To dialog.

■ The Daily view also displays the day's active tasks in the right-hand pane; click the word "Tasks" to send completed tasks to the bottom of the list.

■ In the Daily and Weekly views, pressing Command and the right or left arrow key advances or goes back one day. Hold down option or Shift to move in one-week increments.

■ In the Monthly view, you can choose to display Appointments, Tasks, or both (or none). Go to the View menu, then choose the options under the Calendar submenu.

■ Palm Desktop for Macintosh has a feature for displaying an alarm onscreen, but be careful: since it's a non-modal dialog box, it stays up until you dismiss it, potentially halting operations in your Mac's background applications. So, I recommend turning off the alert in the preferences (**Figure 4.74**).

■ You can create scheduled to do items easily in the Daily or Weekly views. Simply drag a task from the Tasks pane to a time in the calendar. The item's title becomes the appointment's title, and any attached notes are copied over as well. The text "Work on" appears in the title, and an attachment link is created between the task and the new calendar item (**Figure 4.75**).

ATTACHING NOTES IN MAC PALM DESKTOP

ADDRESS BOOK

5

My first attempt at organizing the contact information I had collected over several years was a slick (I thought at the time) system involving a Personal Information Manager (PIM) program on my desktop computer and a cheap little three-ring notebook. I would print my addresses onto standard copy paper, cut the pages into 6.5-inch by 8.5-inch sections, and punch holes in the sides with a hole-punch I had modified to accommodate the binder's rings. This was my low-cost, no-hassle method of keeping my contacts handy.

Well, my system had more holes than its resulting pages. Whenever an address changed, or I added someone to my list, that information would get written in barely-legible pen in the margins. Every week or so, I'd update the PIM and have to print out fresh copies of the whole thing.

The Visor's built-in Address Book, by comparison, is such a dramatic improvement that I can only look back and blame the inexperience of my youth. With Address Book, you can store more than just names and addresses: office and home phone numbers, email addresses, driving directions, birthdays, and more.

Viewing Addresses

The Address List is another example of how Visors can store and present a great deal of information without cluttering up the limited screen.

Address List and Address View

◆ Contacts are listed alphabetically either by last name or by company name down the left side of the screen (**Figure 5.1**).

◆ The right-hand column lists each person's primary contact information; the letter at the end of each line indicates which type of information is displayed (for example, W equals Work, H equals Home, and E equals E-mail).

◆ A note icon (**⌐**) at the far right indicates that the record includes an attached note.

◆ The triangular arrows in the lower-right corner scroll up and down the contact list. You can also use the scroll buttons on the Visor's case, which move through the list one screen at a time.

◆ When you tap a record to view it, the Address View shows you that contact's details (**Figure 5.2**). Scroll up or down to view the details by tapping the arrows or pressing the scroll buttons.

✔ Tip

■ If you use the physical scroll buttons to move up and down within a record in the Address View screen, you can jump to the previous or next record by pressing the buttons when you're at the beginning or the end of the current record.

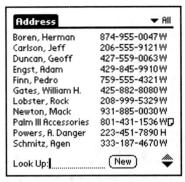

Figure 5.1 The Address List displays names and preferred phone numbers— you may not even have to tap on a name to get the number you need.

Figure 5.2 Tapping a name brings up the contact information; fields left blank (such as Fax number) are hidden to conserve space.

Figure 5.3 Two options are available for sorting the Address List, depending on whether you're looking for companies or people's names.

Figure 5.4 Sorting by Company, Last Name reorders the list alphabetically by company, and truncates longer names to show more information.

Figure 5.5 Specify a preferred number by using the Show in List popup menu.

Changing the Sort Order

Since there isn't much space on the screen, you can't tell if, for example, Thomas Silvestri was the guy you met at last month's conference, or if he's your genius financial adviser. Fortunately, you can choose how you want the records listed.

To change the sort order:

1. Select Preferences... from the Options menu.

2. Choose either Last Name, First Name or Company, Last Name from the List By box, then tap OK (**Figures 5.3** and **5.4**).

Specifying a Preferred Number

Suppose you want to view someone's home number instead of their work phone in the Address List. The Address Book provides a way to do it, although it's slightly buried.

To specify a preferred number:

1. Tap the record you wish to change. This takes you to the Address View screen.

2. Tap the Edit button, or tap anywhere within the Address View to go into the Address Edit screen.

3. Tap Details....

4. Choose the field you want to appear in the main list by tapping the Show in List popup menu (**Figure 5.5**). Tap OK to return to the edit screen, then tap Done.

✔ Tip

■ If you know ahead of time which field you want to appear in the Address List, write that number first when you're entering the address. By default, the contact information shown in the Address List is the first contact field entered.

Changing the Display Font

You have three options for changing fonts: within the Address List, within the Address View, and within the Address Edit screen (**Figures 5.6a** and **5.6b**).

To change the display font:

1. Select Font... from the Options menu.

2. Tap one of the three font styles in the Select Font window (**Figure 5.7**). Tap OK.

Figure 5.6a Choose the font to display contact information. The large font is more readable, but shows less data.

Figure 5.6b The smallest font is easier on the eyes, though probably not as readable at arm's length.

Figure 5.7 The font styles are also available separately for the Address View and Address List screens.

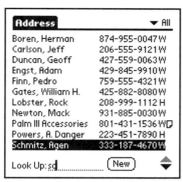

Figure 5.8 No more rustling through pages of contacts to find a number. Begin writing the last name of your contact in the Look Up field to jump to the closest match.

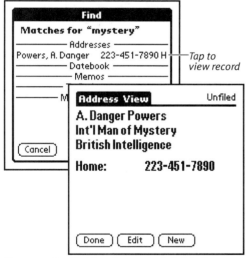

Figure 5.9 The Find function can be helpful when searching for text located within a record.

Looking Up Contacts

There's a better way to find the person you're looking for than scrolling through the list.

To search using Look Up:

1. In the Look Up field, write the first letter of the last name (or company name, depending on the sort order) you're looking for using Graffiti; the first match will be highlighted (**Figure 5.8**).

2. If the first letter doesn't match the intended name, keep writing letters until you get a match. If you know you're close, use the arrows in the lower-right corner to scroll through the list by individual record, or the plastic buttons on the case to scroll by screen.

To perform a find:

1. If you're looking for a word located within a record or a record's attached note, tap the silkscreened Find icon.

2. Enter the text you're searching for, then tap OK. The results (including matches in other programs) appear in a new window. Tap the match you want (**Figure 5.9**).

✔ Tips

- Find will begin its search within the application you're currently running.

- To quickly clear the Look Up field, press the up or down scroll button.

- My work phone has Caller ID to let me know who's calling before I answer it. If there's an unfamiliar number displayed, I do a quick Find for part of the number to see if it's someone in my Address Book.

- Unimpressed with the built-in Find? Install FindHack, a HackMaster utility that greatly expands Find's capabilities (see Chapter 8).

Using Fast Lookup

The Visor Edge introduced a new twist to searching for contacts in the Address Book: Fast Lookup. The typical Look Up feature requires writing a name with the stylus; Fast Lookup, on the other hand, enables you to keep the stylus tucked away by using the application buttons to search for names. As of this writing, the Edge is the only device to feature Fast Lookup, but I'm sure it will find its way to other Visors in short order.

To use Fast Lookup:

1. With the Address Book active, press the scroll up button to enter Fast Lookup.

2. The dotted areas at the bottom of the screen indicate which button corresponds to which range of letters. Start entering the person's last name using the Date Book and Address Book buttons. For example, writing the first three letters of "Tolbert" would mean hitting the Address Book button twice, then the Date Book button once (**Figure 5.10**). If your list is sorted by company name, the left-most buttons apply to the company name. Names that don't match the pattern are hidden from view.

3. If the letters you input point to only one record, it is displayed. If you still have a few matches in the list, press the scroll down button ("Stop"), then use the scroll buttons to highlight the name you want. Press either the Address Book or To Do List buttons to open that record, or one of the other buttons to exit Fast Lookup (**Figure 5.11**).

Figure 5.10 Fast Lookup lets you search your contacts without lifting a stylus.

Figure 5.11 When you've narrowed the list, press the Stop button to interrupt the search of the full Address Book. That brings you to this screen, which navigates among the remaining items.

Figure 5.12 After tapping New, write the contact's information in the fields.

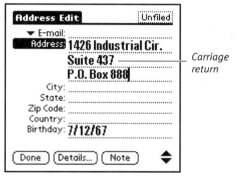

Carriage return

Figure 5.13 Don't worry if there aren't enough fields (such as a second address field): simply write a carriage return to make a new line.

Figure 5.14 With more screen space available, Palm Desktop is able to display a contact's information in the window's right pane.

Entering and Deleting Address Records

Graffiti is a great method for entering text into a handheld, but I won't pretend it's always the best option. If you need to create lots of new records, you're better off typing them into Palm Desktop on your PC. But for one or two, here's how to enter them quickly (I hate asking people to repeat things when I can't keep up with them on my spiffy gadget).

To create a new record:

1. From the Address List or the Address View screen, tap the New button.

2. Fill in the fields using Graffiti or the built-in keypad (**Figure 5.12**). Tap Done.

✔ Tips

■ Write the next field Graffiti character (❚) to go to the next field without moving the stylus from the Graffiti area.

■ You can enter more than one line of text into each field. Write a carriage return (╱) and add another line of information; it stays in the same field (**Figure 5.13**).

To create a new record using Palm Desktop (Windows):

1. Click the Address button, or press F3 to view the Address Book (**Figure 5.14**).

2. Click the New... button, select New Address... from the Edit menu, or press Control-N.

3. Enter the text in the appropriate fields, then click OK.

✔ Tip

■ To quickly switch between tabs, press Control-Tab.

To create a new record using Palm Desktop (Macintosh):

1. Click the View Contact List button from the toolbar, or press Command-Shift-C.

2. Click the Create Contact button, select Contact... from the Create menu, or press Command-Option-C (the keyboard shortcut works anywhere in the program, not just with the Contact List viewed).

3. Click on an information area to access the entry fields (**Figure 5.15**). When you're finished, close the window or press Command-W.

✔ Tips

■ You can jump between the information fields by pressing the Tab key.

■ If you're typing something that's been entered before, such as a city name, Palm Desktop will automatically complete the word for you.

To delete a contact (Palm):

1. Tap the contact to select it.

2. Select Delete Address... from the Record menu, or write ╱-D.

    You can also tap Edit, then Details..., then the Delete... button—but who has that kind of time?

3. If you want to store the record in the PC's Palm archive files, be sure to check Save archive copy on PC. Click OK to delete (**Figure 5.16**).

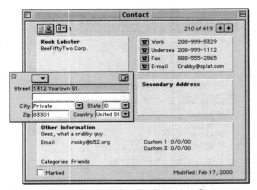

Figure 5.15 The Macintosh Palm Organizer features information areas that pop up entry fields when you click on them.

Figure 5.16 Sometimes we lose track of people who were once dear to us. Check Save archive copy on PC to save deleted records at the next HotSync.

ENTERING AND DELETING ADDRESS RECORDS

Figure 5.17 Palm OS 3.5 adds the capability to duplicate records.

Figure 5.18 When a record is duplicated, Address Book adds the text "Copy" to the First name field.

Duplicating Records

Palm OS 3.5 introduced a welcome change to the Address Book: the ability to duplicate existing records.

To duplicate an existing record:

1. Select an Address Book record from the Address List or tap it to open the Address View screen.

2. Select Duplicate Address from the Record menu, or write ╱-T (**Figure 5.17**). The new record adds the word "Copy"at the end of the text in the First name field (**Figure 5.18**).

✔ Tip

- Need to duplicate a record but aren't running Palm OS 3.5? You can make a copy by beaming it to yourself! In any text field, write ℛ- • -T (shortcut stroke, period, T). Then, select the record to duplicate and select Beam Address from the Record menu. Write ℛ- • -T again to deactivate the beaming feature.

Changing and Editing Phone Field Labels

Although there are five fields for contact numbers such as work and home phones, many of us have more access numbers than that. Address Book includes eight labels accessible via popup menus.

To change phone field labels:

1. Tap on a record to view it, then tap the Edit button (**Figure 5.19**).

2. Tap the popup menu next to the number you want to change. With the menu active, choose from Work, Home, Fax, Other, E-mail, Main, Pager, or Mobile.

3. Tap Done to exit the Address Edit screen.

To edit phone field labels in Palm Desktop (Windows):

◆ Click the field name next to the number you want to change, and choose the desired label from the popup menu.

◆ Set the preferred number in the editing screen by selecting the Show in list button to the left of the popup menu. This number will appear in the Address List.

To set default phone field options in Palm Desktop (Windows):

1. Set the phone field options as you'd like them to appear. The desktop software allows you to specify the fields that will be used for new records.

2. Mark the Save as default checkbox beneath the fields to specify which field is used for new records (**Figure 5.20**).

Figure 5.19 The popup phone label options provide for more than just work and home numbers.

Figure 5.20 Changing the phone field names in Palm Desktop for Windows works the same as in the Palm OS, with the added ability to set the record's preferred number. Marking the Save as default checkbox uses these settings for each new record created in Palm Desktop (but not on the handheld).

Figure 5.21 The Phones box under Palm Desktop for Macintosh features popup menus to label the fields, plus an option for adding numbers to the Instant Palm Desktop menu.

Figure 5.22 A phone field in Palm Desktop for Macintosh can have any name, though it shows up as Other on the Visor if it's not one of the existing labels.

Figure 5.23 Email shows up in the Other Information field instead of in Phones like on the Palm OS and under Windows.

To edit phone field labels in Palm Desktop (Macintosh):

1. Click the Phones box within a Contact window to edit the phone fields.

2. Choose a label from the popup windows to the left of each field (**Figure 5.21**).

3. If you want that contact's name and a number to appear in the Instant Palm Desktop menu, mark the box to the far right of the desired number.

To customize phone field labels in Palm Desktop (Macintosh):

1. Choose Other... from the popup menu to create a custom field name.

2. To permanently add a custom label to the menu, choose Edit Menu... (**Figure 5.22**).

3. Enter a new name and click OK.

✔ Tips

- If you enter an extension into the Ext. field, it appears on the same line as the number under the Palm OS.

- Only a maximum of four fields appear in a contact's Phones section, but there are five on the Visor. The fifth field is the Email field, found in the Other Information area (**Figure 5.23**). An Email option appears on the phone field popup menu as well, giving you a way to record multiple email addresses for contacts.

- You can use any name to describe a phone field, but keep in mind that anything not matching the predefined labels will appear as Other on the Visor.

CHANGING AND EDITING PHONE FIELD LABELS

Renaming the Custom Field Labels

In addition to standard fields like Address and City, four custom fields are available for text input. Since "Custom 1" is a boring label, you can change the names to anything else.

To rename custom field labels:

1. Choose Rename Custom Fields... from the Options menu to display the Rename Custom Fields dialog box (**Figure 5.24**).

   In Palm Desktop for Windows, select Custom Field Labels under the Tools menu. The Custom Field labels dialog box appears (**Figure 5.25**).

   If you're using Palm Desktop for Macintosh, getting there is a little more tricky: open a contact by double-clicking on it, then click in the Other Information area. Choose the field you want to edit, click the popup menu to the right, and select Field Options... (**Figure 5.26**).

2. Type the words or phrases you'd like to use. I find that Birthdate, Web, and Anniversary are essential labels; other possibilities include Spouse, Children (remember, you can type more than one item in the fields by writing a return character in the edit screen), or even Known Allergies.

3. Tap OK to exit.

✔ Tip

- Remember that if you beam a contact to another Palm device, your custom label names won't transfer with the record. So, any data in these fields might confuse someone who uses different labels.

Figure 5.24 Name the custom fields according to the information that's most important to you.

Figure 5.25 Palm Desktop for Windows calls this dialog box Custom Field Labels, not Rename Custom Fields... as in the Palm OS, but the idea is the same. Changing these labels applies them to every record in the Address Book.

Figure 5.26 Change the field names from within an active record by selecting Field Options... from a field's popup menu.

Figure 5.27 From the Address Edit screen, attach a note by tapping the Note button.

Figure 5.28 An attached note appears in the record as if it was a regular field. Use the scroll arrows to read more.

Attaching and Deleting Address Book Notes

The Palm OS's notes feature gives you a blank slate to add all sorts of information about a person or company, from a favorite movie to invaluable driving directions.

To attach a note to a contact:

1. Tap a contact to select it.

2. Tap the Edit button to bring up the Address Edit screen, then tap Note (**Figure 5.27**). Or, select Attach Note... from the Record menu, or write ╱-A.

3. Compose your note using Graffiti or the onscreen keyboard.

4. When you are finished, tap Done.

✔ Tips

- To edit the attached note later, follow the steps above to access the note. If you want a quicker method, however, tap the note icon (▯) to the right of the contact's preferred phone number.

- You don't have to open the note separately to view it. The text appears at the bottom of the contact's Address View, and can be read using the scroll arrows (**Figure 5.28**).

- A quick way to scroll, though harder to navigate, is to "select-scroll" through long notes. Position your cursor somewhere in the text and, without lifting the stylus from the screen, drag down the screen.

ATTACHING AND DELETING NOTES

To delete a note:

1. In the Address View or Address Edit screens, select Delete Note... from the Record menu, or write /-O.

2. If you're on the note editing screen, tap the Delete... button.

3. You will be asked to confirm your choice. Click Yes or No (**Figure 5.29**).

To attach a note (Windows):

1. Double-click a contact or click the Edit button to view the Edit Record screen. Or, click the blank space to the right of the record (where the note icon normally shows up) to bring up the Note Editor.

2. If you accessed the Edit Record screen, click the Note tab, or press Control-Tab to switch to it.

3. Type the text of your note, then click OK.

To attach a note (Macintosh):

1. Create a new note by clicking the Create Note button, or pressing Command-Option-N.

2. Write "Handheld Note: Address Book" in the Title field.

3. Type the text of your note.

4. Link the new Note record to the desired Contact by dragging the gripper ( ) to the Contact window (**Figure 5.30**). (See later in this chapter for information on linking records.)

✔ Tip

- I'll never be lost again! I used to keep a tattered library of paper scraps containing driving directions to people's homes and businesses in my car. Now, I store directions in notes attached to their addresses (**Figure 5.31**).

Figure 5.29 When you delete a note, you will be asked to verify your action.

Figure 5.30 On the Mac, create a new attached Note by dragging the gripper to the intended contact.

Figure 5.31 Attach driving directions to contacts and impress your relatives.

Figure 5.32 The option to edit your categories is strategically placed at the bottom of the popup category list.

Figure 5.33 Create or rename categories using up to 15 characters.

Figure 5.34 Address Book prefers to show you every contact whenever it's launched, unless you select Remember last category in the Preferences dialog.

Setting Up Custom Categories

The categories that are preset in the Palm OS barely hint at the value of organizing records by category. In addition to preventing data confusion, it makes it easier to view your data in comprehensible chunks, rather than one big list.

To create a custom category:

1. Select Edit Categories... from the category popup menu in the upper-right corner of the screen (**Figure 5.32**).

2. Tap New and give your category a name (**Figure 5.33**).

3. Tap OK to return to the list.

To specify the last category viewed:

1. Select Preferences... from the Options menu, or write ╱-R (**Figure 5.34**).

2. Mark the Remember last category box, then tap OK.

✔ Tips

■ To quickly switch to the next category, press the Address Book button on the handheld's case. If you've created a category that currently has no records assigned to it, Address Book skips to the next category containing records. Highly annoying, however, is that the Unfiled category is skipped using this method.

■ Create several records that share the same category by displaying that category and tapping New from the Address List; each new record will remain assigned to the current category.

■ The Macintosh Palm Desktop doesn't store categories for each built-in application, so you can only have a total of 15 categories shared among those programs.

Marking Contacts as Private

It's fun to show off your handheld some-times, but you don't want everyone to have unlimited access to your private information. It's easy to hide records from wandering eyes.

To mark contacts as private:

1. Tap the record you wish to change, then tap the Edit button.

2. Tap the Details... button.

3. Mark the Private checkbox, then tap OK (**Figure 5.35**).

4. Tap Done when finished (**Figure 5.36**).

Changing the Security Setting

Palm OS 3.5 introduced a new way of display-ing private data: masking. Although the pro-cedure below changes the display option throughout the system, you can change the Security setting from within any of the built-in applications.

To change the security setting:

1. Select Security... from the Options menu, write /-H, or tap the Security icon in the command toolbar.

2. Select an option from the Current Privacy popup menu: Show Records, Mask Records, or Hide Records (**Figure 5.37**).

3. Tap OK.

✔ Tip

- For more information about protecting the data on your Visor, see Chapter 12.

Check here for privacy

Figure 5.35 It takes a few taps to get to the Address Entry Details dialog, but it's worth it if you want to ensure that your private records are hidden or masked.

Private record

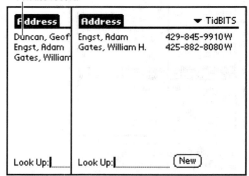

Figure 5.36 When you set the Security application's settings to Hide, private records are suppressed in the Address List.

Figure 5.37 Change the Security setting from within any application.

Figure 5.38 Choose the record you want for your business card (preferably the one with your name on it), then activate it from the Record menu.

Figure 5.39 The record designated as your business card displays a "beaming file card" icon next to the Address View tab. The best way to zap it to another IR-equipped Palm device is to just hold down the Address Book button on the front of the Visor case.

Beaming Addresses

Every Visor includes an infrared (IR) port for beaming data from one device to another. The most common usage of IR is to swap electronic business cards directly into other people's Address Books. If you've ever returned from a conference or trade show with a stack of business cards (and then lost them), you'll appreciate how useful beaming can be. Simply create a record for yourself and be prepared to amaze onlookers.

To specify your business card:

1. Find yourself (in the Address List—we can talk more about philosophy later). Tap the record to select it.

2. Choose Select Business Card... from the Record menu (**Figure 5.38**).

3. If you're sure, tap Yes in the confirmation dialog. A special icon appears next to the Address View and Address Edit tabs (**Figure 5.39**).

To beam your business card:

Choose Beam Business Card from the Record menu, or just press and hold the Address Book button on the handheld's case.

To beam an Address record:

1. Tap the record you wish to beam.

2. Choose Beam Address from the Record menu, or write ∕-B. Private records become public when beamed individually.

To beam a category:

1. Make your chosen category visible in the Address List.

2. Choose Beam Category from the Record menu. All records in that category, except Private records, will be transferred.

BEAMING ADDRESSES

✔ Tips

- You don't have to view a record before beaming it. Use the Look Up field to find a record, which highlights the match in the Address List (**Figure 5.40**). Write the command stroke (✓) to view the command toolbar, then tap the Beam Address icon (📡).

- When you transfer a category, the category's name does not appear on the recipient's Palm device. However, if they're running Palm OS 3.5 or later, they can choose which of their categories to assign to the group of incoming records, or they can create a new category.

- Some people prefer to leave the Beam Receive option off in the Preferences application to conserve battery life (see Chapter 2). If you fall into that camp, but need to receive beamed business cards from other Palm users, there are two ways to activate Beam Receive without making a side trip to the Preferences application (**Figure 5.41**).

  In a text field, write ℛ- · -I to temporarily enable Beam Receive for five seconds.

  The other option is to press and hold the plastic Address Book button as if you were going to beam your business card. After you beam your information (or tap Cancel), you'll be asked if you want to turn Beam Receive on.

- It's possible to "spread-beam" records to multiple handhelds at once. This is great if you're in a small group of Palm and Visor users and exchanging business cards; as long as the recipients are in range of the IR beam, they will all receive your business card even if you send it only once.

Figure 5.40 Find a record and beam it from the Address List using the Beam Address icon on the command bar.

Figure 5.41 You can choose to keep the Beam Receive option turned off, knowing that there's a shortcut for turning it on without coming back to Preferences.

Figure 5.42 In Windows Palm Desktop, drag the field names to match the record's field-mapping order.

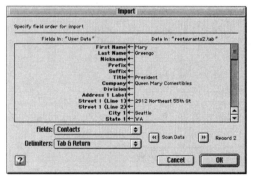

Figure 5.43 The Mac Palm Desktop takes a similar approach to Windows. This step can be slightly monotonous, but you'll appreciate it later on.

Importing Contacts into Palm Desktop

There's a good chance that you already have a stash of contact information stored in a desktop PIM program, or maybe even a customized database or Excel spreadsheet. If so, you should be able to transfer your records into Palm Desktop with a minimum of fuss.

To import contacts from a PIM:

1. In your existing PIM, select the export function—most programs include something like Export under the File menu.

2. Export the file as a tab-delimited text file; if you are presented with the option to include field names (such as "Last Name" or "City"), go ahead.

3. In Palm Desktop, choose Import... from the File menu.

4. Click and drag the field labels in the left-hand pane of the Specify Import Fields (Windows) or Import (Macintosh) dialog box to match the data in the right pane (**Figures 5.42** and **5.43**).

5. When the data looks right to you, click OK to begin the import process. After a few seconds, the records will be available to use.

✔ Tips

- If you have the option of including field names when you export the data from your original PIM, do it—you can save some time by matching the label names instead of guessing the order.

- If you select a category from the Contact List's category popup menu before you import, the new records will belong to that category after being imported.

Palm Desktop Special Features

In general, the desktop software mirrors the Palm OS in functionality. However, there are also a few features of Palm Desktop that add functionality, such as dialing phone numbers (if your PC is connected to the phone line you use for making calls), printing records, and sharing data with other applications.

To dial phone numbers:

1. In the Address List, click the contact you wish to call.

2. Choose Dial... from the Edit menu, or right-click the contact and select Dial... from the popup menu that appears. The Dialing dialog box opens (**Figure 5.44**). Under Palm Desktop for Macintosh, open the contact's information and click the dial button ( ).

3. Pick up the phone after the number begins dialing, and press the Talk button (Windows) or the Release button (Mac).

To print records:

1. Choose which records you want to print. If you want only a few, select them by Control/Command-clicking their names. To print an entire category, select it from the category popup menu. To print all records, select the All category.

2. Choose Print... from the File menu, or press Control/Command-P. The Print dialog box appears (**Figure 5.45**).

3. Set the print range to either Viewed category or Selection, and specify full records or just phone numbers printed (**Figure 5.46**).

Figure 5.44 Let the computer do the work for you—never memorize a phone number again!

Select which records to print
Choose how much information will be printed

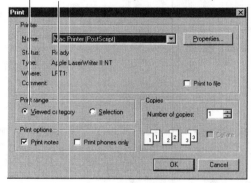

Figure 5.45 Printing Address Book records requires only two specialized fields in the standard Print dialog.

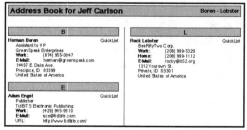

Figure 5.46 Printing from Address Book yields a readable (but not exciting) page of contact information.

Word   Excel   Clipboard

Figure 5.47 The Drag To feature copies the selected addresses to Microsoft Word, Microsoft Excel, or to the Clipboard for use with other applications.

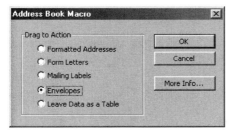

Figure 5.48 Dragging records to Word lets you choose the format of the final data.

Figure 5.49 A contact has been copied into Envelopes format using the Drag To Word feature.

To share data with other desktop applications using "drag to" (Windows):

1. Select the records you wish to copy.

2. Drag the selected records to the Drag To icons in the lower-right corner. Palm Desktop runs a set of instructions (called macros) that copy and format the data (**Figure 5.47**).

   If you drag to Word, you're presented with a dialog box asking in which format you'd like the data: Formatted Addresses, Form Letters, Mailing Labels, Envelopes, or Leave Data as a Table (**Figure 5.48**). Click the button to choose, then click OK.

3. Word or Excel will create a new file formatted with your data. If you copied the records to the Clipboard, go to your selected program and paste the contact information (**Figure 5.49**).

Macintosh Palm Desktop Special Features

Palm Desktop for Macintosh includes several features not found in the Windows software. For example, it offers the ability to attach not only notes to records, but also to create links between related records. Unfortunately, the links don't transfer over to the handheld, but they do save time and effort on the Mac.

To link records:

1. Open a Contact record by selecting it and pressing Return, or double-clicking it.

2. Grab the gripper () in the upper-left corner and drag it to the contact you wish to link. You can drag contacts onto events, to do items, and memos as well (**Figure 5.50**). You can also just drag one record in the Contact List onto another without viewing the details of either.

   Alternately, click the attachment popup menu (🖼️) and choose an item from the Attach To submenu.

To set Contacts preferences:

1. Choose Preferences… from the Edit menu. The Preferencecs dialog box appears (**Figure 5.51**).

2. Click the Contacts button on the left.

Notable preferences here include:

◆ **Phone popup menu.** No matter how you type the number, it will be formatted according to this selection.

◆ **Auto-capitalization.** Similar to the Palm OS, Palm Desktop capitalizes information within Contacts fields.

◆ **Auto-completion.** Palm Desktop stores lists of field contents; when you're entering information, it searches for a match and displays the likely result as you type.

Figure 5.50 Create relational links between records by dragging them onto one another.

Figure 5.51 Palm Desktop offers several options for working with Address Book (Contact) data.

Figure 5.52 The Find command displays matches containing the entire text in the Starts With field. Type more letters to narrow the search if several items appear.

Click name to sort...   ... or choose popup menu item.

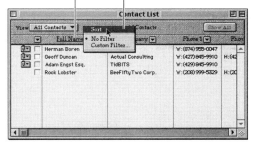

Figure 5.53 Sort the list by any column's contents by either clicking on the column's name, or choosing Sort from the popup menus.

Click and hold here

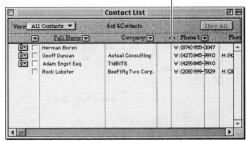

Figure 5.54 Click in the title area and drag to change the order of the visible columns.

To find contacts:

1. Choose Find... from the Locate menu, or press Command-F to display the Find dialog box (**Figure 5.52**).

2. Begin typing the name you're searching for. If you're looking for text within a contact, but it isn't a name or company name, click Display Results in List Window.

3. Click Display when it's found.

To sort records:

◆ To sort each list according to a column's contents, click the column's title (it will become underlined to indicate it's the active method) or choose Sort from each title's popup menu (**Figure 5.53**).

◆ You can also edit the columns to customize your display. Click and drag a column's right border to change its width. To rearrange the columns' order, click and hold in the area next to a column name, then drag left or right to position it (**Figure 5.54**). To choose which columns are displayed, select Columns... from the View menu and mark the ones you want.

✔ Tips

■ Palm Desktop has the added ability to sort using secondary criteria as well. For example, if you want to sort a list of people within a specific company, click the Company column title, then Shift-click the Full Name column title.

■ The Mark checkbox (**Figure 5.55**, next page) enables you to mark records from multiple categories, then quickly view them without creating a filter by choosing Marked from the popup menu in the column head. When printing, you can opt to print only the marked records without first locating them in the Contact List.

MACINTOSH PALM DESKTOP SPECIAL FEATURES

To filter specific data:

You can also configure the sorting method by choosing Custom Filter... from the popup menus, which displays only the items that meet the filter's criteria. For example, if you want to list only the phone calls you need to make, set up a filter that searches for the words "call" or "phone" (**Figure 5.56**).

To save memorized views:

When you've set up a sort order and specific filters, choose Memorize View... from the View popup menu to save it. This way, you can see related tasks and notes without repeating the sorting steps above. To see the full list again, click the Show All button.

To create a pre-addressed email message:

1. In a record's Contact window, click the Other Information area.

2. Click the email button () beside the Email field. A blank email message is created in your email program with the contact's email address in the To: field.

✔ Tip

■ You can change the email client that's tied into the Email field's button. Choose Field Options... from the field's popup menu, then choose your email client from the Script File popup menu (**Figure 5.57**). (If you use Qualcomm's Eudora Pro, you should download the Create Eudora Pro Message AppleScript, found at http://www.palmgear.com/.)

Figure 5.55 Mark records that you use frequently to view and print them quickly, without creating a filter.

Figure 5.56 Create custom filters to display only the contacts matching specified criteria.

Figure 5.57 The custom fields can be customized even further. Here, the Email field is set to create a pre-addressed message in Eudora Pro.

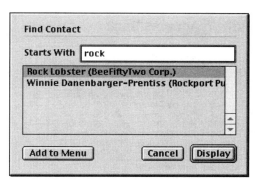

Figure 5.58 Search your Address Book using the Instant Palm Desktop's Find Contact feature.

Figure 5.59 All the information of Palm Desktop—without the RAM overhead—is available when you select a record from the Instant Palm Desktop menu.

Using the Instant Palm Desktop Menu

The Instant Palm Desktop menu resides in the upper-right corner of your screen, next to the Mac OS's Application menu, and allows you to access contacts and other records without having to launch Palm Desktop.

To access contact information using the Instant Palm Desktop:

◆ Click the menu and highlight a contact to view or edit its details; or, choose Open Palm Desktop to launch the program.

◆ Search for an address by selecting Find Contact (**Figure 5.58**). To make a contact appear permanently on the menu, click the Add to Menu button. You can also dial phone numbers directly from the contact detail window (**Figure 5.59**).

◆ Create new addresses, events, To Do items, memos, and event banners from the Create submenu.

To add contacts to the Instant Palm Desktop:

In a record's Instant Palm Desktop contact view, or the Contact window within Palm Desktop, check the box to the right of the phone number you want to appear in the Instant Palm Desktop menu.

To remove contacts from the Instant Palm Desktop:

In the Contact window, uncheck the box to the right of the phone number.

✔ Tip

■ If you find yourself writing your address frequently in letters or email, put yourself in the Instant Palm Desktop menu, then click the Copy All button to get the info.

Alternatives to Using the Built-In Address Book

The Address Book offers a lot of power in a svelte package, but what if you want to supercharge your contact list? Although there are plenty of alternatives, the two I'm most impressed with are Super Names (http://www.standalone.com/) and PopUp Names (http://www.benc.hr/popnames.htm). Both programs use the Address Book's database as their data source, which means your contacts are still synchronized with your PC.

Super Names

I was dubious of Super Names at first, mostly because I respond strongly to interfaces. A quick look at the Super Names main screen shows how crowded it can be (**Figure 5.60**). But notice what's there: categories appear as tabs across the top of the screen; an alphabet running beneath the tabs lets you tap a letter to jump to that range of contacts; an optional panel below the Address List previews the highlighted name, with icons to specify which info appears.

In addition to cramming a lot of useful information on one screen, Super Names lets you link contacts to other contacts, or even to records from Date Book, the To Do List, or the Memo Pad (**Figure 5.61**). Linked records can be displayed by tapping a paper-clip icon at the top of the screen.

PopUp Names

PopUp Names shows more contact information on its main screen, but it has the distinction of being viewed from within any application on your Visor. PopUp Names is actually a system hack (see Chapter 8); when enabled, write a stroke in the silkscreened area (the default is to draw a line from the Calculator icon to the Find icon) to bring up the PopUp Names window (**Figure 5.62**).

You can even perform Address Book functions like beaming your business card or other contacts just as if you've launched the Address Book application itself.

Figure 5.60 Once you get the hang of the Super Names interface, you'll like how easy it is to view contact info.

Figure 5.61 Link contacts or other records to view them quickly next time.

Figure 5.62 PopUp Names is available from any application on your Visor.

To Do List & Memo Pad

When I tell people about the Visor, most seem to get excited about the Date Book and Address Book, two applications that can greatly decrease the amount of paper they carry. But when I was first considering whether to buy a handheld, it was the To Do List that thrilled me. I need to *see* tasks that must be accomplished, or else I risk forgetting about them until it's too late. A digital to-do list that keeps reminding me of tasks not yet finished was irresistible.

The Memo Pad, on the other hand, was low on my list of required features. I mean, it's a necessary element (what's the point of having a palmtop device if you can't jot down quick notes?), but light bulbs are also necessary elements, and you don't see me drooling over the latest 100-watt GE soft-white bulb.

Now, both applications are essential to me: I can track my tasks with the To Do List (and make them disappear when completed), and I can use Memo Pad to store information that I had never considered before.

Viewing Options

The To Do List (**Figure 6.1**) can be as sparse or as detailed as you want. Tap the Show... button to access the To Do Preferences window, which provides the following options (**Figure 6.2**).

◆ If you prefer to see the items you've accomplished, mark the Show Completed Items checkbox.

   If you uncheck this option to hide completed items, the records are still held in the device's memory until you manually purge them (see "Purging Records" later in this chapter).

◆ The To Do List, by default, displays all upcoming tasks, even if they're several years away. If you would rather live for today (as I do), mark Show Only Due Items.

◆ Marking Record Completion Date changes an item's due date to the date it was checked off when finished.

◆ Show Due Dates, when marked, adds a date column to the right of the task names; items with no due date specified are represented by dashes.

◆ Marking Show Priorities displays a column of numbers, representing the importance of each task (1 is highest, 5 is lowest), between the checkboxes and item names.

◆ As with the Address Book and Memo Pad, To Do List records can be assigned to categories. Show Categories adds a category column to the right side of the screen.

Priority | Task name | Due date | Category

Figure 6.1 The To Do List, with all aspects visible, includes each task, plus its priority, due date, and category.

Figure 6.2 Depending on your tolerance for visual clutter, you may want more options visible.

Figure 6.3 Choose how your private records are displayed.

Figure 6.4 The Sort by popup menu organizes tasks to fit your preferences.

Figure 6.5 Sorting by Category, Due Date can do funky things with dates: the task for "Invent... device" is really set for January 2, 2002, eleven months after "Make reservations..." because they belong to different categories.

Changing Security View

Beginning with Palm OS 3.5, private records can be displayed, masked (grayed out), or (as in previous versions) hidden.

To change the Security view:

1. Select Security... from the Options menu.

2. Tap the Current Privacy popup menu to choose from one of three methods: Show Records, Mask Records, or Hide Records (**Figure 6.3**).

3. Tap OK to exit.

Setting the Sort Order

Once you've decided which elements will be visible, you need to figure out how to sort the To Do records. Feel free to experiment with each setting for a few days to get a sense of what works best for you.

To set the sort order:

1. Tap Show... to bring up the To Do Preferences window (**Figure 6.4**).

2. Tap the Sort by popup menu to choose from one of four methods: Priority, Due Date; Due Date, Priority; Category, Priority; or Category, Due Date (**Figure 6.5**).

3. Tap OK to exit.

✔ Tip

■ I can't stress how much I love to check off a To Do item and have it *disappear*. In college, I carried spiral notebooks filled with to-do lists—or rather, I carried notebooks filled with scribbles and marked-out scribbles. Ick. I can understand that people like to see what they've accomplished, but to me it's all just clutter. Show Completed Items is therefore never marked on my Visor.

Entering To Do Items

Creating new To Do items takes more than just having someone say, "Do this!" over your shoulder. But not much more.

To create a new To Do item:

1. Tap the New button. A flashing cursor will appear on a blank line.

2. Write the name of your task—feel free to use multiple lines (**Figure 6.6**). Tap anywhere in a "null" area of the screen (such as the lower-right corner) to deselect your new task.

✔ Tips

- You don't have to tap the New button to create a new To Do item. With nothing selected, start writing in the Graffiti area; a new record will be created automatically (**Figure 6.7**).

- The default settings for new To Do items are Unfiled, no date, with a priority of 1. If you want a new task to share attributes of an existing item, you can maintain category, priority, and/or due date by highlighting an existing record and then tapping New.

- If one category is displayed (versus viewing All), any new records are assigned that category.

Figure 6.6 Tapping the New button creates a blank record for you to name.

Figure 6.7 If you know what you want to add, just write it! Entering Graffiti characters with nothing selected creates a new To Do List item.

Figure 6.8 You can edit most aspects of a task without leaving the To Do List by tapping these areas.

Figure 6.9 Tap the Details... button to bring up a dialog box where you can change any aspect of a To Do item.

Figure 6.10 The only aspect of a task you can't edit from the main list is an item's privacy state.

Editing To Do Items

Depending on which options you've chosen to show, almost every aspect of a To Do item can be changed from the main To Do screen. However, if you prefer a cleaner window, the options are no more than two taps away (**Figure 6.8**).

To prioritize a task:

1. If visible, tap the priority column to the left of the task name and choose a different priority level. Or, tap the To Do item, then tap the Details... button.

2. Choose a priority from the buttons at the top of the To Do Item Details window. Tap OK to make the change.

To change a task's category:

1. If visible, tap the category column at the far right of the screen and choose a new category. Or, tap the To Do item, then tap the Details... button.

2. Tap the Category popup menu and select a new category (**Figure 6.9**). To add or edit categories, see "Categorizing To Do Items and Memos" later in this chapter. Tap OK.

To make a task private:

1. Tap the To Do item, then tap the Details... button.

2. Mark the Private checkbox (**Figure 6.10**). If you've chosen Hide Records or Mask Records from the Security application, the record's text will not be visible when you tap OK. (See Chapter 2 for information on hiding and showing private records.)

To change a task's due date:

1. If visible, tap the due date column and choose a new date. Otherwise, tap the To Do item, then tap the Details... button.

2. Tap the Due Date popup menu. The frequently used commands Today, Tomorrow, and One week later make it easy to reschedule tasks (**Figure 6.11**).

3. If you need to switch to a specific date, tap Choose Date... and select a new day (**Figure 6.12**). Tap OK.

To mark a task completed:

The moment you've been waiting for—tap the checkbox at left to mark the task completed (**Figure 6.13**).

✔ Tips

■ The To Do application indicates a missed deadline by displaying an exclamation point in the due date column (see "Take out trash" in **Figure 6.13**).

■ Despite my best intentions, sometimes I don't complete all of today's tasks by the end of the day. (See Chapter 16 for strategies to avoid this type of situation.) Rather than manually tap the Due Date popup menus on the past due items to reflect today's due date, I use the shareware utility Plonk (http://www.alcita.com/palmpilot/) to update them all for me with one touch.

Figure 6.11 Your Visor knows how you work: four common date options are included in the popup menu.

Figure 6.12 If you select Choose Date... from the popup menu, you can tap your intended date on the calendar.

Completed task

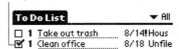

Figure 6.13 Tap the checkbox to mark a task completed. Feels good, doesn't it?

Figure 6.14 Tap the Note button to add important information to a task.

Figure 6.15 Navigating a note attached to a To Do item is identical to notes in the other built-in applications (unless you're running Palm OS 3.5).

Adding and Deleting Notes to To Do Items

To attach a note to a task:

1. Tap an item to select it.

2. Tap the Details... button, then tap the Note button (**Figure 6.14**).

   Alternately, select Attach Note... from the Record menu, or write ╱-A.

3. Compose your note using Graffiti or the onscreen keyboard. Tap Done when you are finished.

✔ Tip

■ To edit the attached note later, follow the steps above to access the note. If you want a quicker method, tap the note icon (**⬚**) to the right of the task's name.

To navigate a note:

Use the scroll bar on the right side of the screen or the physical scroll buttons to move through the text.

If you're using Palm OS 3.3 or earlier, select Go to Top of Page or Go to Bottom of Page from the Options menu to jump quickly to the beginning or end (**Figure 6.15**).

To delete a note (from main list):

1. Tap the To Do item to select it.

2. Select Delete Note... from the Record menu, or write ╱-O. Confirm its deletion by tapping Yes or No.

To delete a note (standard method):

1. Tap Details..., then the Note button.

2. Tap Delete... in the Note window. Confirm whether you want to delete it by tapping Yes or No.

Purging Records

It may bring you a measure of satisfaction to know there are dozens, maybe hundreds, of completed tasks in your Visor. Unfortunately, that means they're also taking up RAM. To free up some memory, purge those aging To Do items (**Figure 6.16**).

To purge old records:

1. From the To Do List, select Purge... from the Records menu, or write ∕-E.

2. If you want to remove the items from your Visor, but keep them stored on your computer's hard drive, mark the Save archive copy on PC checkbox (**Figure 6.17**). They will be transferred at the next HotSync operation, and removed from your handheld.

3. Tap OK.

Figure 6.16 You can see how much space your completed and pending To Do items are filling by going to the Applications screen and selecting Info... from the App menu. Here, the amount of free memory has increased dramatically following a purge.

Figure 6.17 The urge to keep all those successfully completed To Do items can be overpowering, but at some point you'll need to free up some memory on your Visor. Mark the Save archive copy on PC to ensure that the tasks aren't lost forever.

PURGING RECORDS

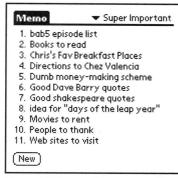

Figure 6.18 Memos let you store all those random scraps of information.

Figure 6.19 The text on the first line of your memo becomes its title. From there, write your memo, or paste the text in from the clipboard.

Creating and Editing Memos

The Memo Pad is straightforward, yet surprisingly useful. Imagine all of your Post-it notes—plus the crumpled papers discovered in last week's laundry—stored in one location (**Figure 6.18**). The power here is not in the number of features the Memo Pad offers, but in its overall utility.

To create a new memo:

1. Tap the New button.

2. Start writing. The first line of your memo will become its title, so don't write something generic like "Note" (**Figure 6.19**).

3. Tap Done when you're, well, done.

✔ Tip

■   With nothing selected from the Memo Pad list, begin writing in the Graffiti area. A new memo will be created containing what you've written.

To edit a memo:

1. Tap once on the title of the memo you want to edit.

2. To change the memo's category, select one from the category field in the upper-right corner. Or, tap the Details button.

3. Tap Done.

To make a memo private:

1. After tapping the memo you want, tap the Details button to display the Memo Details dialog box.

2. Mark the Private checkbox. If your Security preferences are set to hide private records, the memo will not appear in any of the Memo Pad category lists.

3. Tap Done.

Sorting Memos

Information, unlike dark socks, begs to be sorted. Some prefer alphabetical listings, while others are quite content with chaos. Although the Memo Pad doesn't claim to be the storehouse of the world's information, its sorting capabilities—though limited—can appeal to both extremes.

To sort memos:

1. Select Preferences... from the Options menu, or write ╱-R, to display the Memo Preferences dialog box (**Figure 6.20**).

2. Choose a sorting method from the Sort by popup menu. Alphabetic lists items based on their first letters; Manual gives you the power to list items randomly, or by your own secret sorting code. Tap OK.

Note that you must first select Manual sorting before you can begin moving items within the Memo List (**Figure 6.21**). If you've been manually sorting and want to switch back to Alphabetic, you will lose your sort order. Unfortunately, the sorting method you choose applies to all memos, so you can't have some categories sorted manually and others sorted alphabetically.

✔ Tips

■ Several utilities have been written to make it easier to manipulate text. Under Palm OS 3.1, SelectHack (http://www.jeffjetton.com/) lets you tap twice to select a word, and three times to select a sentence. Drag and Drop Hack (http://www.wakuwaku.ne.jp/shuji/) lets you move text without using Copy and Paste.

■ If you want to type on the road, consider two keyboard solutions: Landware's GoType Pro (http://www.landware.com/), or the Targus Stowaway Keyboard (http://www.thinkoutside.com/). See Chapter 1 for more on these keyboards.

Figure 6.20 The Memo Pad gives you two options for sorting the Memo List.

Memo will end up here

Figure 6.21 With sorting set to Manual, tap and drag a memo to a new location. A gray line indicates where it will end up when you lift the stylus.

Figure 6.22 Jump quickly within a memo using the Options menu (Palm OS 3.1 only).

Is Memo Pad Good Enough for Taking Notes?

You'd think that having a palm-sized device to write with would make people want to ditch paper forever. Although there are some people who use their handhelds as note-taking machines, I've found that writing longer texts takes more effort and headache than regular ink and wood pulp.

The advantage of writing longhand is that you can write several letters with one stroke (depending on your handwriting style, of course), whereas Graffiti requires that each char-acter be a sep-arate entity. Plus, extended Graffiti writing tends to aggra-vate my hands and wrists, which have had their share of repetitive strain injuries (RSIs) in the past (**Figure 6.23**). I prefer to use the Memo Pad as a great place to store information, not necessarily create it.

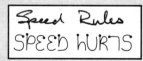

Figure 6.23 Longhand text is a little easier on the hands and wrists than Graffiti.

Navigating Memos

Moving around in memos isn't much differ-ent than navigating notes (see "To navigate a note" earlier in this chapter), but a few aspects do stand out.

To navigate memos:

1. Use the scroll bar at right (if the memo extends past one screen length) to move up and down the text.

2. Press the plastic up and down buttons on the Visor's case. One added benefit of this approach is that you can jump to the next or previous memo, without returning to the main Memo List.

3. If you're running Palm OS 3.1, jump quickly from the top to the bottom (and vice-versa) by choosing either Go to Top of Page or Go to Bottom of Page from the Options menu (**Figure 6.22**). Unfortu-nately, this capability has been removed in Palm OS 3.5.

✔ Tip

■ Although the Go to Top of Page and Go to Bottom of Page commands have been removed in Palm OS 3.5, there's still an easy workaround to zap through your text: tap and drag up or down to select the text and quickly go to the top or bottom. It may not be the most elegant solution, but it's easy and it works.

Categorizing To Do Items and Memos

To assign a To Do List category:

1. If Show Categories is selected in the To Do Preferences, tap the category name to the right of a record and choose a new category from the popup menu that appears (**Figure 6.24**).

   If categories are not visible, select the record and tap Details.

2. Select a name from the Category popup menu. Tap OK to return to the list.

To assign a category to a memo:

1. Tap a memo to open it.

2. Select a category name from the popup menu in the upper-right corner of the screen. Or, tap Details and choose an item from the Category popup menu there.

To set up custom categories:

1. In both the To Do List and the Memo Pad, tap the category popup menu in the upper-right corner. Select Edit categories... from the bottom of the list to bring up the Edit Categories... dialog box.

2. Tap the New or Rename button and write the category name (**Figure 6.25**) or tap a name and Delete to remove a category.

✔ Tips

- To create multiple records sharing the same category, go to that category's screen, then create your records there.

- You can merge categories without changing each record individually. Simply rename the categories so they share the same name; you will receive a dialog box confirming your action (**Figure 6.26**).

Figure 6.24 Assign categories quickly by tapping the category column.

Figure 6.25 You can specify up to 15 categories for each of the four built-in applications.

Figure 6.26 Instead of manually reassigning a category to multiple records, merge two existing categories into one.

Figure 6.27 Selecting a font changes the setting for all memo records, not just the one currently viewed.

Figure 6.28 Tap the Beam icon in the command bar under Palm OS 3.5.

Changing the Font

In the To Do List and Memo List, you can set a different font for list and record views.

To change the font:

1. In either the list view or the record view, select Font... from the Options menu, or write ✓-F. The Select Font dialog box appears.

2. Choose the font from the boxes provided, and tap OK (**Figure 6.27**).

Beaming Records

Save a friend some writing time and transfer your to do items or memos via infrared.

To beam a To Do item or memo:

1. Tap the record that you want to beam. The Memo Pad will display the entire memo; the To Do List will position your cursor in the record's text.

2. Select Beam Item (To Do List) or Beam Memo (Memo Pad) from the Record menu, or write ✓-B; you can also choose the Beam icon (☎) from the command toolbar under Palm OS 3.5 (**Figure 6.28**).

To beam a category:

1. With no records selected, select the category you wish to beam from the category popup menu at the top-right corner. To beam all categories, choose All.

2. Select Beam Category from the Record menu. Note, however, that your categories will appear as Unfiled on the recipient's Visor. (Palm OS 3.5 lets them choose a category for the received files.)

Working in Palm Desktop for Windows

Using the To Do List and the Memo Pad within Palm Desktop is, for the most part, the same as working on the Visor. Creating records, specifying viewing options, and using categories are all accomplished using the main screen (**Figure 6.29**). However, there are also a few features that can only be accessed on your PC.

To print records:

1. Choose the items you want to print, or choose the category to print.

2. Choose Print... from the File menu, or press Control-P.

3. Specify how you want the data to appear in the Print Options box. Click OK to create a printout (**Figure 6.30**).

You can easily transfer your memos directly to Microsoft Word or other applications via the Clipboard by dragging them to the "Drag to" icons in the lower-right corner of the Palm Desktop window.

To share memos with other applications using "Drag to":

1. Select the memos you wish to transfer.

2. Drag your selections to either the Word or Clipboard Drag to icons.

3. Format your information either in Microsoft Word (which would have launched after you dropped the memos onto the Word icon), or the program of your choice.

Figure 6.29 The To Do List within Palm Desktop presents all of your options on one main screen.

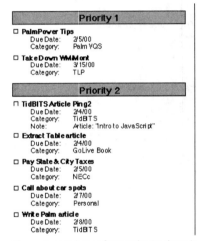

Figure 6.30 Printing from Palm Desktop isn't sexy, but it works. The layout of tasks depends on the sort order you've specified using the Show button.

Figure 6.31 Memo contents are displayed in the pane at right. Dragging memos to the Drag to icons at lower right copies them to Word or the Clipboard.

Figure 6.32 Dropping tasks on the Microsoft Word Drag to icon activates a set of macros that formats your data using handy templates.

To share To Do items with other applications using "Drag to":

1. Select the To Do items to transfer, and drag the selections to one of the icons at the lower right (**Figure 6.31**).

2. If you chose Word, you are given the option to format the data as a Task Progress Report, a Task Delegation Form, or just Leave Data as a Table. When the transfer is complete and the data is formatted, it will be available in Word (**Figure 6.32**).

✔ Tips

■ In addition to clicking the application buttons at left, you can press the F4 key to view the To Do List, and the F5 key to bring up the Memo Pad. F1 launches the Palm Desktop online help.

■ To quickly access the Note Editor from the To Do List, click either a note icon (🗐) to the right of a task, or the blank space where the icon would appear, which will take you to the Note Editor.

■ When adding records, you can press the Apply button to deactivate the current record. If you're adding multiple records, however, forget about the Apply button and instead just press New to begin the next record—your previous entry will be added automatically to the list.

Working in Palm Desktop for Macintosh

In essence, the To Do section of Palm Desktop for Macintosh (referred to as the Task List) provides the same functionality and features as its Windows counterpart, even though it looks quite a bit different. However, because of the program's lineage as Claris Organizer, the Mac Palm Desktop works a bit differently.

To view the Task List or Note List:

◆ Select Task List or Note List from the View menu, or press Command-Shift-T or Command-Shift-N.

◆ Click the View Task List or View Note List button on the Toolbar (**Figure 6.33**).

To create new To Do items and memos:

◆ Double-click an unused portion of the Task List window or Note List window (**Figure 6.34**). You can also double-click the Task pane of the Daily calendar view.

◆ Choose Task... or Note... from the Create menu, or press Command-Option-T (To Do item) or Command-Option-N (memo).

◆ You can also click the Create Task or Create Note button on the Toolbar.

✔ Tips

■ The Daily calendar window also displays tasks for that day only. The only time I ever need the full Task List is if I'm looking ahead at future To Do items.

■ In the Daily calendar window, set aside a block of time to work on a task by dragging it to the day's schedule. Palm Desktop adds "Work on" to the task name—or "Celebrate" if it's a birthday reminder created by Palm Desktop!

Create Task   View Task List

View Task List

Create Note   View Note List

Figure 6.33 The Toolbar offers quick access to the Task and Note controls.

Figure 6.34 Double-clicking in the Task List brings up a new Task window.

Click name to sort... ... or choose a popup menu item.

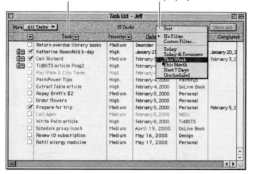

Figure 6.35 Sort the list by any column's contents by either clicking on the column's name, or choosing Sort from the popup menus.

Click and hold here

Figure 6.36 Click in the title area and drag to change the order of the visible columns.

Figure 6.37 Create custom filters to display only the tasks or memos that match specified criteria.

To sort records:

◆ To sort each list according to a column's contents, click the column's title (it will become underlined to indicate it's the active method) or choose Sort from each title's popup menu (**Figure 6.35**).

◆ You can also edit the columns to customize your display. Click and drag a column's right border to change its width. To rearrange the columns' order, click and hold in the area next to a column name, then drag left or right to position it (**Figure 6.36**). To choose which columns are displayed, select Columns... from the View menu and mark the ones you want.

To filter specific data:

You can also configure the sorting method by choosing Custom Filter... from the popup menus, which displays only the items that meet the filter's criteria. For example, if you want to list only the phone calls you need to make, set up a filter that searches for the words "call" or "phone" (**Figure 6.37**).

To save memorized views:

When you've set up a sort order and specific filters, choose Memorize View... from the View popup menu to save it. This way, you can see related tasks and notes without repeating the sorting steps above. To see the full list again, click the Show All button.

✔ Tips

■ You can sort a list according to multiple criteria. Click a column name to perform the first sort, then Shift-click another column name to then sort the sorted results.

■ In the Daily calendar view, sort the day's Task List according to completion by clicking the word "Tasks" above the list.

WORKING IN PALM DESKTOP FOR MACINTOSH

You can attach related records to other records (such as memos attached to To Do items or records). Although this linkage does not carry across to the Visor, it can be a valuable way of working with your data on the desktop.

To attach records to To Do items and memos:

◆ If both records are visible, drag and drop one to the other. A link is created in both records (**Figure 6.38**).

◆ Click the folder icon (🔲) and choose Attach To from the popup menu.

As I mentioned in Chapter 1, the biggest confusion arising from Macintosh Palm Desktop is the way it handles notes belonging to records (such as in the Date Book or Address Book). Whereas the Windows Palm Desktop treats attached notes as separate entities, the Mac software uses its Notes feature to handle attached notes.

Each note attached to a To Do item exists as a separate record in the Mac Palm Desktop Note List, and each is titled, "Handheld Note: To Do List." It is then linked to its associated record using the Palm Desktop's attachment feature explained above. With that in mind, it becomes relatively easy to attach new notes on the desktop.

To attach notes to To Do items:

1. Click the Create Note icon or press Command-Option-N.

2. Type "Handheld Note: To Do List" exactly as shown in the Title field.

3. Write the text of your note.

4. Link the note by dragging its Gripper (🔲) to its associated task (**Figure 6.39**).

Figure 6.38 Drag and drop records onto each other to create links, indicated by the folder icon that appears to the left of records.

Figure 6.39 Be sure to use the title "Handheld Note: To Do List" to ensure that your note will appear as an attached note on your handheld.

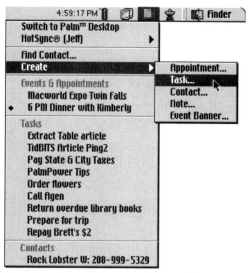

Figure 6.40 You don't even need to open Palm Desktop to access its features; the Instant Palm Desktop menu is a quick method of accessing or creating records.

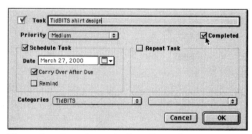

Figure 6.41 Experience the joy of completing a task without even launching Palm Desktop to mark it done.

Instant Palm Desktop menu

The day's current tasks are also listed in the Instant Palm Desktop menu (**Figure 6.40**). From here you can edit or create tasks—without even launching Palm Desktop.

◆ Highlight an item to view or edit its details, or choose Open Palm Desktop or Switch to Palm Desktop (if it's already running) to launch the program.

◆ To mark an item as done, highlight it to open the Task dialog box. Click the Completed checkbox and click OK (**Figure 6.41**).

◆ Create new To Do items by selecting Task... from the Create submenu.

CALCULATOR & EXPENSE

Remember when having one of those calculator watches was the coolest? Imagine! A whole calculator on your wrist—and if you could just sneak it into math class without anyone suspecting....

The screen is now bigger than the old calculator watches (and the buttons are certainly larger!), but the utility of having a calculator on my handheld has been helpful for those times when this former English major has found himself awash in numbers.

The number fun doesn't stop at the calculator, though. If you have to keep track of expenses for work, the included Expense application should save you a headache at month's end when you're trying to explain to your boss where that $100 went in Las Vegas.

Using the Calculator

Admittedly, the Palm OS's built-in calculator isn't what you'd call comprehensive (especially if you're a real number cruncher). It adds, subtracts, multiplies, and divides. It has big buttons so you can use your finger instead of the stylus if you want to. And it reinforces the Palm philosophy that something doesn't have to be complicated and bloated with features in order to be useful.

Still, there are several things lurking just below the surface of the Calculator application that make it better than a cheapo math machine hiding somewhere in the back of your desk drawer.

To perform calculations:

1. Launch the Calculator application by tapping the silk-screened icon, or the Calculator icon from within Applications (**Figure 7.1**).

2. Tap the buttons to enter numbers and basic mathematical operations.

3. Tap the percentage button to convert a number to a decimal percentage (for example: ❷ ❺ 🔘 = 0.25).

4. Tap the 🔘 button to make a number either positive or negative.

To clear the results field:

1. Tapping 🔘 clears the entire calculation.

2. Tapping 🔘 clears the last number you entered without wiping out everything.

✔ Tip

■ You can operate the calculator by writing in the Graffiti area (**Table 7.1**). I'm not sure why exactly you'd want to, but at the very least it's good Graffiti practice!

Figure 7.1 There's no mistaking that this is a calculator, right down to the finger-friendly buttons.

Table 7.1

Graffiti Calculator?
Yes, it's true! Use the Calculator without tapping any buttons by writing numbers and symbols in the Graffiti area.

BUTTON	GRAFFITI	BUTTON	GRAFFITI
❶	|	CE	ε
❷	2	C	C
❸	3	MC	M
❹	L	MR	R
❺	5	M+	P
❻	6	%	·/
❼	7	+/-	·\
❽	8	÷	\⅔
❾	9	×	·⅔
❿	O	−	·—
•	..	=	\Z
		+	\α

Figure 7.2 View the last several steps in an operation by bringing up the Recent Calculations screen.

Recent Calculations ⓘ

2437.607	=
2437.607	+
339.	*
452.	M+
452.	-
263.147	+
452.	MR
452.	-
-2.	+/-
-2.	=

1255217.2	=

(OK)

Figure 7.3 The Calculator's "tape" makes it easier to see where mistakes are made, although it only stores one screen full of information.

To memorize calculation results:

1. Tap the 🔵 button to store the current result in memory; a small "m" will appear in the number field. If you tap the button again later, the new result is added to the stored number, instead of replacing it.

2. Tap 🔵 to display the stored number; you can use it as part of a calculation in progress.

3. Tap 🔵 to clear the contents of the stored memory.

To view "the tape":

1. You can access a list of the most recent numbers in a calculation by choosing Recent Calculations from the Options menu, or by writing ╱-I (**Figure 7.2**).

2. You'll see the numbers of the current calculation in a list running down the right side of the screen (**Figure 7.3**). Note that only what you see is stored; you can't scroll up to an earlier number. Also, tapping the equals button (🔵) ends an operation, so the next number you press will create a brand new "tape."

USING THE CALCULATOR

159

Copying and Pasting Calculations

Being able to take your calculation results to another application is one of the reasons I said that Calculator is more useful than most calculators. Sure, you can write the numbers on paper, but that's just *so* 1995.

To copy and paste calculations:

◆ On the main screen, choose Copy from the Edit menu (or write ╱-C) to copy the current number to the Palm OS's Clipboard for pasting into other programs. Similarly, you can copy a number from another application and choose Paste (or write ╱-P) to add it to your calculation.

◆ In the Recent Calculations screen, choose Copy from the Edit menu (or write ╱-C) to grab the visible list of calculations for pasting elsewhere (**Figure 7.4**).

✔ Tips

■ If you make a calculation, then switch to another application, the calculation result is held in memory. However, the last set of operations normally viewed by the Recent Calculations screen gets erased! If you're going to need the full transcript of a calculation later, copy it first before exiting the Calculator. You may want to set up a Memo Pad record to paste in your results before moving on to the next task.

■ There are several calculators you can download that should be able to handle whatever you throw at them (**Figure 7.5**). For example, RPN (http://www.nthlab.com/) is an advanced calculator that also accepts plug-ins written by other developers. FCPlus Professional (http://www.infinitysw.com/) specializes in financial calculations.

Figure 7.4 Paste calculations or results into other applications, like Memo Pad shown here.

Figure 7.5 Other calculators, such as RPN (top) and FCPlus Professional (bottom) take over where the built-in Calculator leaves off.

Figure 7.6 Handspring's Advanced Calculator mode requires a calculator just to count all of its features.

Figure 7.7 The View popup menu switches between the different modes.

Advanced Calculator Mode

One of the attractions of the Visor is the work that Handspring's engineers put in to enhance some of the built-in applications. At first glance, the Calculator is the same as on any other Palm device. It isn't until you switch to Advanced mode that you see just how much calculation power is at hand (**Figure 7.6**).

The Advanced Calculator features nine built-in views, accessible by tapping the View popup menu: Math, Trig, Finance, Logic, Statistics, Weight/Tmp, Length, Area, and Volume. The top two rows of buttons change depending on the view.

To switch to Advanced mode:

1. From the Options menu, choose Change Mode..., or write ╱-M.

2. Tap the Advanced button, then tap OK.

To change calculator views:

1. Tap the leftmost popup menu below the calculator's number field.

2. Select a view name; the calculator's buttons change depending on the view (**Figure 7.7**).

✔ Tip

- Okay, disclaimer time: as Chevy Chase said (in a *Saturday Night Live* skit as former President Gerald Ford), "I didn't know there would be math involved."

  I'm not a mathematician, so I won't waste pages going through every function that the Advanced Calculator offers. Instead, consult the Visor manual (in PDF format on the CD-ROM) that came with the device; Handspring has put together a good overview of each function.

Creating Custom Views in the Advanced Calculator

I may not be the sharpest slide rule in the mathematician's toolbox, but I know a cool feature when I see one. The Visor's Advanced Calculator comes with nine built-in views, but that's not the limit. You can create a custom view that operates according to your whims, changing the functions of the view-specific buttons.

To create a custom view:

1. First, export an existing view to use as a template. Choose Export from the Program menu, or write ╱-E.

2. Select a view style to export from the popup menu that appears, then tap Export (**Figure 7.8**).

3. Switch to the Memo Pad, then choose Calculator from the category popup menu.

4. Tap the record you exported (**Figure 7.9**). The first line is the title; each subsequent line corresponds to one of the view-specific buttons.

5. To change a button's title, write the new title at the beginning of the line. Edit the last number in the line to specify the calculation amount to be applied when the button is pressed. To make the button blank, replace the line with "Unused."

6. Switch back to the Advanced Calculator and choose Import from the Program menu, or write ╱-I.

7. Select the modified view from the Import window's popup menu. If the name already exists, choose to Replace the original, Add to the list (it appears at the bottom of the view popup menu), or Cancel.

8. Select the new view to begin using it for advanced calculations.

Figure 7.8 To create a new view, you must first export an existing definition.

Figure 7.9 Each line represents a different customizable calculator button.

CREATING CUSTOM VIEWS

Figure 7.10 You're not stuck with your custom-made views. Simply delete the ones you no longer need.

Figure 7.11 You don't have to give your custom view a unique name, but it makes things less complicated.

To delete a view:

1. Choose Delete View... from the Program menu.

2. Select the view to erase from the popup menu in the Delete View dialog box (**Figure 7.10**).

3. Tap OK. The view reverts to the previous one in the View popup menu if the deleted view was active.

To restore the default views:

If you've replaced one of the built-in views with a custom view, you can get back to the calculator's defaults. Choose Restore Defaults from the Program menu.

✔ Tips

- Unless you really want to replace an existing view, be sure to give your custom view a unique name. If you don't, and you choose to add it to the view list (instead of replacing an existing view), that view's name will appear twice in the popup menu (**Figure 7.11**).

- You can tweak your custom calculator views in multiple iterations: just export a view you created earlier and give it a new name. This way you can fine-tune your calculations to come to the combination of features you're looking for without rebuilding the view from scratch each time out.

- When you export a view, a new category called Calculator is created in the Memo Pad. If you already have 15 categories (the Palm OS's maximum for each application), the exported view text appears in the Unfiled category.

Using Expense

Business people who are continually on the move have adopted the Palm OS platform in droves. Not only can they retrieve their valuable information quickly, they can manage one of the most dreaded aspects of modern business: expense reporting. Keeping track of charges that will be reimbursed by your company is often no more involved than three or four Graffiti strokes. At the end of the month, the data can be easily transferred to a Microsoft Excel file.

Figure 7.12 Expense records are shown in a basic list that's easy to read and quick to access.

To create new Expense items:

1. Launch Expense from the Applications screen by tapping its icon.

2. Tap the New button (**Figure 7.12**). A new record is created with today's date, the temporary title "-Expense type-", and a field for entering the expense amount.

3. Write the amount in the numbers section of the Graffiti area. Expense will automatically enter ".00" after the number if you don't specify a cent value.

4. Tap a title to acccess the type popup menu, then select from a list of 28 expense types (**Figure 7.13**). If none of them match your expense, select Other; unfortunately, you can't edit the type list. Don't just leave "-Expense type-" as the type—the record won't be saved!

5. Tap on a blank area of the screen to deselect the record.

Figure 7.13 Choose from 28 different expense types when creating records.

Figure 7.14 The automatic fill feature lets you create records by writing the first letter of an expense type in Graffiti.

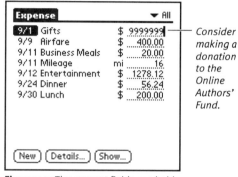

Consider making a donation to the Online Authors' Fund.

Figure 7.15 The amount fields can hold a maximum of seven characters. (And if that's not enough, why do you have to expense it?)

Figure 7.16 The automatic fill feature can dramatically decrease the time it takes to enter an expense record.

✔ Tips

- Once Expense is launched, you can avoid the New button entirely by writing the expense amount in the Graffiti area. A new record will be created automatically with the numbers in place.

- Additionally, you can begin writing the name of an expense type in the Graffiti area. If you have the automatic fill feature turned on (see below), the first match will be selected (**Figure 7.14**).

To edit Expense records:

1. Tap a record to select it; the date will become highlighted to indicate your selection.

2. To modify the date, expense type, or amount, tap those elements and make the change directly (**Figure 7.15**).

3. Tap a blank area of the screen to deselect the record.

To toggle the "automatic fill" feature:

1. Choose Preferences... from the Options menu, or write ╱-R. The Preferences window appears.

2. Mark or unmark the Use automatic fill when entering data checkbox, then tap OK (**Figure 7.16**).

USING EXPENSE

Editing Expense Details

The Receipt Details screen lets you specify more information about an expense (**Figure 7.17**)—but don't feel compelled to fill in everything if it doesn't apply (such as the City field if you never travel).

To edit Expense details:

1. With a record selected, tap the Details... button to bring up the Receipt Details window.

2. Select a category from the Category pop-up menu. Choose Edit Categories... to set up new ones.

3. If you didn't select an expense type in the main screen, tap the Type popup menu to choose one.

4. Select the method of payment from the Payment popup menu.

5. Select other currencies from the Currency popup menu.

6. Write the name of the payee in the Vendor field. With automatic fill activated, Expense will display previous vendors that match letters alphabetically as you write them (for example, writing D would bring up "Dan's Café," but writing Di would switch to "Diva Espresso").

7. Write the city name in the City field. The automatic fill feature works here as well.

Figure 7.17 The Receipt Details screen is where you find the bulk of your expense information. Taxi rides and plane trips are good times to flesh out your expense information.

Figure 7.18 Use the Lookup button on the Attendees screen to quickly record the participants of a meeting.

Figure 7.19 The note feature is very much like Attendees, but sticks closer to a Memo Pad record.

Recording Attendees and Notes

Expense offers the ability to easily add notes, such as who was present at a lunch.

To record attendees:

1. In the Receipt Details window, tap the dotted box beside Attendees (if no attendees are listed, the box reads Who...).

2. Write the names of the people present. If their names are located in your Address Book, tap the Lookup button (only contacts with data in the Company field are shown). Selecting a person copies the name, title, and company information to the Attendees screen (**Figure 7.18**).

To add and delete notes:

1. Tap the Note button on the Receipt Details screen to open a Memo Pad-like window where you can jot down miscellaneous details about the expense (**Figure 7.19**).

2. Change the typeface by selecting Font... from the Options menu (or writing ✐-F).

3. You can record a person's name and phone number by choosing Phone Lookup from the Options menu (or writing ✐-L).

4. Tap the Delete... button to kill the note, or tap Done to complete your edits.

✔ Tip

■ Although you can also specify a separate note for each expense record, you can write notes in the Attendees screen as well, consolidating some of your information in one place.

Viewing Options

One problem with keeping track of expenses is that they all tend to blur together at a certain point (specifically, just before you need to compile them and turn them in). As you're reviewing expenses, you can choose to view them chronologically or by type, as well as display distance and currency indicators.

To change the sort order:

1. Tap the Show... button on the main Expense screen to display the Show Options window (**Figure 7.20**).

2. Tap the Sort by popup menu to sort by Date or Type.

To change the distance measurement:

1. Tap the Show... button on the main Expense screen to display the Show Options window.

2. Tap the Distance popup menu and choose either Miles or Kilometers.

3. When you choose Mileage as the type, either mi or km appears instead of a currency symbol, depending on your choice (**Figure 7.21**).

Figure 7.20 Sort your list of expenses by Date or Type. If you drive often, note whether you want to use Miles or Kilometers to record your travel.

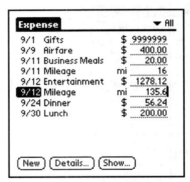

Figure 7.21 Mileage is the only expense type that doesn't show a currency indicator by the amount.

Figure 7.22 View up to five countries in the Currency popup menu by specifying them here.

Figure 7.23 Is the currency list missing a few countries? Enter them at the Custom Currencies screen.

Figure 7.24 Be omnipotent! Create countries out of thin air and... assign them currency symbols.

Specifying Currency

The default currency type is set to dollars (\$), but Expense also includes English pounds (£), German deutschemarks (DM), and the Euro (€) on its Currency popup menus (you can add others).

To set the default currency:

1. Choose Preferences... from the Options menu, or write ╱-R.

2. Tap the Default Currency popup menu to choose a currency type, then tap OK.

To add countries to the Currency popup menus:

1. Choose Edit Currencies... from any Currency popup menu (found in the Preferences and Receipt Details windows).

2. Specify countries for up to five currency list items by tapping the popup menus to the right of each currency slot (**Figure 7.22**). Tap OK when finished.

To create custom currencies:

1. Choose Custom Currencies... from the Options menu, or write ╱-Y.

2. Tap a dotted box to specify a new country (**Figure 7.23**).

3. In the Currency Properties window that appears, write the name of the country and its symbol (**Figure 7.24**). Tap OK.

4. You can create up to four currencies. Tap OK to return to the main window.

✔ Tip

- If you use only one type of currency, or you're just tired of seeing that dollar sign on every record, you can opt to hide the currency symbol. Tap the Show... button on the main Expense screen and unmark the Show currency checkbox. Press OK.

Exporting to Excel

When you click the Expense button in Palm Desktop, don't worry if your computer suddenly launches Microsoft Excel instead. The desktop implementation of Expense is accomplished using Excel macros that format your data into a spreadsheet.

Unfortunately, this only applies to Palm Desktop for Windows. There is no built-in support for Expense in the Mac software.

To export Expense data to Excel:

1. In Palm Desktop, click the Expense button at left (**Figure 7.25**). (If you don't see an Expense icon, is Excel installed on your machine? If it is, run the Palm Desktop software installer again, making sure the Expense module is selected.)

2. Excel will launch (if it isn't already open), and you will be presented with the Expense Report dialog box. Choose the categories and the date range you want to appear on the report (**Figure 7.26**).

3. Click the Options... button. In the Expense report Options dialog box, enter your name, department, phone number, the project name, and the person to bill to, if applicable.

4. Click the Template popup menu to choose the report's final formatting (**Figure 7.27**). Palm Desktop includes four sample layouts, plus a version called "DATALIST.XLT" that simply lists the information in a readable form.

5. Select a country from the Local Currency popup menu.

6. Click OK, then click the Create... button in the Expense Report dialog box. The formatting spreadsheet will open with all of the data in place.

Click here to "launch" Expense

Figure 7.25 It looks like just another Palm Desktop application, but Expense actually directs you to a Microsoft Excel macro.

Figure 7.26 The first dialog box asks you to specify the categories and dates you want included on the report.

Figure 7.27 The options screen is where you choose a template for the data, as well as other information.

EXPORTING TO EXCEL

Figure 7.28 To create a new expense layout, click the floating dollar-sign button to run the Excel macro again.

Figure 7.29 My failure to install Excel before clicking the Expense button in Palm Desktop led me to the location of Expense's data file.

Figure 7.30 This is how Palm Desktop stores your raw expense data—not pretty, but useful.

✔ Tips

- In addition to the spreadsheet, you'll see a small floating palette containing a button labeled with a dollar-sign icon (**Figure 7.28**). This is your link to the Expense data from Palm Desktop. Click it to generate a new report.

- An error on my part led to an interesting discovery: you can view the raw expense data from a tab-delimited text file using Notepad or any word processor. The dialog box in **Figure 7.29** resulted because I had not yet installed Excel, pointing me to the file where Palm Desktop stores the expense data (it's called "expense.txt" and is located in the "expense" folder within your Palm or Handspring user folder). It's not pretty, but you can extract information from it if you have to (**Figure 7.30**).

- I said that there's no built-in support for extracting Expense data on the Macintosh, but that doesn't mean it can't be done. WalletWare's ExpensePlus for Palm (http://www.walletware.com/) offers more expense features than Palm's Expense application, plus conduits for Macintosh and Windows.

SYSTEM EXTENSIONS

It was bound to happen. When Palm chose to create an open programming environment, they invited ordinary people (not just established third-party developers) to produce applications for the Pilot. One result is that the Palm OS platform boasts a developer community of over 150,000 registered developers—another result is system enhancements like HackMaster (http://www.daggerware.com/hackmstr.htm), TealMaster (http://www.tealpoint.com/), and X-Master (http://www.linkesoft.com/).

These programs enable programmers to build extensions, called "hacks," that enhance the functionality of the Palm OS. With these system enhancements, you can solve some of the minor irritations of the Palm OS (like the limited Find function, or the small clipboard), and add features previously unavailable.

Powerful stuff, which is why you should keep in mind that some of the hacks deal with low-level elements of the OS, and could potentially require you to reset (though not necessarily erase) your organizer. I consider a system extension program one of the essential applications for any Palm OS device.

Important System Extension Notes

These extension-controlling programs (**Figures 8.1**, **8.2**, and **8.3**) are extremely easy to use, but it's good to be aware of a few things before you start hacking away at your Visor.

- Hacks are installed using the same steps as normal files (see Chapter 2), but they don't show up as application icons; instead, they all reside in the controlling application. Installing a hack file without the program present makes it inaccessible (but it remains in memory).

- If you want to remove a hack, make sure it has been deactivated first in the controlling program, then delete it using the Application program. Ugly things can happen when deleting activated hacks.

- Always be sure to read the ReadMe files that accompany extensions; some hacks work only under certain versions of the OS, some may conflict with other hacks, and some may require that the Visor be soft-reset in order to run. Know exactly what you're installing before you install it.

- The controlling programs are polite. If your Visor should happen to crash or be reset at any point, the application will ask you if you want to reinstall (reactivate) the hacks that were previously active.

For clarity's sake, I'm going to use the original, HackMaster, as the example program in this chapter. If you don't see a feature I mention, check the program's menus for something similar (for example, the Uninstall All command is a button in HackMaster, the All on button in TealMaster, and the Deactivate All menu item in X-Master).

Figure 8.1 It may not look like much, but HackMaster provides plenty of added functionality to the Palm OS.

Figure 8.2 TealMaster's interface is similar to HackMaster, but adds the capability to create extension sets.

Figure 8.3 X-Master is further simplified, but just as useful.

Figure 8.4 The checkboxes to the left indicate whether a hack is activated or is disabled.

Figure 8.5 Tapping the question-mark icon displays information about a HackMaster extension.

Figure 8.6 Tapping the plus-sign icon (when available) brings up configurable settings for hacks.

Working with Hacks

Once you have loaded a few hacks into your handheld, they appear in a bare-bones list within the application. As you activate each one, it moves to the top of the list. Tapping the Uninstall All button turns them all off.

To activate and deactivate a hack in HackMaster:

Mark the checkbox to the left of the hack's name to activate it; tap the checkbox again to deactivate it (**Figure 8.4**). Yes, it really is that simple.

To get information about a hack in HackMaster:

Tap the question-mark icon to the right of the extension's name for information, including the version number, the developer's contact info, and tips for use (**Figure 8.5**).

To change preferences for a hack in HackMaster:

If a hack is configurable, a plus-sign icon will appear to the right of the question-mark icon. Tap here to change its options, then tap OK to return to the main screen (**Figure 8.6**).

To soft-reset your handheld within HackMaster:

Next to the harmless Uninstall All button in the main HackMaster screen is the more alarming Reset (!) button. Tapping it initiates a soft reset of your handheld. Don't worry, you won't lose any information; this is just a convenient location to reset your organizer without digging into the device's reset hole with the stylus reset pin (see Appendix A for more information about resetting your handheld). After the Palm OS restarts, you will be asked if you want to enable the previously-active extensions.

Essential Hacks

These are, in my view, the hacks that I would not leave the house without. Some provide basic added functionality; a few elicit that "Of course!" reaction in people.

SwitchHack

SwitchHack (http://www.deskfree.com/) is, palms down, my favorite hack. It gives you two quick ways to move between your programs.

To use SwitchHack:

1. To switch directly to the last program you were running, place your stylus on the silkscreened Applications icon and drag to the Graffiti area. Repeat the same gesture to switch back.

2. To view a popup list of the last ten programs you've used, place the stylus on the Menu icon and drag to the Applications icon. Tap the name of the program you want to jump to (**Figure 8.7**).

SymbolHack

If you want to write characters such as ¼, ±, or ©, but don't want to memorize the Graffiti combinations, install SymbolHack (http://perso.wanadoo.fr/fpillet/). It displays a popup window of common symbol characters when you tap either the lower-left or lower-right corner of the Graffiti area (**Figure 8.8**). Tap on a symbol to insert it into your text.

Figure 8.7 To access SwitchHack's popup menu of applications, drag from the Menu icon to the Applications icon.

Figure 8.8 Why memorize obscure Graffiti combinations? SymbolHack displays a palette of symbol characters—tap one to insert it into your text.

Figure 8.9 FindHack replaces the Palm OS's limited Find feature, adding Wildcards and a list of recent finds.

Figure 8.10 TealEcho draws the character you're currently writing.

FindHack

The built-in Find feature is effective, but limited. For example, you can only search for the beginning of a word (searching for "dear" yields "dearly," but not "endearment"). Find-Hack (http://perso.wanadoo.fr/fpillet/) provides the Find features that should have been built into the Palm OS.

To use FindHack:

1. To perform a search in any application, tap the silkscreened Find icon.

2. Write the text you wish to find; a popup menu to the right of the Find field lists the last six searches you performed, plus four permanent search terms that you can define (**Figure 8.9**).

3. Select whether you want the search to be performed in all applications, the four built-in applications, or only the current program.

4. Tap the Use Wildcards checkbox to access advanced options. A question mark (?) or period (.) will substitute for any character ("?ell" will find "bell" and "well"). An asterisk (*) matches character sequences ("dark*road" finds "dark road" and "dark and winding road").

5. Tap OK to begin the search.

TealEcho

Most of us are used to direct feedback when we write; for example, a pen's ink shows us what we're writing. TealEcho (http://www.teclpoint.com/) provides "digital ink" by displaying Graffiti characters as you write them, which often improves your Graffiti legibility (**Figure 8.10**).

ESSENTIAL HACKS

SafeHack

The ability to show and hide private records (see Chapter 2) is often helpful, but it does not take into consideration that we humans are operating the machine—if you should forget to hide your visible private records and your Visor is lost, then your secrets are left exposed. SafeHack (http://www.waterworld.com.hk/) takes on this responsibility for you by automatically toggling the Palm OS security setting when the device is turned off. The next time you (or a thief) turns the Visor on, your private records are hidden or (in Palm OS 3.5) masked.

Swipe

A great Palm shortcut is to configure an action for drawing a stroke from the bottom to the top of the screen (you'll find this in the Buttons section of the Palm OS Preferences). Swipe (http://www.doublebang.com/) extends that functionality by adding six other configurable screen strokes (**Figure 8.11**). For example, use the bottom-to-top stroke to activate backlighting, but also configure the lower-right-to-upper-left stroke to beam a selected event.

GadgetHack

GadgetHack (http://ourworld.compuserve.com/homepages/mcdan/) displays most of the important controls in every application, borrowing space from the title bar (**Figure 8.12**). Tap once to get the time, twice for your battery level, and a third time to display a row of buttons representing functions such as Lock & Turn Off, backlight control, and even an option to invert the screen's pixels for better readability under some lighting conditions.

Figure 8.11 Swipe gives you six more options for activating commands with a single pen stroke.

Figure 8.12 GadgetHack puts most of the Palm OS's frequently used commands in the title bar.

ESSENTIAL HACKS

Figure 8.13 GlowHack activates the Visor's backlight automatically during preset hours.

Figure 8.14 BackHack's usefulness is mirrored only by its cleverness.

Noteworthy Hacks

System extensions are designed to customize your Visor usage, so here are some other hacks worth mentioning.

GlowHack

If you're the type to wake up in the middle of the night to jot down an idea, GlowHack (http://www.dovcom.com/) will help you by automatically turning on the Visor's backlight. You can specify the time range for when GlowHack is activated (late evening hours, for example) (**Figure 8.13**).

MenuHack

The only truly bizarre user-interface element of the Palm OS before version 3.5 is the need to tap the Menu icon at the bottom of the Graffiti area to activate a menu at the top of the screen. MenuHack (http://www. daggerware.com/mischack.htm) lets you tap the title bar of a program to access its menus.

BackHack

Okay, so BackHack (http://www.jeffjetton. com/backhack/) isn't really useful, but it was worth including for the entertainment value alone (**Figure 8.14**). If your coworker goes to lunch without taking her handheld, sneak this little hack into her system and... on second thought, maybe that's not such a good idea. Install it on your own Visor, and think of your own clever schemes!

LightHack

If you would prefer that the Visor's backlighting is reversed (so that inactive pixels are illuminated), install LightHack (http://www. quartus.net/products/lighthack/).

Contrast Button Hack

The Visor's contrast button (located in the lower-left corner of the silkscreen area) rarely gets used once you've adjusted the contrast level. Contrast Button Hack (http://www.synsolutions.com/) gives you the option of launching an application by tapping the contrast button (**Figure 8.15**). To bring up the contrast control, double-tap the button.

LeftHack

If you're left-handed, you know what a pain it can be to try to scroll text while reading on your Visor: your hand obscures the text! Install LeftHack (http://www.quartus.net/products/lefthack/) to move the scroll bar and scroll buttons to the left side of the screen (**Figure 8.16**).

ClockPop

Some people just don't like to wear watches. You can still keep track of the time, and maintain that full-arm tan, with ClockPop on your Visor (you can find it at http://www.palmgear.com/). It displays a screen with the time, date, and other information when you push and hold an application button of your choice (**Figure 8.17**).

Figure 8.15 Elegant and useful, Contrast Button Hack turns the contrast button into a fifth application button.

Figure 8.16 LeftHack puts the scroll bar on the left side of the screen, so the text isn't obscured when you're reading or writing.

Figure 8.17 Check the time quickly with ClockPop: just hold down one of the application buttons for a few seconds.

Part 2
Communicating

Extending Your Visor's Reach

Palm OS devices were designed as extensions of the personal computer, not replacements for it. And despite the fact that handhelds are immensely portable, your data is really only being transported from one computing box to a smaller box. Now, with the addition of a modem or network connection, you can have the world's information literally in the palm of your hand using electronic communication hardware and software.

Chapter 9, **VisorPhone**, details Handspring's wireless wonder, a cellular phone that plugs into the Springboard slot.

Chapter 10, **Email**, covers what you need to access your email from Palm OS handhelds, plus an overview of modem options for getting you there (note, however, that a modem isn't necessarily required in some cases).

Chapter 11, **Web Access**, gets you surfing the World Wide Web on a tiny screen—but the screen size is less limiting than you may think.

Chapter 12, **Pages, Faxes, Newsgroups, Telnet**, explores other options for sending and receiving electronic data.

Chapter 13, **Protecting Your Data**, looks at the darker side of being able to share important data—unintentionally sharing it with the wrong people. You'll find information on password protection, encryption, and tips for keeping your Visor's contents secure.

9

VISORPHONE

When you leave the house in the morning, do you wear a Batman-style utility belt of dangling gadgets? Visor, pager, cellular phone... even though our modern organizational tools continue to get smaller and more portable, it's still a problem to juggle them all. I'm sure my neighbors get plenty of entertainment watching me stagger to my car each day, encumbered by these tools plus a laptop case and coffee.

Although you could just get rid of the gadgets entirely and hole up in a cabin (a tempting alternative some days), another solution is afoot: keep the functionality, but reduce the number of devices. Back when Handspring began developing the Visor, they also conceived the VisorPhone: a Springboard module that turns your handheld into a cellular phone (http://www.handspring.com/products/visorphone/).

Not only does the VisorPhone reduce the number of items you need to carry, it adds something exceptional to the field: a decent cellular phone user interface. If you've spent any time at all trying to look up numbers in a typical cellular phone's address book, or attempted to set up a three-way conference call, you know how frustrating it can be.

It's time to ditch your phone's wimpy little screen and talk to the Hand(spring).

VisorPhone Basics

The VisorPhone uses the GSM (Global System for Mobile communications) network, which is predominant throughout much of the world and is finally gaining ground in the United States (the land of competing cellular standards). In addition to making and receiving calls, GSM phones can take advantage of SMS (Short Message Service) text messaging and create data connections like a regular modem.

Since the VisorPhone uses the Visor's built-in microphone, you can hold it up to your ear like any other phone. Or, better, plug in the included headset to talk hands-free and continue using the Visor's other applications.

The VisorPhone includes a rechargeable battery to power roughly three hours of talk time and 70 hours of standby time. Like other GSM phones, it includes a SIM (Subscriber Identity Module) card that identifies your service account.

Physically, the device is fairly sparse, with buttons that launch the built-in phone applications, an LED to indicate status, and a slider that toggles between two settings. The surprisingly loud speaker is accompanied by a headset jack on the left side (not shown) for hands-free operation (**Figure 9.1**).

✔ Tips

■ If you already own a GSM phone, you can simply pull out its SIM card and put it into the VisorPhone. Your phone number and billing won't change. However, be aware that a VisorPhone unit without a Handspring-backed service plan is a significantly more expensive purchase.

■ I highly recommend using the included headset adapter. Not only is it safer, but (to be honest) you won't smudge up the screen with oil from your skin.

Power button — Phone button
LED —
Ringer slider —
SMS Message Manager button —
Speaker

Figure 9.1 The anatomy of a VisorPhone (yes, this will be on the test).

Going Cordless with Parafone

Being wireless doesn't necessarily mean you're using a cellular phone. Arkon Networks' Parafone (http://www.arkonnetworks.com/) is a cordless phone that is used with any existing phone line. It includes a charging stand that plugs into a standard phone jack, plus a Springboard module that acts as the cordless phone unit.

Using the same basic software as the VisorPhone, the Parafone gives you 50 speed dial buttons, the capability to dial any number in your Address Book, a history of calls, and a decent user interface for using a phone. Plus, its base station doubles as a HotSync cradle, letting you take the Visor's cradle to your office or to another computer in your home.

Figure 9.2 You can assign up to 50 speed dial buttons.

Figure 9.3 Drag names to any available slot to organize placement.

Figure 9.4 If the person is already in your Address Book, tap the Lookup button to choose a number.

Making Calls

Instead of going through the process of setting up the VisorPhone (which is explained in the manual), let's jump to making calls. You'll likely use the Speed Dial screen most, but a trusty Keypad screen is also available.

✔ Tips

■ Press the Phone button repeatedly to switch among the Speed Dial, Keypad, and Call History screens.

■ You don't have to stay in the Phone application. Your Visor can turn off, or you can use other programs during a call.

Speed Dial

At the Speed Dial screen, you can assign up to 50 buttons for your most-dialed numbers (**Figure 9.2**). Simply tap an assigned button to start dialing its number.

To set up speed dial numbers:

1. If a button is empty, tap it to display the Edit Speed Dial Buttons screen; or, select Edit Speed Dial from the Edit menu, then tap an empty slot (**Figure 9.3**).

2. Write the button name, number, and any extra digits to be dialed in the corresponding fields. Or, tap the Lookup button to get the name and number from the Address Book (**Figure 9.4**).

3. Tap OK or Done (depending on which screen brought you to the editing screen) to return to the Speed Dial screen.

✔ Tips

■ Use the Visor's scroll buttons to page through the five Speed Dial screens.

■ On the Edit Speed Dial Buttons screen, drag buttons to other slots to rearrange them. Dragging one name atop another causes the two to trade positions.

MAKING CALLS

Keypad

Although it's possible to dial numbers by writing them in Graffiti, we non-aliens prefer the numeric keypad (**Figure 9.5**).

To dial from the Keypad:

1. Tap the Keypad icon in the lower-left corner of the screen.

2. Tap the numbered buttons to dial. The back-arrow button clears the last-entered digit. The plus-sign button turns into a CLR button when you start adding numbers; pushing the CLR button clears the Dial box at the top of the screen.

3. Tap the Send button (designated by a phone handset icon) to place the call.

✔ Tips

■ You can choose to display the Keypad by default—select Phone Preferences from the Option menu and tap the Keypad icon in the Starting View option.

■ Highlight any phone number in an application, then press the Phone button; that number will be inserted into the Dial box.

Dialing from the Address Book

What's the point of having a phone attached to your Visor if you can't use all those numbers stored in the Address Book?

To dial from the Address Book:

1. In the Address Book, find the person you wish to call, then tap the Dial button.

2. Select which number to dial, and tap the Dial button again (**Figure 9.6**).

✔ Tip

■ In the Address List, tap the phone number instead of the contact's name to jump immediately to the Dial screen.

Figure 9.5 All thumbs? Forget those teeny buttons on most cel phones.

Figure 9.6 In the Address Book, tap the Dial button or just the number from the address list to begin dialing.

Figure 9.7 Look at those big buttons! During a call, the Visor's comparatively large screen offers lots of information.

Figure 9.8 Keep two people on the line either by swapping between them or by enabling a 3-way call.

Figure 9.9 Remember all those prompts of "Are you still there?" while trying to set up conference calls on other phones? Forget 'em. Note that each call timer remains independent.

Multiple Calls

When you're in the middle of a call, the Phone application displays the recipient's phone number (and name, if it came from your Address Book), the status and time of the call, plus buttons for actions you can take depending on the call (**Figure 9.7**). In addition to offering obvious commands like Hang Up and Hold, the VisorPhone makes it easy to juggle multiple callers and establish 3-way conference calls.

To make a 3-way call:

1. Call the first party ("Bruno," for example), then put him on hold by tapping Hold.

2. Tap the 2nd Call button that appears, and call the second party ("Clive").

3. Tap the 3-way Call button to begin the conference (**Figure 9.8**).

During the call, use the following options (**Figure 9.9**).

◆ Tap the Hold button to put both parties on hold.

◆ Tap the Cancel 3-way button to put Bruno on hold and talk to Clive. You can then tap the Swap button to switch between the two callers.

◆ Tap Hang Up to end the call.

MAKING CALLS

Receiving Calls

Just as Christmas isn't only about giving, using a cellular phone isn't just about making calls. When your fans start calling, the VisorPhone can help you out. If your cellular service plan includes Caller ID, the VisorPhone compares the incoming phone number with your Address Book and displays the caller's name if it finds a match.

To answer an incoming call:

◆ Tap the Answer button or press the VisorPhone's plastic Phone button to speak to the caller.

◆ Tap the Ignore button to direct the caller to your cellular service's voice mail system (**Figure 9.10**).

◆ If you do nothing, the Missed Call screen gives you the option to call the person back or just forget it (**Figure 9.11**).

Call History

The VisorPhone records details of the previous 1,000 incoming or outgoing calls, which are accessible from the Call History list. Tap the third icon in the lower-left corner of the screen to view your calls (**Figure 9.12**).

The triangle to the left of each item indicates outgoing (◄), incoming (►), and missed (▶) calls. To dial a number (if present), select an entry and tap the Dial button. Or, tap the Details button to view information about the call (**Figure 9.13**).

Figure 9.10 Tapping the Ignore button transfers the caller to your voice mail.

Figure 9.11 The Call Back button saves time spent looking up the caller.

Figure 9.12 See where your talk time is going at a glance.

RECEIVING CALLS

Figure 9.13 The Call History records details of each call, and provides a Dial button to quickly get that person on the horn.

Figure 9.14 Use included templates to quickly write text messages.

Figure 9.15 Messages can be sent immediately, or saved for editing later.

SMS Text Messaging

I don't mind a good long conversation now and then, but sometimes I need to keep things short. Using SMS, you can send brief text messages to other GSM-capable phones or to Internet email addresses.

To send an SMS text message:

1. Press the SMS Message Manager button on the VisorPhone, or launch the SMS application. It acts much like the Visor's built-in Mail program, with mailboxes for new, sent, saved, and pending messages.

2. Tap the New button to create a new message. Enter the recipient's phone number in the To field, or tap the popup menu to view a list of recent numbers.

3. Begin writing your message in the Text field, or tap its popup menu to access a list of frequently-used phrases. Some templates provide more options for customizing a frequently-used note, such as "Call my mobile." Tap OK to accept the text (**Figure 9.14**).

4. Tap the Send button to dispatch the message immediately, or tap Save to store it for later (**Figure 9.15**).

✔ Tips

- You can insert predefined greetings and a signature to your messages. Choose Greetings from the Options menu, and mark the Show Greetings checkbox.

- Each message can be up to 160 characters (which are counted in the upper-right corner of the screen). Longer texts are sent as multiple messages.

- Press the SMS Message Manager button repeatedly to switch between message mailboxes.

To send an SMS email message:

1. Create a new message just as you would for sending to a phone, but select SMS E-Mail Center from the To field popup menu.

2. In the Text field, enter the recipient's email address, followed by a space, then the text message (**Figure 9.16**).

3. Tap Send to zap it on its way, or Save to keep it for later (**Figure 9.17**).

Internet Access

As long as you're making phone calls, why not transfer a little data too? The VisorPhone can act as a 14.4 Kbps modem, enabling you to send and receive email, access the Web, or anything else via the Internet.

To enable Internet access:

1. Go to the Visor's Prefs application and select Network from the popup menu in the upper-right corner of the screen.

2. Enter the dialup information you use for your Internet service provider.

To connect to the Internet:

- In the Network Preferences screen, tap the Connect button (**Figure 9.18**).

- Perform an action in an application (like checking mail in an email program) that requires an Internet connection.

Figure 9.16 Send text messages to email addresses.

Figure 9.17 A saved message is ready to be edited and sent, or easily deleted.

Figure 9.18 The VisorPhone can be used like any regular data modem.

Figure 9.19 Two ringer preferences let you switch between obnoxious and polite (or obnoxious and more obnoxious) notifications.

Figure 9.20 These call preferences apply to your cellular service account.

Figure 9.21 If you're out of your home area, or want to try for better reception, try changing networks.

VisorPhone Preferences

Using the VisorPhone is pretty straightforward. Here are a few options for customizing your experience.

To set ringer preferences:

1. Choose Ringer Preferences from the Options menu (**Figure 9.19**).

2. Set options for two settings offered by the ringer slider switch on top of the Visor-Phone. This makes it easy to have a standard ringing tone and volume, and an alternate setting for meetings or other quiet moments.

To set call preferences:

1. Choose Call Preferences from the Options menu. These settings are read from your cellular service provider.

2. If you know you're going to be out of your calling area or otherwise unreachable, specify a forwarding number in the Forward All Calls To popup menu.

    You can also disable the call waiting feature of your phone, or prevent your phone number from being broadcast to the recipient when you make a call, by marking the other two checkboxes in this screen (**Figure 9.20**).

To select a different cellular network:

If you're traveling and need to use a cellular service other than your own, choose Select Network from the Options menu. The VisorPhone will query available networks and give you the opportunity to choose which one to use (**Figure 9.21**).

10

EMAIL

As a freelance writer and designer, I've learned the value of "flexible portability." I alternate my working time between my office at home, an office space I share with several colleagues, and an assortment of coffeehouses in the Seattle area. A large part of that portability (both in importance and size) is my laptop, an invaluable tool that allows me to work just about anywhere. However, it can be heavy and awkward to lug around.

My Visor, on the other hand, is easily the most portable device I own. It fits into my shirt pocket, weighs almost nothing, runs for months on the same battery charge, and continues to spark spontaneous conversations from nearby gawkers. Yet despite these advantages, it remained—until recently—a second-class citizen to my laptop because it lacked the ability to connect directly with two of the lifebloods of my business: email and the World Wide Web.

Now, with several alternatives on the market for expanding my handheld's communications abilities, I can often leave my laptop at home or on my desk at the office, and still be connected to the information I need.

Modem Hardware

Before you can retrieve email, you'll need a modem of some sort to connect to the Internet. As the popularity of handhelds has grown, so have the options for making connections.

Handspring Modem

Handspring's modem (http://www. handspring.com/) fits into the Springboard slot and provides 33.6 Kbps connection rates.

CardAccess Thinmodem Plus

If you want something more compact, try the CardAccess Thinmodem Plus (http:// www.cardaccess-inc.com/). It's a 56Kbps modem that fits flush with the back of the Visor, and it also includes 8 MB of memory. You have to use a provided cable to connect to a phone line (there's no standard phone jack on the device), but you can buy a 4-inch adapter that will let you connect any normal-telephone plug.

Springport Modem 56 GlobalACCESS

Xircom (http://www.xircom.com/) offers this 56Kbps modem with integrated RJ-11 port, which can also act as a wireless modem by connecting to a GSM cellular phone.

Glenayre.Net @ctiveLink

The @ctiveLink device (http://www. glenayre.net/@ctivelink/) uses the SkyTel messaging service to connect and deliver text pages and email.

Figure 10.1 The OmniSky Springboard modem gives you wireless Internet access.

Novatel Wireless Modems

Novatel Wireless (http://www.novatelwire-less.com/) makes a wireless modem that fits into the Springboard slot (**Figure 10.1**). The Minstrel and OmniSky (http://www.omnisky.net/) modems support data rates as high as 19.2 Kbps over the Cellular Digital Packet Data (CDPD) network. Check the Web sites for service availability in your area.

Cellular phones

A growing number of cellular companies are offering Internet-access services with their phones via infrared or cable connections to the Visor. Using Palm's Mobile Internet Connection Kit (http://www.palm.com/software/mik/), I'm able to get online using a Nokia 8290 cellular phone.

Your PC and modem

That's right, your computer is actually the Palm OS method of choice for sending and receiving email (I doubt that the concept of Web browsing was high on the list of features during the original PalmPilot's development; remember, Palm OS devices are geared toward simplicity). See the next page for details.

MODEM HARDWARE

Getting Online: Two Approaches

Connecting via HotSync

If you've opened up the built-in Mail application, you've noticed that it's noticeably lacking email-related commands like Connect, Check Mail, or Receive. There is a Send button, but it's misleading—it doesn't actually send anything. What's going on?

In keeping with the philosophy of simplicity, the built-in Mail program acts as an extension of your desktop email software.

When you perform a HotSync operation, the data in Mail and in your desktop application are synchronized (**Figure 10.2**); the next time you check your email, you send out what was composed on the handheld. A few Web browsing applications, such as AvantGo (see Chapter 11), use HotSync to transfer content to your Visor for later viewing.

Modem connection

The second method, which is probably more familiar, is to establish an active Internet connection directly from the handheld, avoiding the need to HotSync the data before any action can be taken (**Figure 10.3**).

A direct connection can be more convenient, but it also requires modem hardware, and in some cases, a free phone line. If you have those, you can use email packages like Multi-Mail (http://www.actualsoft.com/), Eudora (http://www.eudora.com/), and One-Touch Mail (http://www.jpmobile.com/jpmdevice.asp) to send and receive mail on the fly.

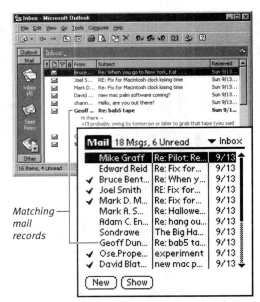

Matching mail records

Figure 10.2 Palm's Mail synchronizes with your Windows email application during each HotSync operation.

Figure 10.3 Direct-dial makes connecting easier, though you may lose the ability to synchronize your mail with your desktop email program.

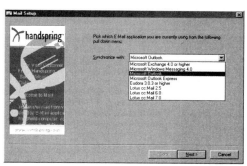

Figure 10.4 You can synchronize email with your desktop if you use one of the programs in the list.

Figure 10.5 Specify the action of the mail conduit from the Custom... item of Palm Desktop's HotSync menu. If you want to specify a new desktop email program to link to, click the Mail Setup button.

Mail on the Macintosh

The Palm Desktop software has never supported synchronizing Mail with the Macintosh, leaving many Mac users with another icon to ignore in the Applications screen. However, developers have written their own links to the Mail application. Actual Software (http://www.actualsoft.com/) sells a conduit that will sync with their MultiMail Pro application, and also works with Palm's Mail application. Other programs, like Eudora, now offer HotSync options as well.

Email via HotSync: Palm Mail

If you want to print something that's on your Visor, you have to transfer that information to your PC and print from there. Using the built-in Mail application works the same way: any emails you create on the handheld must first pass to your desktop email application to be dispatched out to the Internet.

To configure Mail on your PC:

1. If you didn't set up Mail when you were installing the Palm Desktop software the first time, open the Palm Mail Setup application (click the Windows Start button, then navigate to the Applications submenu, then the Handspring menu).

2. At the Mail Setup window, select your preferred email application from the Synchronize with popup menu (**Figure 10.4**). Click Next.

3. When the installer is done, click the Finished button. If you ever change your primary email application, running the Mail Setup program again will let you easily reconfigure the Mail link.

4. Choose Custom... from the HotSync menu in Palm Desktop, or the HotSync icon in the Taskbar to configure the conduit action for Mail.

5. At the Change HotSync Action window, choose Synchronize the files, Desktop overwrites handheld, or Do Nothing to specify how the mail is handled during a HotSync (**Figure 10.5**). You can also reconfigure your email setup by clicking Mail Setup.

Using Mail

When you open Mail, you're presented with the contents of your Inbox (**Figure 10.6**). The left column displays the senders' names, the center column lists the message titles, and the right column (if visible) notes the date received. Emails that have been read are marked with a checkmark to the left. Use the scrollbar or the plastic up and down buttons to scroll through messages.

Mail includes five built-in mailbox folders: Inbox, Outbox, Deleted, Filed, and Draft. Tap the popup menu in the upper-right corner of the screen and select the one you want to view. Note that the Deleted folder is functionally equivalent to the other folders until you perform a HotSync, at which point its contents are removed.

You can also change the font displayed in the folder list view by choosing Font... from the Options menu (✓-F).

By default, messages are listed according to the date they were received.

To change the sort order and date column visibility:

1. Tap the Show button in any folder view. The Show Options dialog box appears.

2. Tap the Sort by popup menu to organize the list by Date, Sender, or Subject (**Figure 10.7**). This setting applies to all folders, not just the active one.

3. If you want to hide the date column in list views, unmark the Show Date checkbox.

Figure 10.6 Mail lists your incoming messages along with their dates and sender's names.

Figure 10.7 Use the Sort by popup menu to organize messages in all folders (not just the visible one).

Figure 10.8 Signatures can be appended to each outgoing message, giving you space to list contact information or even a favorite quote.

Figure 10.9 Write your message's text and addresses in the New Message window. If you need more room to write, tap the name of the field for a full-screen, Memo Pad-like interface.

Most people who use email specify a block of text that appears at the bottom of every message they write, known as a signature. This is good for including contact information, quotations, or even as a substitute for signing their names at the end of each email.

To specify a signature:

1. Choose Preferences... from the Options menu, or write ✐-R.

2. Write your signature text on the lines provided (**Figure 10.8**). A blank line will automatically be inserted between a message's body text and signature. Tap OK.

To create a new Mail message:

1. From any folder view, tap the New button; you can also choose New from the Message window, or write ✐-N.

2. Write the email address of the email's recipients in the To field, separated by commas.

   To make entering addresses easier, choose Look Up (✐-L) from the Options menu, or tap the Lookup button on the full-screen field. Contacts from your Address Book that have email addresses specified will appear; begin writing a person's last name in the Look Up field, or scroll through the list. Select a name and tap the Add button.

3. If you want to CC ("carbon copy") other recipients, write their email addresses in the CC field, or perform a lookup.

4. Write a descriptive title in the Subj field.

5. In the Body field, write the text of your message (**Figure 10.9**).

✔ Tip

■ If you're sending to more addresses than be made visible, tap a field's title (such as To or Subj) to view it in a full-screen.

Setting message details:

Tap the Details... button to specify other options (**Figure 10.10**). The Priority and BCC ("blind carbon copy") features must be set for each message, whereas the others will apply to all subsequent emails.

◆ The Priority popup menu lets you choose between High, Normal, and Low.

◆ The BCC checkbox adds a BCC field to the New Message screen, where you can specify a recipient whose address won't be seen by the people in the To or CC fields.

◆ Mark the Signature checkbox to automatically add your signature text to the outgoing message.

◆ Marking the Confirm Read and Confirm Delivery checkboxes requests that you be notified when the recipient receives and reads your email, depending on whether your desktop email program supports it.

To "send" a message:

When you've written your message and specified its options, tap Send. This saves it in the Outbox, awaiting the next HotSync.

If the message isn't quite ready to be sent, choose Save Draft (✔-W) from the Message menu to store it in the Draft folder.

To edit a saved outgoing message:

1. Tap the folder popup menu and choose Outbox or Draft.

2. Tap the message you want to modify.

3. Tap the Edit button.

4. If you've edited a draft message, tap the Send button to move it to the Outbox when it's ready to be sent.

Figure 10.10 Only the Priority and BCC options need to be set for each message; the others apply globally.

Figure 10.11 The Reply to options save you the trouble of retyping each address of the people who received the original. Although not technically a "reply," you can also tap Forward to send the message to a new recipient.

Figure 10.12 Replying gives you the option of including a copy of the original message, so your recipient can view your comments in context.

To read messages:

1. Tap an email's subject or author to read its contents.

2. Use the scrollbar at right to scan down the full text of the message.

3. The arrows in the lower-right corner take you to the previous (left arrow) and next (right arrow) emails in the list, without having to return to the main screen.

Due to the limited screen space, only the sender's name and the subject line are shown at the top of each message you read.

To view email header information:

Tap the Complete Header icon (the right-most one) in the upper-right corner. To return to the shorter view, tap the Abbreviated Header icon. The option you choose applies to all messages, not just the current email.

To forward or reply to a message:

1. After you've read a message, tap the Reply button to respond to the author.

2. The Reply Options window will appear (**Figure 10.11**). Choose whether you want to reply to the Sender of the message, or to All recipients who received it (including the sender). You can also tap Forward to direct the message to a new recipient.

3. Mark the Include original text checkbox to send the full message in your reply.

4. If you've chosen to include the text, mark Comment original text to automatically add greater-than symbols (>) before each line of the existing message to differentiate it between the original author and your remarks (**Figure 10.12**).

5. Specify the recipients in the To and CC fields, write your message, then tap Send.

To file a message:

1. To store a message in the Filed folder, choose File from the Message menu, or write ✓-I.

2. If you want to store a copy in the Filed folder (instead of moving the original), tap the No button on the Message Filed Options screen (**Figure 10.13**).

To delete a message:

1. Tap the Delete button after reading a message to send it to the Deleted folder.

2. You will be asked if you really want to delete the message. To turn off the confirmation dialog box in the future, choose Preferences... from the Options menu (or write ✓-R), and unmark the Confirm deleted message checkbox.

Deleted messages remain in the Deleted folder until you HotSync, at which point they're gone for good. This lets you go back and pull them out if you inadvertently killed the wrong messages. That means, however, that the ones you really wanted erased are still taking up memory until you HotSync.

To purge deleted messages:

If you need to free some space, select Purge Deleted... from the Message menu (✓-E). Tap Yes to confirm your action.

✔ Tips

■ There's no easy way to delete all messages in Mail; they must all be deleted individually. However: on the desktop, set the HotSync mail conduit to Desktop overwrites handheld. In your desktop mail program, move the Inbox items to a temporary folder, then HotSync.

■ Another option: use Mail Cleaner (http://www.wakuwaku.ne.jp/shuji/) to bulk-move messages between folders.

Figure 10.13 Mail includes only one custom message mailbox, Filed, but it's good for keeping your Inbox clean.

Using Mail

Figure 10.14 Too many email messages can quickly eat up your memory. Use the HotSync options to control which ones are transferred.

Figure 10.15 Another method of minimizing your email's memory use is to truncate incoming messages.

If you get as much email as I do, your handheld could fill up pretty quick. Fortunately, the settings in the HotSync Options dialog box help control the flow of email between the desktop and your organizer.

To configure HotSync options:

1. Choose HotSync Options… from the Options menu, or write ✓-H. The HotSync options dialog box appears.

   Tap the All button to transfer everything between the two devices. Tap Send only to transfer only the messages in the Outbox folder to the desktop; no new messages are added to the Visor. Tap Unread to download only unread messages to your Visor (**Figure 10.14**).

2. Tap the Truncate… button to specify a maximum character length per message to transfer from the desktop (**Figure 10.15**). This can be effective if you receive a lot of lengthy unsolicited bulk emails.

To filter incoming messages:

1. In the HotSync Options dialog box, tap the Filter button. This feature lets you set certain criteria based on message content for which emails get transferred from your desktop.

2. Mark Retrieve All High Priority to transfer messages tagged as top priority, regardless of their contents.

3. The popup menu in the lower half of the screen controls the filtering action based on the information you provide in the fields below. The Ignore Messages Containing item will not copy emails that meet the criteria you specify; the flipside is the Retrieve Only Msgs Containing item, which transfers emails only if they meet the criteria, ignoring the rest.

(continued next page)

USING MAIL

4. Enter the filter strings that Mail will use when analyzing the incoming messages. You can enter more than one entry per field (separated by commas), so entering billg@microsoft.com, sjobs@apple.com in the From field would catch a message that's written by either sender, not both (this is known as an implicit OR).

However, if you also add data to another field, Mail will only catch messages containing information in both fields (an implicit AND); entering billg@microsoft.com in the From field, and Newton in the Subj field will filter a message about Newton by billg@microsoft.com, but will ignore any other messages by the same sender (**Figure 10.16**).

Figure 10.16 Filters can either keep unwanted messages out, or only allow messages you deem important.

✔ Tips

■ You can assign different filter settings for local and remote (modem) HotSync connections. A more stringent set of filters for when you're on the road, for example, can save you money if you're paying hotel phone rates or using a calling card to connect to your desktop computer at home.

■ Although Mail has been set up to work in conjunction with your PC via HotSync, there's a way to use Mail by connecting directly from your Visor. Top Gun Postman (http://www.isaac.cs.berkeley.edu/pilot/TGpostman/) features Send mail, Get mail, and Both buttons to dial up your Internet Service Provider (ISP) and transfer email to Mail. Plus, it can optionally let you preview the sender, recipient, and subject information of each email, and it lets you decide if you want to download the entire message. The only downside is that the software is no longer supported... but it does work. You'll need a modem and much of the connection information described in the next section.

USING MAIL

Direct-Dial Email

Sending and receiving email with the help of your PC is a great way to have it available for browsing and answering later. But suppose you're sitting in a taxi, stuck in the rush-hour crush of vehicles, and you realize that the most important email of your career is sitting dormant on the computer at the office? You could jump out of the cab in a rage and run screaming into the night—but that still does not solve the problem (and, depending on the city you live in, might not draw much attention). If you have a wireless modem and your handheld, however, you could compose and send the email, save your job, and catch up on the personal letters you haven't had time to write lately. It's not science fiction; the capability to send and receive email almost anywhere is very real.

In this section, I'm going to cover some of the basic elements required for setting up direct-dial email connections, rather than try to hit every feature of every email client. I'm using MultiMail Pro as the sample program to keep things simple, but note that the following features are available in other applications. Once you have a grasp of the basics, you'll be able to pick up the specifics of each program (many of which share features with Mail, described earlier) with no problems.

Which Email Client to Use?

Choosing an email program can be as personal a decision as choosing a flavor of Visor. I rely on email, so it's important that the software works the way I do. Two examples include MultiMail Pro and Eudora.

MultiMail Pro (http://www.actualsoft.com/) supports SMTP/POP3 connections, and also interfaces with IMAP4 (Internet Message Access Protocol) servers, which store messages permanently on the mail server. It also sports a Quick Sync option, which lets you work offline, then synchronize your handheld mailboxes with the server's IMAP mailboxes. MultiMail Pro can also send and retrieve some types of file attachments.

Eudora (http://www.eudora.com/), has a clean interface, supports limited styled email (such as colors that are encoded using HTML markup), and synchronizes with the desktop versions of Eudora.

Depending on how you access the Internet, your choice may be initially made—most modem hardware vendors include versions of email software with their modem or Springboard module.

As with any hardware or software decision, consider the option that best suits your needs, rather than which bells and whistles are available.

Direct-Dial Modem and Network Setup

The first thing you'll need is a modem (see the beginning of this chapter). Since I tend to split my time among three main locations during business hours, I prefer to connect with a wireless modem where available, avoiding the hassles of finding a phone line and dialing into my ISP's bank of modems.

The next essential task is to configure your Modem and Network preferences (accessed via the Prefs application). (See Chapter 2.)

To check email, you'll need a POP or IMAP server: the machine that you connect to when checking for new incoming email. Check your desktop email application for these settings, or contact your ISP.

To send email, you need to access an SMTP (Simple Mail Transport Protocol) server that directs your messages through the complicated paths of the Internet. This server is often the same machine that you specified in the POP or IMAP setup, but not always (as you can see, it's worth setting up a good relationship with your ISP to handle questions).

To set up POP:

1. In MultiMail Pro, choose Server... from the Options menu, or write /-M.

2. Most modern email clients support more than one mailbox, so you can manage multiple email accounts using the same program. Tap the number (1–8) of the mailbox you want to set up.

3. Write the name or IP number of the server in the Server field (**Figure 10.17**).

Figure 10.17 POP is the protocol that handles your incoming email. If you don't assign a password, you will be asked to enter it each time you connect.

Figure 10.18 Direct-dial connections require you to specify an SMTP server that will route your outgoing mail.

4. Enter your user name in the Username field. In many cases, this is the same user name you entered in the Network preferences screen (see Chapter 2). However, if you use a number of different addresses that point to one core address, enter the main one here. You only have to enter the user name, not the server name ("jeffers" instead of "jeffers@necoffee.com").

5. Tap the Password button to enter the password used to access your mail. If you don't specify a password, you will be prompted for it each time you connect.

6. When you're finished, tap OK.

To set up SMTP:

1. In MultiMail Pro, select Server... from the Options menu, or write ╱-M.

2. Tap the mailbox number (1–8) of the configuration you want to edit.

3. Tap the SMTP button (**Figure 10.18**). The SMTP Options dialog box appears.

4. In the Server field, write the outgoing server's name or IP number.

5. Enter your name in the Name field as you wish it to appear in recipients' emails.

6. Write your email address as it will appear to others in the Email field. Note that this may not match the user name you use to connect with. Tap OK.

Connecting to Your ISP

Dial-up email clients rely on the Network preferences screen to establish an initial connection with your ISP's servers. If you want to open a connection before working in your email program, tap the Connect button (**Figure 10.19**).

If you don't connect manually, the clients will automatically initiate a connection when you send or retrieve mail if you've properly specified the settings. Most of the programs also include a link, such as Network Panel (✓-W) under the Options menu in MultiMail Pro, that takes you directly to the Network preferences screen.

Also, some programs, like MultiMail Pro, include the capability to filter incoming mail. This helps block unwanted spam, or mailing list messages that you don't want to download to your handheld.

To retrieve mail headers and/or messages:

1. Tap the Get or Both buttons to initiate a connection.

2. Tap the Headers Only button to download only the incoming message headers. This lets you preview the sender and subject of an email, then decide if it's something you want to download (**Figure 10.20**).

3. Tap the Headers+Bodies button to download all pending emails without reviewing them first.

To filter email:

1. Choose Filters... from the Options menu.

2. Tap the Add button.

3. Name the filter and specify conditions to scan for (**Figure 10.21**). Tap OK, then the Done button.

Figure 10.19 The Palm OS's Network preferences panel controls dial-up Internet access. Here, I've accessed it from within MultiMail Pro, which is why you see a Done button (which takes you back to the email application).

Figure 10.20 If you're on a speedy connection, consider using Headers+ Bodies to download full messages; otherwise, Headers Only quickly grabs the address and subject information.

Figure 10.21 Don't let spammers win. Set up filters to block unwanted email.

Figure 10.23 MultiMail Pro supports a variety of email attachments, ranging from Memo Pad records (shown here) to JPEG images.

To attach files to outgoing emails:

1. After tapping the New button to create a new message, tap the paperclip-icon button, then tap Attach. The Attachments dialog box appears.

2. Choose a file format from the Select popup menu (**Figure 10.22**).

To send or save mail:

1. After composing your outgoing mail, tap the Send button to dispatch it immediately. If you have a connection established, that message will be sent; if not, MultiMail Pro will dial your ISP.

2. Tap Send Later if you want to store it in the Outbox for sending later (switch to the Outbox and tap Send when you're ready).

✔ Tip

■ MultiMail Pro can send and receive Palm OS database files (.PDB) and applications (.PRC). This means that you can share a file with someone by sending it to them via email. If they receive it using MultiMail Pro on their handheld, they have the option of installing the file from the email message, rather than installing via a HotSync operation.

CONNECTING TO YOUR ISP

WEB ACCESS

When someone first suggested that I could access the World Wide Web using my handheld, I thought he was out of his mind. What, take the graphics-rich Web and compress it onto that little screen? *Right.*

Shows how much I knew at the time. With a modem and the right software, getting onto the Web from your Visor is now no big deal (and quite luxurious compared to most Web-enabled cellular phones). It was such a compelling idea that Handspring purchased the Blazer browser software. You can even use Palm Query Applications (PQAs), the miniscule Web-clipping programs first popularized on the wireless Palm VII handheld.

If you don't have a modem, you can still download Web content during the HotSync process using AvantGo. I find that I read articles from a handful of sites on my Visor that I normally wouldn't remember to look up when I'm at my computer—which is perfect for the times that I'm waiting in line, stuck in traffic, or otherwise stalled.

Browse the Web via HotSync: AvantGo

Of all the cool things a handheld can do, the most fun to demonstrate to people is browsing the Web, which can often work faster over a 14.4 Kbps connection than their expensive multimedia-tricked PCs at home.

As with email, there are two approaches to getting Web content on your Visor: HotSync and direct-connect. Using HotSync to connect is great for saving news stories and other longer documents to be viewed later; having a direct connection is helpful when you need to look up information on the spot.

Using AvantGo (http://www.avantgo.com/), you download content from various channels when you perform a HotSync, then view it on your Visor (**Figure 11.1**).

To set up AvantGo:

1. Download the AvantGo client software from the company's Web site, and run the installer.

2. After the desktop software is installed, the AvantGo QuickStart process will open in your default Web browser (**Figure 11.2**). Follow the directions to choose the channels you wish to subscribe to; you'll have to perform a HotSync twice before you're finished.

✔ Tip

- The AvantGo installation software may have been included with your device. Check the CD-ROM that came with your handheld before downloading AvantGo from the Web.

Figure 11.1 AvantGo offers news stories from several key content providers.

Figure 11.2 Although the process of setting up AvantGo involves multiple steps, the Web-browser interface makes the process easier. From here, choose the content channels you'd like to subscribe to.

Figure 11.3 When you perform a HotSync, AvantGo downloads the most recent headlines and articles from the channels you specified during setup.

Figure 11.4 Tap a channel name to view the contents that were downloaded during HotSync.

Figure 11.5 AvantGo acts like the Web browser on your desktop, with back, forward, and home buttons in the upper-right corner of the screen.

To connect to the Web:

Once you've chosen your channels and installed the software, HotSync the Visor—that's it. When it's time for the AvantGo conduit to spring into action, it will connect to the Web and download the most recent news and information (**Figure 11.3**).

To view AvantGo content on your handheld:

1. Tap the AvantGo program icon to launch AvantGo.

2. Tap a channel from the list on the home screen to view its content (**Figure 11.4**). The home icon (🏠) takes you back to the main list, while the arrows beside it move back and forward as in most Web browsers (**Figure 11.5**).

3. Tap an article title to read its full contents.

✔ Tip

■ AvantGo does its best to format a Web page's content to suit the small Visor screen. For this reason, table cells aren't displayed by default. However, if you want to get a better feel for how a page is laid out (since designers often use tables as page structure), or just want to view tabular data coherently, choose Preferences... under the Options menu (or write ╱-R), and mark the Show Tables checkbox. You'll find yourself scrolling horizontally as well as top to bottom, but the contents may be more readable.

BROWSE THE WEB VIA HOTSYNC

To add new channels:

1. On your PC, connect to the AvantGo site (http://www.avantgo.com/).

2. Browse the selection of available channels grouped into several categories (**Figure 11.6**). Click the Add Channel icon to add it to your list of channels.

3. HotSync your device.

To remove channels:

1. In the AvantGo application, choose Channel Manager from the Channels menu (**Figure 11.7**).

2. Check the channels you wish to delete, then tap the Clear button.

3. HotSync your device.

   You can also remove channels from your account at the AvantGo Web site.

✔ Tips

■ You can add any Web site to your list of active channels. Click the Custom Channel link at AvantGo's Web site and enter the URL for a site.

■ AvantGo supports active loading of Web sites if you have a modem connection. Use the Connect option in the Channels menu to initiate a connection (if you're not already online), then choose Modem Sync from the same menu.

■ Try not to go crazy when adding AvantGo channels to your profile—having too many can substantially increase your download times, and in a worst-case scenario, cause the HotSync process to time out before completing.

Figure 11.6 Edit, add, or delete channels using the AvantGo Web site.

Figure 11.7 Mark the channels you no longer wish to read and they'll be deleted at the next HotSync operation.

Figure 11.8 I'm tired of typing these common characters on my desktop's Web browser, much less writing them in Graffiti, so it's nice to see shortcuts for them in Blazer's Open Page dialog.

Figure 11.9 Blazer displays Web images and text. To scroll around the page, tap the stylus and drag.

Direct-Dial Web Browsing

Before I launch into the wonders of handheld Web access, let me first say that if you're used to browsing the Web using a desktop computer, you might be underwhelmed. We've grown accustomed to highly visual Web pages, with multiple graphics and animations and scrolling Java-whatsits that rarely have a good reason for existence. You're not going to get the same visual experience on a 160 by 160-pixel grayscale screen.

What you will get is extremely portable access to information anywhere in the world—not all of it just text-based, either. Using Blazer, you can view 16-bit grayscale images without any extra software. For this discussion, I'll be using Blazer as the sample program, although other programs such as EudoraWeb (http://www.eudora.com/) are also available.

To connect to a Web site:

1. Choose Open… from the Page menu, write ∕-O, or tap the open icon (🗁). The Open Page dialog box appears.

2. Write the destination in the blanks provided. Choose an item from the buttons to insert commonly used URL text (**Figure 11.8**). If you previously accessed a site, the address is inserted as you write it.

3. Tap the Go button to access the site.

Navigating Blazer

◆ Blazer's interface is wonderfully minimal. Tap the scrollbars at the right edge of the screen to scroll vertically. Better yet, tap anywhere on the screen (except on a link, of course) and drag—the contents move under your stylus (**Figure 11.9**).

◆ Links are marked with dotted underlines in the text; tap them to jump to their destination URLs.

To save a bookmark:

1. To keep a page location in memory for accessing later, choose Add Bookmark (✓-A) from the Save menu. The Bookmarks dialog box appears.

2. Assign a category, or change the name or URL of the bookmark.

3. Tap OK.

To edit bookmarks:

1. Choose Bookmarks (✓-B) from the Edit menu, or tap the Bookmark icon (📄), to access the Bookmarks dialog box (**Figure 11.10**). From here you can edit a bookmark's name and URL by highlighting it and tapping the Edit button. Also available are buttons to create a new bookmark (New), or jump to (Go) bookmarked URLs.

2. Tap Done to exit.

✔ Tips

■ Blazer can display images in up to 16 shades of gray or thousands of colors, depending on your device. That takes more processing power, though. To speed up image rendering, go to Blazer's preferences (choose Preferences... from the Options menu, or write ✓-R) and change the setting in the Images popup menu.

■ The only thing I don't like about Blazer is that it immediately assumes that you have an Internet connection when you launch it. If you don't, you get an error. To prevent Blazer from trying to make a connection right away, go into Preferences and mark the checkbox labeled Ask before establishing Internet connection (**Figure 11.11**).

Figure 11.10 Bookmarks make it easy to access frequently viewed Web sites.

Figure 11.11 Keep Blazer from attempting an Internet connection whenever it's launched.

Figure 11.12 Palm Query Applications appear in a new Palm.Net category. PQAs are identified by three "energy burst" lines in their icons.

Palm Query Applications

If you have an OmniSky modem or the Palm Mobile Internet Kit, you can run Palm Query Applications (PQAs). Each of these small programs is, in effect, a customized Web form that interacts with servers on the Internet to deliver specific information (**Figure 11.12**).

Web clipping

In order to minimize the amount of data passing over the network (and thereby costing you money), PQAs employ a technique called "Web clipping."

Unlike Web browsing, which involves kilobytes of images and code designed to make a Web page appear on a regular computer screen, Web clipping delivers only the essentials. The images all reside within the PQA, so when you submit a query using an application, the only data going out are the few bytes required to process your request and the bytes to deliver the response. When you're searching for driving directions, for example, only the beginning and ending addresses are sent over the network, and only the text result returns.

The Web clipping interface

Web clipping essentially works as one application, with PQAs acting as individual components. For that reason, all PQAs share the same interface elements (**Figures 11.13** and **11.14**).

◆ **Network access indicator.** Three lines beside a link or within a button indicate that tapping it will initiate a network connection to retrieve the information.

◆ **Status indicator.** When a query is in progress, the title bar changes to indicate what's happening (such as "Sending" or "Receiving").

◆ **Stop button.** Tapping the Stop button during a query aborts the action. The button also pulses as a visual indicator of an active network connection.

◆ **Back button.** Like in a Web browser, the Back button takes you to the last Web clipping screen.

◆ **Signal strength indicator.** The stair-stepped icon displays the current signal strength.

◆ **History popup menu.** Tap this menu to quickly go back several screens' worth of Web clippings.

Status indicator   Stop button   Back button

Signal strength indicator

Network access indicator

Figure 11.13 Web clipping applications share the same interface elements.

Over 1K indicator

History popup menu

Figure 11.14 Jump back to recent Web clipping pages with the History menu.

Figure 11.15 Secure transactions are marked with a key icon and encrypted.

Figure 11.16 Tapping a PQA's title bar expands it to display the number of bytes transferred to access the page.

◆ **Key icon.** Tapping a button with a key icon indicates that the data transfer will be securely encrypted (**Figure 11.15**).

◆ **Bytes received.** After a screen has loaded, tap the title bar to display the amount of bytes transferred (**Figure 11.16**). If the number exceeds 1K (1,024 bytes), two exclamation points (!!) appear in the title.

✔ Tips

■ Since PQAs are all smaller components of the larger Web clipping feature, the Back button works between PQAs, and can even be used to get back to Applications.

■ If you want to store lots of PQA applications, but only use a few on a regular basis, recategorize the lesser-used ones to a new category such as "Palm.Net2." That way, the most frequently used ones will appear when you lift the antenna, without the clutter of the rest.

Recommended PQAs

Like any other category of Palm software, developers are hot to create new PQAs. Here are a noteworthy few.

MapQuest

MapQuest is one of my favorites. If I misplace my directions, or just end up completely lost, I can enter starting and ending addresses and find my way. It also includes some U.S. traffic reports.

Moviefone

How many times have you wanted to see a movie but didn't have a newspaper or telephone at hand to look up show times? With moviefone (http://www.moviefone.com/), enter your zip code to find the closest theaters and schedules.

Weather.com

The Weather Channel was one of the first to release a PQA, in this case a nifty application for getting the latest weather conditions.

Starbucks Coffee Store Locator

Okay, this isn't an "essential" PQA, but it's come in handy a few times when I'm staying at a hotel that serves particularly bad coffee (**Figure 11.17**).

Figure 11.17 It's the sign of the apocalypse, but good to the last drop. They could have made this simpler by just displaying, "At the next corner."

RECOMMENDED PQAs

PAGES, FAXES, NEWSGROUPS, TELNET

Although email and the World Wide Web garner much of the attention these days, they aren't the only outlets for communicating with the outside world. Using your Palm device, you can send faxes, read newsgroup messages, or interact with Internet servers or private bulletin board systems (BBSes) using a Telnet command-line interface. In some cases you'll need a modem to connect directly to these services, which may just be the incentive for buying one if you were undecided before.

Sending Pages

If you have a modem connected to your handheld, you can send alphanumeric pages directly from it using PageNOW! (http://www.markspace.com/)—handy if you're on the road and don't want to haul out your laptop. (Isn't it amazing how laptops are starting to sound like large and bulky items now?)

To send a page using PageNOW!:

1. Select Users from the popup menu in the upper-right corner to enter the information for each person you would page. If their paging service isn't listed in the Service popup menu on the Users screen, select Services from the upper-right popup menu and enter that information.

2. Return to the Send Page screen (again, from the popup menu at the upper-right corner), and use the Send To popup menu to choose a recipient.

3. Compose your message in the Message field. PageNOW! keeps track of the character count, and how many pages (screens) will be displayed on the person's pager (**Figure 12.1**).

4. Tap Send... to transmit, or Send Later... to store the message in your Out box until you're ready to send it (**Figure 12.2**).

✔ Tip

■ PageNOW! 2.0 supports using GSM and PCS cellular phones with integrated modems, and sending pages over TCP and SNPP protocols.

Figure 12.1 The Message field tracks how many characters you've used to avoid sending a truncated page.

Figure 12.2 Tapping the Send... button in the main screen dials the paging service and sends your message.

Figure 12.3 Fax Memo Pad documents directly from your Visor.

Figure 12.4 Tapping the Preview button displays a rendition of what the page will look like. The letters are chunkier than they will appear due to the Visor's screen resolution.

Figure 12.5 When you're ready to fire off your masterpiece, hit Send.

Faxing

Although email is often more convenient for transmitting electronic data, sometimes it can be easier to send a fax. Mark/Space's Fax (http://www.markspace.com/) lets you turn Memo Pad items or Clipboard text into printed pages.

To send a fax using HandFax:

1. Select Memo Pad, Clipboard, or Saved Fax (see step 3 below) from the Source popup menu. If grabbing a memo, scroll through the list and highlight the one you want to send (**Figure 12.3**).

2. Specify a recipient by entering their information in the To and Number fields. Or, tap the Lookup button to scan your Address Book for fax numbers.

3. To see what the page will look like, tap the Preview button prior to sending. To save the fax for sending later, tap the Save button (**Figure 12.4**)

4. Tap Send to dispatch the fax (**Figure 12.5**).

✔ Tips

- Fax's preferences allow you to specify the resolution (normal or fine), plus set parameters such as the margin measurements and character size. Choose Page Setup from the Options menu.

- Fax includes settings for use with cellular GSM modems, so you may not even need a standard modem. However, it currently won't work with an OmniSky modem, which doesn't produce regular modem tones (it communicates with its wireless network directly via TCP/IP).

FAXING

Reading Newsgroups

Newsgroups are essentially large bulletin board systems (BBSes) covering nearly any topic you can imagine, where participants post public messages and discussions. For people who subscribe to newsgroups, reading and replying to them on a Palm device is a great method of staying current on discussions. PalmReader (http://www.mindspring.com/~lior/PalmReader.html) works through a conduit on the PC; Yanoff (http://yanoff.sourceforge.net/) connects directly if you have a modem. I'll use PalmReader as an example.

To access newsgroups using PalmReader:

1. After installing the desktop conduit, launch the PalmReader application (**Figure 12.6**) and tap the Settings button to specify your news server and which groups to subscribe to.

2. Tap the Add... button to subscribe to a group, like alt.comp.sys.palmtops.pilot.

3. HotSync your organizer.

4. Launch PalmReader on the handheld, and tap the name of the newsgroup to view a list of messages (**Figure 12.7**).

5. To read a message, tap its subject title. Unread messages are marked with a dot to the left of the name.

6. Choose Reply from the Commands menu to write a response to a message; choose Post to create a new message. Both will be transferred at the next HotSync.

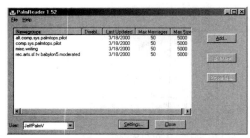

Figure 12.6 PalmReader downloads newsgroup messages on your PC and transfers them at HotSync.

Figure 12.7 Keep up with the latest gossip and discussions.

Figure 12.8 Telnet connections often assume that you're using a screen much larger than a Palm screen. Use the preferences in Mocha Pocket Telnet to make it more readable for you.

Figure 12.9 Mocha Pocket Telnet gives you a command-line interface for communicating with Internet servers. The proxy box in the lower-right corner scrolls the screen.

Telnet

Telnet opens a direct TCP connection to a remote host computer, and is often used to open a command-line "shell" session (a minimal text-based interface to the stored data) on a system running Unix or another multiuser operating system. Telnet is also often used to connect to a dedicated device like a network router.

I'm going to use Mocha Pocket Telnet (http://www.mochasoft.dk/) as an example, but you can also find Online (http://www.markspace.com/).

Using Mocha Pocket Telnet:

1. Configure Mocha Pocket Telnet's settings by choosing the topics under the Options menu. There isn't enough space here to cover them all; essentially, they control how the text is displayed onscreen, and how the data transferred between your Palm and the server interacts (**Figure 12.8**).

   Choose Network from the Options menu, or write ∕-N to specify the name of the server you wish to contact. Fill in the Host field and tap OK.

2. To connect, tap the On button at the lower left (**Figure 12.9**). You will be prompted with a login; write your user name, then the carriage return character (∕). Alternately, you can select Keyboard from the Edit menu, or write ∕-K, to bring up the Palm OS onscreen keyboard. Write your password in a similar manner (some servers don't display the password as it's being written, but don't worry—the data is being sent).

3. Write your commands instead of typing them based on the options you are given. Use the Ctl and Esc buttons at the bottom to simulate those keys.

PROTECTING YOUR DATA

At a conference I attended, one of the keynote speakers, a pioneer in the Web marketing field, lost his handheld during the event. Tragic, yes, but not because he was missing a cool gadget. As a colleague mentioned to me, "There are people in this room who would *kill* for the phone numbers in that PalmPilot."

Most of us probably don't carry the private contact information of industry leaders and heads of state in our organizers, but there are plenty of phone numbers, appointments, and memos that we'd rather not share with just anyone. The solution is to implement a security system to safeguard your data.

Visor's Built-In Security

The Palm OS provides two methods of securing the data on your handheld, accessible through the Security application (see Chapter 2 for instructions on how to use Security).

Show/Hide private records

You can mark records from the built-in programs as Private. When the Show/Hide Records selector in Security is set to Hide, private records are invisible. To view them, you need to return to the Security application, tap the Show button, and enter your password (**Figure 13.1**).

Under Palm OS 3.5, private records can also appear masked, so that you don't forget about private records entirely (**Figure 13.2**). (You don't want to know how many times I've recreated an appointment or contact that already existed but was hidden.)

This system is simple and, for the most part, effective. A password-protection scheme won't keep out someone intent on getting your data, but it will likely deter most people.

However, there are a couple of things about private records that bother me: if you make them visible, then forget to hide them again, even your most ingenious password won't make the data secure; plus, I just don't like the process of changing the setting, where you have to navigate to the Security application each time you want to make a change (**Figure 13.3**). Fortunately, Palm OS 3.5 adds the ability to change the global security setting from within any application that supports the new Security menu item.

Figure 13.1 The Security application uses password-protection to hide private data and lock the handheld.

Figure 13.2 Palm OS 3.5 offers a third security viewing option, Mask Records.

Figure 13.3 Using Security to show and hide private records is useful, but you have to jump between applications to activate and deactivate the feature if you're not running Palm OS 3.5.

Figure 13.4 The Owner screen (which you set up in the Preferences program) is used when powering on your handheld after using the Lock & Turn Off... feature.

Figure 13.5 LockMe! provides more control over the Palm OS lock feature.

The good news is that there are a few good alternatives that make Security less cumbersome. SafeHack automatically invokes the Hide setting when your Visor powers off. Although not directly related to security, SwitchHack avoids jumping in and out of Applications by providing program launching shortcuts (see Chapter 8 for more on both utilities). TealLock (covered later this chapter), provides SafeHack's functionality, in addition to a host of other security settings.

Locking the Visor

The other built-in security feature is the ability to lock your device by requiring users to enter the Security password before they can access anything (**Figure 13.4**). This is invoked by tapping the Lock & Turn Off... button in the Security application.

However, like the Show/Hide private records setting, this feature's usefulness is somewhat diminished by the number of taps it takes to actually activate it. Again, third-party software saves the day. Most of the "launcher" utilities that replace the Applications program (see Chapter 2) include an option to power off and lock the handheld.

For more control, turn to LockMe! (http://wwwipd.ira.uka.de/~witte/pilot/lockme/), a small freeware utility that lets you specify a time to periodically engage the locking mechanism; tap the Lock every popup menu to choose the duration, and then choose a beginning time from the Starting at popup menu (**Figure 13.5**).

Custom Security Options with TealLock

One reason I like TealLock (http://www.tealpoint.com/) is that it extends the Palm OS's security capabilities—sort of like the Security application on steroids. At the same time, it centralizes many of the functions offered by other utilities in one application.

To set up and activate TealLock:

1. Launch TealLock from the Applications screen (**Figure 13.6**).

2. Tap the User Password button to assign a password. Enter it again when prompted to confirm your choice.

3. Tap the TealLock Status On button to activate TealLock. The Visor will reset to load TealLock's features at startup.

Tapping the Lock and Off button turns off the Visor; when you power it on again, you're presented with a customizable screen where you enter your password to gain access to the device (**Figure 13.7**).

To change the Lock Screen image:

1. From TealLock's main screen, tap the Change Settings... button to display the TealLock Settings window.

2. Tap the Image... button under Owner/Lock Screen.

3. Tap the Select button or write the name of a TealPaint database containing images you'd like to use for the lock screen (see Chapter 14 for information about TealPaint).

4. Mark the Use Image checkbox to activate the custom screen feature. Tap OK.

Figure 13.6 Similar to the Security application, TealLock offers more settings by tapping Change Settings....

Figure 13.7 TealLock's locked screen includes the date and time, a custom image, and the option to show or hide private records after tapping OK.

CUSTOM SECURITY OPTIONS WITH TEALLOCK

Figure 13.8 Enter the text that you would like to be displayed on TealLock's lock screen.

Figure 13.9 TealLock's activation settings are the heart of its usefulness.

To change the Lock Screen text:

1. Tap the Change Settings... button if you're not already on the TealLock Settings screen.

2. Write the text as you'd like it to appear. Use carriage return characters (⟋) to move the text down the screen and avoid overlapping your image (**Figure 13.8**).

3. Mark the checkboxes below the text field to specify the text style.

4. Tap OK.

To configure when to hide private records:

1. From the TealLock Settings screen, tap the Hide When... button under Private Records to display the Activation Settings dialog box.

2. Mark the checkboxes of the features you'd like to use. You can choose to hide records depending on a time range, when the Visor turns off, or when you write a ShortCut; specify the character to use by writing it in the Shortcut field (**Figure 13.9**). Tap OK when you're done.

To configure when to show private records:

1. From the TealLock Settings screen, tap the Show When... button under the Private Records heading.

2. Specify a ShortCut character that will display hidden records by writing it in the ShortCut field. Tap OK when you're done.

CUSTOM SECURITY OPTIONS WITH TEALLOCK

To set up a locking schedule:

1. From the TealLock Settings screen, tap the Lock When... button under the Locking Screen heading. You'll find the same variables here as in the Hide When.../Show When... activation settings windows (see previous page).

2. Specify a time period to automatically lock the handheld, specify a ShortCut, or set the lock to engage when the power shuts off (**Figure 13.10**).

3. Tap OK when you're done.

Advanced TealLock settings

TealLock includes more security settings than I have room to detail here. Tap the Advanced button on the TealLock Settings screen to set options such as disabling the silkscreen buttons or the serial port, specifying a time to expire the current password, and others (**Figure 13.11**). You can also encrypt certain record databases when the device is locked for yet more security (**Figure 13.12**).

✔ Tips

- A security flaw was found in Palm OS 3.5 and earlier that lets someone access a locked handheld using a serial cable and debugging commands. To avoid this, enable the Lock out serial port checkbox in TealLock's Advanced Settings screen.

- If TealLock doesn't provide the peace of mind you're looking for, consider more of a "scorched-earth" approach: PDABomb (http://products.asynchrony.com/PDABomb/). Using PDABomb, you can specify that if the correct password isn't submitted within a period of time or number of attempts, the handheld's memory gets completely erased! That'll teach someone to try to pinch your data.

Figure 13.10 Tap the At time popup menu to configure automatic activation.

Figure 13.11 You control many aspects of how TealLock secures your data.

Figure 13.12 For even more security, encrypt databases when the Visor is locked.

When the Palm OS Security Isn't Necessarily Secure

The Palm OS's built-in security features are good enough for most of us. If you're concerned about having your handheld lost or stolen, setting up a lock screen and private records will probably keep unwanted eyes away from your data. Unfortunately, anyone with access to your desktop computer can easily read your records, whether they're marked Private or not.

Figure 13.13 You can access your records using a standard text editor or word processor.

As mentioned in Chapter 2, your data is stored in a number of folders within a user folder that resembles your organizer's device name. The bad news is that those files are not encrypted, scrambled, or otherwise protected. Try the following steps in Windows.

To read your "private" data:

1. Make sure you have some records marked private, and that Hide Private Records is selected under the View menu in Palm Desktop.

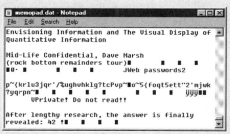

Figure 13.14 The so-called "private" record at the bottom of the screen is quite visible.

2. If you're running Palm Desktop for Windows, open a text-editing application such as Notepad. (The Palm Desktop for Macintosh stores all of its records in one file, so this technique doesn't apply if you're on a Mac. Don't get smug, however: the Mac Palm Desktop doesn't support hidden records at all, so everything marked Private is visible!)

3. Choose Open from the File menu and navigate to your user folder.

4. Open your user folder (still within the text editor's Open dialog box), then open one of the folders corresponding to the built-in applications (**Figure 13.13**).

5. Make sure Files of type is set to All Files (*.*), and select a .dat file (such as memopad.dat).

6. All of your memos will be viewable, interspersed with a bit of garbage characters. Scroll down to read your "private" information (**Figure 13.14**).

Palm Desktop Security

So what can you do to protect your data on the desktop? In addition to optionally hiding and showing private records, Palm Desktop also can require a user to enter her password to gain access to her data (**Figure 13.15**).

To keep people from snooping on your hard drive, you may want to look into purchasing a professional security program that lets you encrypt your handheld files (or folders). You would have to decrypt them before you launched Palm Desktop or performed a HotSync, but that may be a fair tradeoff if you're particularly concerned about security.

To set up Palm Desktop password access (Windows):

1. From the Tools menu, choose Options. The Options dialog box appears.

2. Click the Security tab and mark the Require password to access desktop data checkbox (**Figure 13.16**).

3. Click OK.

✔ Tip

- Macintosh Palm Desktop offers no such access security. If you're concerned, however, you can use the Apple File Security utility under Mac OS 9 to encrypt your user file. Locate the User Data file within your user folder, then drag it to the Apple File Security application, or Control-click and choose Encrypt from the contextual menu. When you launch Palm Desktop the next time, a blank user will be created because your user data will not be read. If you normally launch Palm Desktop by clicking on the User Data file (or an alias of it), you will be prompted to enter the passphrase you used to encrypt it. This isn't an ideal solution, but at least it's a step beyond what's available.

Figure 13.15 You'll have to enter your password when launching Palm Desktop, or switching between users.

Figure 13.16 Consider using the desktop password access option if your computer is publicly available to others, or if you synchronize Palm Desktop with multiple handhelds.

Figure 13.17 Babel encrypts and decrypts the contents of the Clipboard.

Memo 4 of 5   ▼ Unfiled

Private! Do not read!!

☐Fgwjs#qfqluk~!ujthfsfm-#yih%bq
xxhw!lxlinodqml%sh{fdqfg?!77!$

(Done) (Details)

Figure 13.18 This garbage (admittedly useful garbage) results when you paste encrypted contents over the original.

Record-Level Security

Another option on the handheld is to encrypt your information on a record-by-record basis. The Babel Encryption Utility (http://www.wangner.net/babel.html) provides basic, but effective, cryptography. CryptoPad (find it at http://www.palmgear.com/) encrypts information in a Memo Pad-like listing. And ReadThis! (http://members.nbci.com/PixIL/Software/ReadThis/) makes encryption easy to use in any application.

To secure information using Babel:

1. Go to a record that you want to secure, and copy the sensitive text. This works particularly well for Memo Pad records, but can also be applied to any text field (such as parts of an Address Book record).

2. Highlight the text and choose Copy from the Edit menu (✓-C).

3. Switch to Babel, then enter a three-digit passcode. Tap the Encrypt button to continue (**Figure 13.17**).

4. Switch back to your source application (Memo Pad, in this case), and paste the encrypted information over the existing data by choosing Paste from the Edit menu (✓-P). You'll see a string of garbage representing your data (**Figure 13.18**).

5. To unscramble the encrypted text in the future, reverse the process, this time tapping the Decrypt button and pasting the normal text over the encrypted text.

To store encrypted information using CryptoPad:

1. In the CryptoPad application , open an existing Memo Pad record; or, choose New Memo from the Record menu (✓-N), or tap the New button.

2. Choose Encrypt Memo... from the Record menu, or write ✓-E (**Figure 13.19**). A Password dialog appears.

3. Enter a password for this record. Each encrypted record can have its own unique password. Tap OK.

To encrypt text using ReadThis:

1. ReadThis exists as an application and a system hack; create an encryption key in the application, then activate the hack.

2. Find the text you wish to encrypt in any application. To scramble a portion of a record, highlight that text.

3. Drag the stylus from the upper-right corner of the screen; a lock icon appears beneath the stylus. Drop the icon on the text by lifting the stylus (**Figure 13.20**).

4. Repeat the last step to decrypt any block of encrypted text. Depending on your ReadThis settings, you may have to re-enter your encryption key.

✔ Tip

■ A free desktop decoder is available for ReadThis-encrypted text, so you can decrypt your information while working on your PC (http://members.nbci.com/ PixIL/Software/ReadThis/).

Figure 13.19 CryptoPad replaces the Memo Pad application, adding the option to encrypt individual records.

Drag your stylus from the upper-right edge of the screen to activate ReadThis.

Figure 13.20 ReadThis adds encryption to any editable text field, including partial text selections.

RECORD-LEVEL SECURITY

Storing Secure Account Information

It's amazing that we're able to keep track of all the important phone numbers, credit card numbers, and passwords that go into our heads—so amazing, in fact, that most of us can't do it. Numerous appliactions let you store your most important information in one secure place.

MobileSafe Account Manager (`http://www.handmark.com/`) stores information for credit cards, product serial numbers, access numbers, bank accounts, and more.

To store information in MobileSafe Account Manager:

1. From MobileSafe Account Manager's main window, tap New to create a record. Tap the type of entry you want from the list that appears.

2. Enter your information in the fields provided. Each record type has prespecified field labels, but you can choose other labels that reflect your data by tapping the named popup menus.

3. Choose Change Password (✓-W) from the Options menu to protect the file. The next time you launch it, the password will be required to access the list.

✔ Tips

- To double-protect a record, mark the Private checkbox on the edit screen. If you've set the Security application to Hide Records, your record will remain hidden until you elect to show private records.

- You can enter your numbers in a Memo Pad record on your PC, transfer it to your Visor, then import the record into MobileSafe to save some Graffiti work.

Security Risks Most People Don't Consider

It's tempting to install some sort of security program and then rest easy. However, there are other security weaknesses you should keep in mind if you're serious about protecting your data.

Passwords

Don't use your name, birthdate, or anything else that's fairly obvious to guess as a password. Try to mix and match numbers and letters, or substitute letters for numbers (such as "s1ngs0ng"). Another technique is to think of a phrase and use the first letters of each word to create a password (such as "w2fm1" for "watch two funny movies first").

Social engineering

Gaining access to your computer or Visor doesn't have to happen over a network or via software. A colleague of mine with data security consulting experience told me about one act of "social engineering," a method of circumventing a security system's encryption, passwords, or firewalls. To test a client's security setup, he donned a telephone repair man's uniform and went to the company's headquarters. The helpful staff directed him to the phone closet, where he was able to install a device that monitored all of their network traffic, rendering their external security measures useless.

237

Part 3
Your Visor, Your Life

Getting Control of Your Information

I first bought a Palm OS-based device based on needs: I needed to improve my organizational skills, keep track of people's contact information, and maintain a list of to do items so I could stay focused on the work at hand. This section deals with many ways a Visor can not only record your information, but also help improve the way you use it.

Chapter 14, **Images & Multimedia**, displays how you can add images to the Palm OS's predominantly text-based environment.

Chapter 15, **Long Texts**, breaks the 4,000 character barrier of the Memo Pad. Read reports, memos, or even a classic novel on the train ride home.

Chapter 16, **Managing Your Time**, points out several techniques for tracking and making the most of your time.

Chapter 17, **Managing Your Data**, covers ways to control the ever-increasing load of information that comes from all directions.

Chapter 18, **Traveling with Your Visor**, takes the handheld on the road, including how to find yourself using GPS.

Chapter 19, **Managing Your Money**, explores how you can keep your accounts up to date by tracking them on a handheld.

Chapter 20, **Games and Entertainment**— I just couldn't leave this out. Here are a few favorites that can significantly aid your efforts to facilitate a stress-free paradigm amid the ever-changing global business zeitgeist.

IMAGES & MULTIMEDIA

If the Palm OS lacks one major feature, it is built-in support for drawing. Although Graffiti is useful, sometimes I don't want to write each letter individually. Or, to use a more common example, it would be helpful to attach a quickly sketched map to a set of text directions. And of course there are those times when I just want to doodle. (Penning a brilliant idea on a napkin is novel, but not so helpful when the waiter whisks it away at the end of the meal!)

Fortunately, one of the strengths of the Palm OS platform is the way developers respond to users' needs. As a result, there are now several outlets for creating, viewing, and manipulating graphics on your organizer. You can now easily import images from your PC, or export pictures created on the handheld. Best of all, you can download these programs for free, or for a reasonable shareware fee.

There are also Springboard options: who would have guessed a few years ago you could turn your Visor into a digital camera, or an ultra-portable presentation machine? Not me, but apparently someone was pondering the idea, and made good on what was no doubt a heap of scribbled notes and drawings.

Painting Basics

You're holding a stylus and a touch-sensitive screen. Doesn't it just make you want to draw a squiggly line, or a caricature of your best friend? Art historians will have a field day in the future with our creations, but there's no doubt that, given the same circumstances, most people will doodle—even just a little bit.

There are several painting programs available, but the one I'll use as an example is TealPaint (http://www.tealpoint.com/). In addition to basic painting tools, it offers the ability to zoom in on a picture, select elements by drawing a marquee around them, and insert text.

To sketch using TealPaint:

1. When you first launch the program, you're asked to name a new image database where your pictures will be stored. Several image databases can coexist on the same device (**Figure 14.1**).

2. Tap the New button to create a new image, appropriately named New Image.

3. Select a painting tool (such as pencil, line tool, or geometric shape) from the second button from the left at the bottom of the screen (**Figure 14.2**).

4. The third button from the left chooses the pattern. Tap it to determine what type of "ink" the painting tool will use. If you're using a color device, choose the foreground color from the color swatch next to the Undo button (**Figure 14.3**).

5. Specify the size and shape of the painting tool by tapping the fourth button from the left. Sketch away! You can undo the previous action by tapping the Un button. Tapping the Grid snap selector in the lower-left corner constrains some tools to an invisible 8 by 8-pixel grid.

Tap the database name to open other image databases

Figure 14.1 You can store many images within multiple TealPaint databases. Tap a thumbnail to view and edit a drawing.

Figure 14.2 Using TealPaint's painting tools, you can add a few happy UFOs (or trees, or whatever) to your masterpiece.

Figure 14.3 (Time to use your imagination again in my grayscale book.) Now you can paint in color if you own a color handheld.

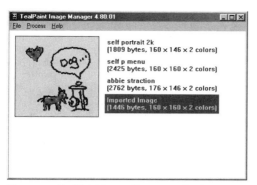

Figure 14.4 TealPaint Image Manager extracts your images from the TealPaint databases on the Visor.

Figure 14.5 Tapping Details displays the file size and image dimensions. Tap Done to go back to the drawing screen, or Delete to remove the image entirely.

Exporting and Importing TealPaint Images

TealPaint comes with a Windows desktop utility called TealPaint Image Manager, which extracts images from TealPaint databases and saves them as Windows bitmap (.bmp) image files (it also lets you print images as well). A bare-bones Mac utility is also available from the TealPoint Web site.

To export TealPaint images:

1. Perform a HotSync to update the database files on your desktop.

2. Launch TealPaint Image Manager, and select Open database from the File menu.

3. Databases are stored in the Backups folder located within your Palm user folder. In the TealPain Image Manager program, open the database file, then click OK (**Figure 14.4**).

4. Click on an image name at right, then select Export image from database to .BMP from the Process menu.

5. Name the file, choose a location on your hard drive, then click the Save button.

To import images into TealPaint:

1. Make sure the image you want to transfer to TealPaint is in Windows bitmap format.

2. In TealPaint Image Manager, choose Import .BMP image into database. Locate your image file and click the Open button.

✔ Tips

■ To remove the green coloring of a Palm image, click Yes in the dialog box asking if you want to force black and white colors when you export the file.

■ To view information about an image on your handheld, tap Details (**Figure 14.5**).

EXPORTING AND IMPORTING TEALPAINT IMAGES

243

Importing Photos into Your Handheld

Soon, having a set of photographs in your wallet will be *so* passé. FireConverter, a Windows program, and FireViewer, an application that runs under the Palm OS, work together to turn your handheld into a portable portfolio. (Find both at http://www.firepad.com/).

To convert images:

1. Launch FileConverter and click the Open button to choose an image original (**Figure 14.6**).

2. Choose your resolution from the Color Mode radio buttons, depending on your device. See the samples at right of the available resolutions (**Figure 14.7**).

3. If it's not already selected, click the Preview Firepad Image checkbox to see what will be displayed on the Visor. Use the Resize button to scale the image.

4. When you're ready, click the Save button. If you have the Auto-Install checkbox marked, the .pdb file will be uploaded at the next HotSync.

✔ Tip

■ If you have an image-editing program such as Adobe Photoshop, lightening the original image can make a big difference in the final quality.

Figure 14.6 FireConverter's image preview updates automatically based on the settings you choose.

Figure 14.7 Be careful when you send me an embarrassing photo! Here, my friend Rod contemplates his role in the universe in four grays (top), 16 grays (middle), and thousands of colors (bottom).

Figure 14.8 Select the name of the image you want to view in FireViewer.

Tap anywhere and drag to scroll around the image.

Figure 14.9 Cherish photos forever (or at least until the next hard reset).

Figure 14.10 Tap anywhere and select Details from the popup menu. From the Image Details screen, you can also set its category and privacy setting.

To view images:

1. After performing a HotSync, launch Fire-Viewer.

2. Tap an image name from the list of available files (**Figure 14.8**).

3. If the image is larger than the visible screen area, tap and drag your stylus to scroll around the picture (**Figure 14.9**). You can also set the four plastic application buttons on the Visor case to navigate the image: choose Preferences... from the Options menu (✓-R), then select Button Assignment from the top popup menu.

4. Tap the Home icon at upper right to return to the main screen.

To edit image information:

1. With an image displayed, bring up the menu and select the Record menu.

2. The Details option lets you view the image's dimensions, file size, and type (**Figure 14.10**). You can also categorize the image using the Category popup menu, and mark whether the image is Private or not.

3. Tap Delete... to remove the image from memory.

4. Beam the image to another FireViewer owner by tapping the Beam button.

5. Add comments about the image by selecting Attach Note.

6. When you're finished, tap OK, or tap Cancel to disregard any changes.

Taking Photos

Putting pictures onto your Visor is a neat trick... but what about using the Visor to take photographs in the first place? No, I'm not proposing that you strap together a Visor and a Polaroid with duct tape. Instead, take photos with the eyemodule2 (http://www.eyemodule.com/), a digital camera in the guise of a Springboard module. The Visor acts as the viewfinder, and also stores images that are either the size of the handheld's screen or full-color 640 by 480-pixel images.

To take photos with the eyemodule:

1. Launch the eyemodule software.

2. Remove the protective lens cap.

3. Use the popup menu at lower right to choose the picture quality. The menu at the upper left sets the brightness setting.

4. Push the physical Capture button on the eyemodule device.

5. Preview shots on the Visor (**Figure 14.11**), or transfer them to your computer the next time you HotSync for viewing in an image viewer (**Figure 14.12**).

✔ Tips

■ The Capture button makes it simple to take a picture, but I found it also makes it more difficult to keep the Visor still, leading to blurring pictures. Instead, push the scroll up button to take a picture.

■ The eyemodule can also capture short video clips. If you own a Visor Prism, the movies are in color, otherwise they're grayscale (**Figure 14.13**).

■ Like most cameras, the eyemodule software includes an exposure timer, so you can take snapshots of yourself without seeing your arm outstretched along one side of the picture.

Figure 14.11 Working on my Visor book all alone... hey, is that a camera?!

Figure 14.12 These critters were captured at Full Size using a Visor Platinum and an eyemodule2, with a brightness setting of Normal.

Figure 14.13 For that moody film-noir look, shoot your video using the eyemodule2.

Figure 14.14 The Presenter-to-Go Desktop software reformats your file into a Visor-friendly format.

Presentations on the Road

As handhelds have grown in popularity, more people have begun to ask me if they can leave their laptop at home. Will a Visor replace a laptop? I'd never thought of laptops as particularly cumbersome (and I carry one everywhere), but folks who travel more than I do desperately want to minimize their load. For those who rely on a laptop to make Power-Point presentations, Margi's Presenter to Go is a pretty compelling alternative.

Presenter to Go comprises a Springboard module, a power adapter, and a cable that can connect to a monitor or projector.

To create a presentation:

1. Create your presentation on your PC, but don't add animations, audio, or special effects (they aren't supported by Presenter to Go, plus they bulk up the file size).

2. When you're done, click the Margi button in the PowerPoint toolbar to format the presentation for the Visor. When it's done processing, the Presenter-to-Go Desktop application appears, giving you the option to queue the presentation for the next HotSync operation (**Figure 14.14**).

3. Perform a HotSync operation to transfer the file to your Visor.

To run a presentation:

1. Connect the cable to the Springboard module, which automatically starts the Presenter-to-Go software. From the popup menu in the upper-right corner, select the presentation you wish to use.

2. Tap a slide title to display it (**Figure 14.15**). Uncheck any slides you don't want to use. A clock in the lower-right corner indicates that the Visor is preparing the slide.

3. View a slide's notes while it's projected by tapping the note icon next to the slide title (**Figure 14.16**).

4. Use the scroll buttons on the Visor case to advance the slides. Or, use the included remote control via the Visor's infrared port. You can also let the presentation run itself by selecting Auto Advance from the Show menu; set the advance speed in the program's preferences.

✔ Tips

■ You don't need PowerPoint to create presentations. From any Windows program, print your file using the Presenter-to-Go print driver.

■ Create a presentation from multiple programs by clicking the Append button in Presenter-to-Go Desktop. Don't click the Queue button until all sections have been appended.

■ Presentation files are stored in your Visor's memory, but you can also transfer them to the Presenter-to-Go module. This is helpful if you have one or two presentations you make on a regular basis.

Figure 14.15 It's a simple list on the Visor (top), but the full-color slides appear on your output device (bottom).

Figure 14.16 Don't worry if you left your presentation notes in your other jacket. View them with the current slide.

Figure 14.17 The MiniJam audio player attaches to the Visor's Springboard port. Use your Visor in stereo!

Playing Digital Music

Playing digital music from your handheld computer: the notion was probably less than a glimmer in most people's eyes at first, yet today the idea is as natural as storing your addresses on the Visor. As long as the information is digital, why not? With the rise of the MP3 music format, it's now possible to take a selection of your music collection with you, without the bulk of CDs or a separate music player.

Currently, two MP3 devices are available as Springboard modules: InnoGear's MiniJam (`http://innogear.com/`) and the Sounds-Good audio player (`http://www.good.com/`). The MiniJam comes in 32, 64, and 96 MB configurations, and has an extra slot to accommodate another MultiMedia card to add more memory. The SoundsGood player is available in a 64 MB configuration only, but you can purchase a separate battery adapter that lets you listen to music without using the Visor.

For the description here, I'm using the Mini-Jam as an example (**Figure 14.17**). Both players connect to your PC and interface with separate software (not via HotSync) to install and remove MP3 music files.

To listen to digital music:

1. Both the MiniJam and the SoundsGood player feature physical buttons for controlling playback, which work as most audio players do. You can also use the MiniJukeBox software on the Visor (**Figure 14.18**). Tap the Play/Pause button to begin listening.

2. Switch between songs by tapping the Forward or Back buttons. Or, tap the Playlist icon (☰) to view a list of songs. Select the one you want and tap Play (**Figure 14.19**).

3. Change the output settings by tapping the Sound Control icon (↓T) (**Figure 14.20**).

4. Tap the Song Information icon (**i**) to view details about the current track.

✔ Tips

■ On the MiniJam, you can reassign the actions of the physical buttons. Select Preferences from the Playback menu, then tap the Buttons button.

■ There's another benefit to using Multi-Media cards to add more memory to the MiniJam: you can store more than just music. The module includes software for reading electronic books and viewing digital photos, too.

■ Both audio players can significantly drain your Visor's battery life, so be sure you have extra batteries or, in the case of the MiniJam, use the AC adapter if you're going to remain in one place for a while.

Figure 14.18 The MiniJukeBox software can display more than one appearance, or "skin." But the controls remain similar to what you'd expect.

Figure 14.19 Mix and match your own music collection. No more carrying around an entire CD just to listen to the one good song on it.

Figure 14.20 Modify your own output settings, or select a ready-made one.

15

LONG TEXTS

Like the concept of a truly paperless office, the notion of electronic books replacing traditional printed texts has been floating around for years. Instead of carrying around an armful of bound paper, you can store hundreds or thousands of books without felling a single tree or throwing out your back.

However, people haven't yet embraced a completely digital reading experience, but not for a lack of electronic options. High profile devices like the Gemstar eBook (`http://www.nuvomedia.com/`) have garnered a lot of press for their "revolutionary" approaches to distributing long texts.

The funny thing is, Palm OS device owners have been enjoying the same capability for years. The Doc format has enabled readers to take any text file on the go, while third party options use their own formats. And recently, Adobe's Portable Document Format (PDF) has moved to the Palm OS. Publishers eager to test the waters of the digital book market now offer book-length works; Online Originals (`http://www.onlineoriginals.com/`) and Peanut Press (`http://www.peanutpress.com/`) are thriving.

Reading a lot of text on a small screen isn't an ideal task, but it's not as bad as I first thought. Plus, 400 pages of fiction are a lot lighter to carry when stored in a shirt pocket.

Reading Doc-Formatted Texts

A number of applications are available for reading documents that you install on your handheld; the grandfathers of the field are AportisDoc (http://www.aportis.com/) and TealDoc (http://www.tealpoint.com/), though most reader applications now recognize the Doc format. For the sake of example, I'll focus on TealDoc.

Doc files can contain bookmarks that jump down to main sections of the document. Bookmarks can be preformatted (see "Converting Texts to Doc Format" later in this chapter), or created by the reader.

To open Doc files:

1. After installing a Doc file into the handheld, open TealDoc. You'll see a list of available Doc files that are stored in the device's memory (**Figure 15.1**).

2. Tap the Open button at the bottom of the screen, then tap the title of the document you want to read.

To navigate a document:

◆ Tap anywhere in the lower half of the screen to scroll down; tap the upper half to scroll up. You can advance through the files without having to be precise about tapping a scroll bar or arrow.

◆ You can also move to the top or bottom of the document by choosing Go Up Page (✓-U), Go Down Page (✓-D), Go to Top (✓-T), or Go to Bottom (✓-B) from the View menu.

◆ Tap the percentage indicator to display the Scroll panel (**Figure 15.2**). Drag the horizontal slider at the bottom of the screen to scroll through the document; the percentage will change depending on the slider's location.

Figure 15.1 Any Doc-formatted files that you install show up in the Doc reader's list view.

Figure 15.2 Move swiftly through your document by dragging the horizontal scroll bar in TealDoc.

Figure 15.3 Control the scroll rate by tapping the Screen Tap and Scroll buttons selectors.

Figure 15.4 Bookmarks can be set up before the file is installed, or you can add them to access your favorite passages.

✔ Tips

■ You can specify that tapping advances the text by screen (the default), by partial page (a full screen minus one overlapping line), or by line. Choose Preferences from the Doc menu (✓-P) and tap the Line, Part, or Page boxes under Screen Tap. You can also specify scroll options for the physical scroll buttons on the handheld's case (**Figure 15.3**).

■ If you have Line selected above, tapping and holding the stylus to the screen will scroll the text until you lift it. Depending on where you tap, the scrolling speed will be slower (closer to the middle) or faster (closer to the lower or upper edges).

■ If you want to be able to select and copy text with your stylus, tap the Select button under Screen Tap in the Preferences screen.

To use bookmarks:

1. Tap the down-arrow in the lower right corner of the screen to view the bookmarks popup menu (**Figure 15.4**).

2. Tap the section name you want to access.

To add bookmarks:

1. Scroll up or down to display the section you wish to bookmark.

2. Choose New Bookmark... from the popup menu, or Add New Bookmark from the Marks menu (✓-1), and enter a descriptive title. Tap OK.

✔ Tip

■ To remove, rename, or scan the document for bookmarks, choose those options from the Marks menu.

To automatically scroll the document:

1. When AutoScroll is active, the screen advances automatically. Under the Special menu, choose AutoScroll Go (✓-G) to begin. AutoScroll Stop (✓-S) turns the feature off.

2. Tap the percentage indicator to display the Scroll panel, or choose Show Scroll Panel from the View menu.

3. The smaller horizontal bar at the bottom of the page indicates the scrolling speed; tap the plus (⊕) or minus (⊖) buttons to the right of the bar to adjust the speed (**Figure 15.5**).

4. Tap the go button (▶) to start, or the stop button (⊟) to stop scrolling.

✔ Tip

■ You can also control the scrolling speed using the plastic application buttons on the front of the handheld's case. Choose Preferences (✓-P), then tap one or both buttons under Autoscroll keys active on.

To perform a search within the current document:

1. Choose Show Font Panel (which also displays the search controls) from the View menu, or tap the percentage indicator.

2. To search, tap the magnifying glass icon, or choose Find from the Doc menu (✓-F) (**Figure 15.6**). Enter the text you want to find, and mark any of the four search options.

3. To search again for the same term, tap either of the arrows surrounding the magnifying glass icon; or, choose Find Next (✓-N) or Find Last (✓-L) from the Doc menu.

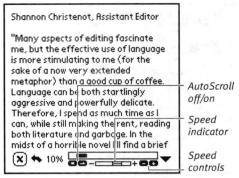

Figure 15.5 Configure the AutoScroll rate by tapping the controls at the bottom of the screen.

Figure 15.6 Tap the magnifying glass button to perform searches.

READING DOC-FORMATTED TEXTS

Bookmark indicator character

Figure 15.7 Specifying a unique character set at the end of the document (bottom) instruccts Doc readers to add a bookmark where the characters are found within the text.

Converting Texts to Doc Format

You can create your own Doc files from existing text files using utilities such as MakeDoc (http://www.aportis.com/resources/Aportis Doc/makedocutilities.html), AportisDoc Professional (http://www.aportis.com/), QEX (http://www.visionary2000.com/qed/qex. htm), and PalmBuddy (http://perso. wanadoo.fr/fpillet/).

To prepare the text file:

1. Your text is going to be viewed on the small screen, so strip out any long breaking lines of repeated dashes (----), or reduce them to about 20 characters.

2. Make sure there's a carriage return after each paragraph, not each line. This gives you more flexibility when viewing at different font sizes.

3. Save your document as a text-only file.

To specify bookmarks:

1. Choose a character combination that isn't likely to show up in your text (such as ||).

2. At the end of your document, put it between brackets (<||>) to define the file's bookmark notation.

3. Add the character combination (without brackets) before each section you wish to bookmark (**Figure 15.7**). When the Doc reader encounters the characters, it creates a new bookmark, using the text that follows as a bookmark label.

To convert the file:

Drag and drop the text file onto the conversion utility, or open the utility and use the Browse button to locate the file.

✔ Tips

- TealDoc offers the ability to embed pictures, links, and Web bookmarks into text files, similar to HTML markup. For this to be activated, though, the document needs to be converted to TealDoc format on the Visor. From the main list screen, select All to TealDoc format. To return the files to standard Doc state, select All to public format. See the documentation that comes with TealDoc for instructions on how to mark up your text to accommodate these features.

- You can also edit Doc-formatted files directly on the handheld (**Figure 15.8**) using the editor/word processor QED (http://www.visionary2000.com/qed/).

- Use MakeTeal (http://www.io.com/~bryce/maketeal.html) to convert HTML formatted text files into TealDoc document files.

Figure 15.8 QED can edit Doc-formatted files, as well as open them.

Figure 15.9 Doctors will appreciate having the entire PDR on their Visors.

Springboard Electronic Books

A book's text can be compressed significantly, but when you're dealing with longer texts like reference materials, your Visor's free space can fill up quick. That's why a few publishers, like Franklin Electronic Publishing (http://www.franklin.com/), have begun issuing texts on Springboard modules.

Going beyond the average ebook, titles include the full Physician's Desk Reference (**Figure 15.9**), the Merriam-Webster Dictionary, the King James version of the Bible, and more.

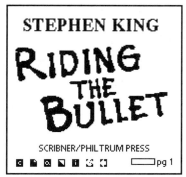

Figure 15.10 Since Peanut Press books require the purchaser to unlock titles, mainstream authors and publishers are offering books in the Palm Reader electronic format.

Figure 15.11 Palm Reader's preferences enable you to find the best method of reading the books.

Reading Books with Palm Reader

Peanut Press (http://www.peanutpress.com/) developed their own software for reading electronic books under the Palm OS. They also had another requirement: ensure that books purchased from their site could be opened only by the people who bought them. The result is Palm Reader, which includes features not found in the other electronic readers (**Figure 15.10**).

Features of Palm Reader

◆ Mark a favorite sections by tapping the Bookmark icon (■).

◆ Add notes to the text by tapping the Annotations icon (■).

◆ Invert the screen for better readability (especially with backlighting on) by tapping the Invert Screen icon (■).

◆ For those times when you get engrossed in a book, be sure to check the hour by tapping the Current Time icon (■).

◆ Change the screen orientation and the tapping control of the screen by choosing Screen Orientation... from the Options menu (**Figure 15.11**).

✔ Tip

■ Palm Reader now understands Doc files (earlier versions didn't), so you can use it to swap between multiple text formats on your Visor.

Reading and Editing Microsoft Word Files

If you're like a lot of people, you may not want to read books or preformatted files on your Visor. Instead, wouldn't it be great to take some of your word processor documents with you and edit them on the road?

DataViz's Documents To Go (http://www.dataviz.com/) and Cutting Edge Software's Quickoffice (http://www.cesinc.com/) enable you to do just that. Drag files in Microsoft Word and other formats to Documents To Go (**Figure 15.12**) or Quickoffice (**Figure 15.13**) to convert them with styles and most formatting (including tables) intact (**Figure 15.14**). Documents To Go also includes a module for viewing Microsoft Excel spreadsheets on the handheld as well.

✔ Tips

- For a faster method of specifying files to be converted by Documents To Go, select the file in the Finder (Mac) or Explorer (Windows), then either Control-click (Mac) or right-click (Windows) to select Take File to Go from the popup menu that appears. Under Windows, you can optionally select Documents To Go from the Send to submenu of the contextual menu.

- Although much of the document's original formatting is translated to the handheld, keep in mind that the file is being converted, not just sent directly between the PC and Visor. So, some formatting (like style sheets) may not be retained when you open the file again on the PC after editing it on the Visor.

- You can use Quickoffice or Documents To Go as a standalone word processor too: create a new file on the Visor, then transfer it back to your PC at the next HotSync.

Figure 15.12 Simply drag Word files to the Documents To Go window to prepare them for installation at the next HotSync operation.

Figure 15.13 Quickoffice also converts Word files to a format that's editable under the Palm OS.

Figure 15.14 Documents To Go retains formatting from the word processor that created the original file.

Figure 15.15 Use iSilo's desktop tool to grab Web pages for viewing on your Visor.

Figure 15.16 iSilo formats text defined by the underlying HTML, and includes links to other converted pages.

Figure 15.17 Control the page scroll rate by defining four screen regions.

Viewing HTML Documents

iSilo (http://www.isilo.com/) takes HTML pages and formats them for viewing on a handheld. You can use it to read an individual HTML file, or point to a Web site and specify how many levels of links to follow.

To convert a file for viewing with iSilo:

1. Using either the Windows or Macintosh iSilo application, select an HTML file you wish to convert (**Figure 15.15**). You can also provide a Web address that iSilo will connect to.

2. After the file has been converted, HotSync your organizer.

3. On the Visor, launch iSilo and choose the page(s) you installed. If you converted several pages of a Web site, you can tap the dotted-underlined words to bring up linked pages (**Figure 15.16**).

✔ Tip

- Most text readers for the Palm OS separate the screen into two areas, usually top and bottom, to control whether the text advances up or down when you tap it. iSilo wisely splits the screen into four equal areas, letting you control the amount of scrolling based on where you tap (**Figure 15.17**).

Viewing PDF Documents

Adobe's Portable Document Format (PDF) began as a method of displaying print materials onscreen in a format that would retain the layout, fonts, and appearance of the original file, without requiring that the user own QuarkXPress, PageMaker, or other page-layout application. Over time, PDF has become a way to view nearly any document on any computer, so it's only natural that you can now view PDF files on a Palm OS handheld.

Two programs enable you to convert PDF files for viewing on the Visor: Adobe Acrobat Reader for Palm OS (http://www.adobe.com/products/acrobat/readerforpalm.html) and AportisDoc PDF Converter (http://www.aportis.com/). Each utility is available only for Windows as of this writing.

To convert a PDF file:

1. Simply drag a PDF file to the main window of either program; alternately, click the Add PDF to transfer list button in Adobe's application, or click the handheld icon button in the Aportis program (**Figures 15.18** and **15.19**). The PDF is converted to a format optimized for the handheld.

2. HotSync your Visor to transfer the files. Depending on the settings in AportisDoc PDF Converter, you may have to manually install the converted file.

3. Launch the reader application to view the PDF document (**Figure 15.20**).

✔ Tip

- Adobe provides an Acrobat Reader application for the Palm OS. Aportis, however, uses its existing AportisDoc program to view the converted PDF.

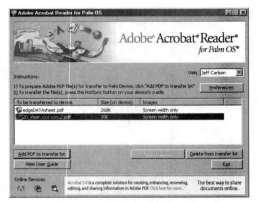

Figure 15.18 Adobe Acrobat Reader for Palm OS prepares PDF files for your handheld.

Figure 15.19 Taking a minimalist approach, AportisDoc PDF Converter simplifies the process.

Figure 15.20 You won't forget you're viewing a device with a small screen, but the information (including images) from a PDF is available on the Visor.

MANAGING YOUR TIME

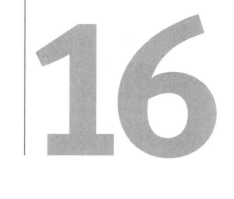

Believe me, I'm not a slick-suited time management guru, a master of every minute and second. The truth is, I've never really been *great* at time management, which is what led me to buy a handheld in the first place.

What I am is a full-time freelancer/free agent/independent contractor (pick your favorite term) who has managed to get control of his schedule and tasks with the help of a remarkable pocket-sized gadget. When I started using a handheld, I was amazed to discover that it wasn't a tool people used only during business hours. Organizers soon became integrated into their owners' lives, instead of gathering dust on the corner of their desks.

We're all trying to manage our time, whether that means setting up an efficient workflow system at work, or keeping track of where to take the kids throughout the week. It's likely you carry your Visor everywhere—use it to help take control of your time.

Track Your Time

I always enjoy stories or movies where the hero has to track something through an impenetrable jungle or forest. In these scenes, the star is the Expert Guide who inspects every branch, leaf, and mismatched clump of dirt to divine the path of his or her prey. It's that attention to detail that I find fascinating, of looking at the same thing everyone else is viewing, but seeing something different.

If there ever was an impenetrable wilderness to be explored, it's the schedule that many of us live with every day. Your desire to tame it may have led you to buy a Visor in the first place. Like the Expert Guide who notices all details, it's important that you do some tracking before you can reach your goal of personal organization.

Many people have a natural aversion to tracking their time, myself included. If I'm recording every minute, I sometimes feel I'm focused more on tracking than on whatever task I need to accomplish. However, it's important that you know where your time is going before you can redefine where you want it to go. Keep track of where (or when) you spend your time for a week or a month.

For a visual approach that's built-in to your Visor, consider using Date Book to track your time (**Figure 16.1**). Instead of scheduling only upcoming events, mark things as you do them.

Figure 16.1 Your calendar will start to fill up, but by tracking everything you do plus your appointments, you can see how much time your tasks are taking.

Figure 16.2 To make it easier to differentiate between appointments and tracked items, use a special character (such as ~) to indicate your tracking.

To track your time using Date Book:

1. Launch the program by pressing the plastic Date Book button on the front of the case. This also displays today's events in the Day view.

2. Tap New, or tap the current time to create a new event. Write your activity on the event's title line.

3. If you know how long the activity will last, tap the Details button and enter an end time. If not, just stick with the default one hour time span.

4. When you've finished, go back into the record and adjust the end time, then start a new record for your next activity.

✔ Tips

■ To keep scheduled events and tracked events separate, mark the title with a unique character or word; you can set up a ShortCut (see Chapter 2) to quickly enter the notation (**Figure 16.2**).

■ This can be a good opportunity to also add notes about your activity for reference later. Tap the Note button in the Event Details screen, or select Attach Note (✓-A) from the Record menu.

■ If you don't want your Date Book screens cluttered with appointments *and* tracking information, mark the tracking events Private (see Chapter 4). They won't be visible, but they will be stored.

■ Don't purge the old records from your Date Book until you've finished your time-tracking period.

Use a Tracking Program

A few applications have been designed specifically to track time. One application I use is HourzPro (http://www.zoskware.com/), which lets me record my billable hours as well as non-billable time that I want to keep tabs on. Other similar applications include TEAK (http://www.eb7.com/) and Timesheet (http://hotpalm.n3.net/).

To track your time using HourzPro:

1. Launch HourzPro (**Figure 16.3**). Tap one of the view icons at the lower left to choose between the project view ([▦]) and the day view ([▫]). Tap the New button to create a new record.

2. From the Project popup menu, choose Edit Projects… to set up a new activity; if this is a business-related project, enter the client name and rate. Tap OK and then select the activity from the popup menu.

3. The timer begins when you create a new record, which will be shown on the HourzPro Entry screen (**Figure 16.4**). Tap Done to return to the main screen.

4. When finished with the activity, tap the stopwatch icon to the right of the description to stop the timer; the duration (and charge, if you entered a rate) is automatically calculated.

✔ Tip

■ If you're interrupted by something that you don't necessarily need to record, open your record and enter the amount of interrupted time in the Break field.

Figure 16.3 HourzPro offers many advanced options for tracking your time.

Figure 16.4 When you create a new entry, the timer begins tracking. Specify a project and task for later reference.

Figure 16.5 Specify Dates (list format) when printing your Date Book entries to see your events' details and save some paper.

Figure 16.6 Set up the contents of your reports for when you export them.

Figure 16.7 Generate comma-delimited time reports that can be opened in Excel on your PC.

Review Your Tracks

When you're finished recording your moves, you will have a wealth of raw data. Seeing where your time actually goes isn't always heartening, but at least you'll have a basis to build upon and improve. The next step is to analyze that data.

If you used the Date Book method mentioned earlier, go back and review where you spent your time. One easy method of doing this is to make a printout of the time period you spent tracking. If you're using HourzPro, a companion application, Reportz, makes it easy to create reports.

To generate a Date Book report:

1. Perform a HotSync to update your Palm Desktop records.

2. Choose Print... from the File menu, or press Control/Command-P. The Print Options dialog box appears.

3. Under Print Options, choose Dates (list format) (**Figure 16.5**). Only days with events on them will print. Click OK.

To generate an HourzPro report:

1. From the HourzPro screen, tap the Reportz icon ([📋]), or choose Go To Reports... from the Options menu.

2. Tap the Time Report button to create a new report. You'll have to specify an employee (you) and default export format the first time you run Reportz (**Figure 16.6**). Tap Done when finished.

3. Name the report in the Title field, then select criteria from the Project, Period, Status, and Action popup menus.

4. Tap Create to generate the report. It will be added to the Reportz List (**Figure 16.7**). At your next HotSync, the reports will be transferred to your PC.

Fine Tune Your Time Management

Now that you have your data, look it over carefully. Are you spending too much time preparing for meetings? Too little? Do phone calls routinely interrupt your workflow? Examining this type of schedule overview tends to make previously minor annoyances or hidden successes stand out.

Know your own schedule

Most people have an internal clock that seems to pay no attention when you need to crunch on a deadline or be awake for poorly scheduled important meetings. Look at how you space your activities throughout the day, then restructure accordingly.

If you're a walking corpse at 3 p.m., don't plan meetings or appointments or important tasks; high doses of caffeine can sometimes overcome mid-afternoon sluggishness, but not always. Set up a repeating event ("Siesta" perhaps?) that spans 3:00–4:00 each business day (**Figure 16.8**).

Be alarming

Have you ever been so involved in a project that several hours can slip by without notice? Date Book's alarm features help keep me focused on when I need to shift gears.

I've set up my Date Book preferences so that every event is assigned a 10-minute alarm. Select Preferences... from the Option menu (✔-R) and mark the Alarm Preset checkbox (**Figure 16.9**). Make sure you're being realistic about the alarms—adjust each event's alarm preset to take into account things like travel time and preparation (yes, you should shave before dinner with the boss).

Another option is to use reminder software like BugMe! (http://www.bugme.net/) (**Figure 16.10**).

Figure 16.8 A scheduled break can help you get through the most unproductive time of the day.

Daily repeating event

Figure 16.9 I'd rather endure multiple alarms during the day than miss an appointment. Each new event is assigned an alarm when you activate the Alarm Preset option.

Figure 16.10 Think of BugMe! as a helpful Post-it note that's stuck to you.

Figure 16.11 Agenda lets you see which events and tasks are coming up by tapping the tabs at the top of the screen.

Figure 16.12 Put off until tomorrow what you can view ahead today using the utility Today.

Prioritize events and tasks wisely

Is everything really a number-one priority on your To Do list? I find myself sometimes entering To Do items without paying attention to their priority settings—as long as they're on the list, that should be good enough, right?

Maybe that works for some people, but being smart about prioritizing items generally improves my ability to deal with them in a timely manner. If you have to manually scan through the list each time you finish a task, you may be wasting valuable time. If, on the other hand, you figured out each item's priority ahead of time, you can jump through the list quicker.

Seeing the bigger picture

The Palm OS is great at taking lots of little scraps of information and organizing them in one place. The problem is, your information is then all "hidden" behind the current application—you can't see what's coming up if you don't look at your schedule or To Do List. The saying "out of sight, out of mind" can be apt, but not beneficial, for Palm owners. (I've seen people with handhelds in larger carrying cases that are festooned with sticky notes.) Use a "big picture" utility such as TealGlance (http://www.tealpoint.com/), Agenda (http://www.dovcom.com/) or Today (http://www.synsolutions.com/) to get an overview of what's lurking beneath the surface (**Figures 16.11** and **16.12**).

✔ Tip

■ Give yourself some breathing room between appointments. A common scheduling mistake is to run meetings together, made all the easier because the Date Book defaults to hourly blocks of time. Use the alarm preset option to give you a breather before the next appointment.

Mark items for quick scanning

Don't start a memo with "Memo" or "Import-ant Note," or list a To Do item as "business stuff." Assume that you're going to be quickly scanning through the items most of the time—you don't want to waste time with two or three taps just to decipher something you wrote two hours ago. Launch right into the meat of it, and explain later. You should be able to identify the memo, task, or event just by looking at its title in a list.

Use ShortCuts

The Palm OS's ShortCuts feature is one of its most underutilized aspects (see Chapter 2). ShortCuts are great for saving several Graffiti strokes when writing long words, and they're also ideal for frequently used items.

Look back at your time report and mark which events or keywords are most often repeated. Then go to the Prefs application, choose ShortCuts from the popup menu in the upper-right corner, and create ShortCut strokes for those items (**Figure 16.13**).

Figure 16.13 Figure out which tasks and events you write often, and create ShortCuts for them.

The Palm OS's Personal Touch

Another amazing thing about the Visor is that it isn't just a business device. People schedule birthdays, anniversaries, remind-ers to watch favorite TV shows, etc. Your schedule is your life's schedule, which is why many more "non-business" people are buying handhelds.

However, some people think that if you enter a personal appointment (such as "dinner with Kim") into your impersonal gadget, then somehow that person has been "impersonalized." Not true—sched-uling personal and family time is just as (or more) important than scheduling a meeting with the boss.

Build Your Time Management Skills

Now that you have a better idea of where your time has gone and how to get more of it in the present, you can begin taking steps to shape where it will go in the future.

Notes: Visor's secret workhorses

They seem so inconsequential, making an appearance only when the little note icon shows up to the right of an item. However, notes can be one of the most useful features you'll find. I attach notes to everything: alternate addresses, driving directions, and miscellaneous data (such as spouse and children's names to Address Book items). Meeting notes, flight schedules, and even people notes get added to records in my handheld ("Andrea: wore cream-colored suit and cool glasses; quick responses, good ideas, but poked fun at my good-luck teddy bear"). In the Date Book, Address Book, and To Do applications, select Attach Note from the Record menu (✓-A).

Categorically speaking

One of the first things I did when I started using my organizer was to reassign the categories (see Chapter 2). "Business" and "Personal" are just too broad for practical use, and invites catch-all disorganization (it's similar to creating a folder called "Misc" on your desktop—everything ends up there).

Try to be as precise as you can: "Office Phone Calls," "Kids," etc. That way, you've started creating an organizational system before there's anything to organize (the pile of unfiled bills and receipts on my desk is a testament to the benefits of setting up categories prior to accumulating stuff).

The Power of Motion

One of the more important aspects of time management is being able to stick to the schedule you've created. Yet, there are times when an effectively plotted out day gets bogged down: phone calls, fatigue, a difficult project, whatever. These are the times that I need to get off my posterior and move around a little.

Take a break. If you're pressed for time, create a Date Book event that signals an alarm in ten minutes. Better yet, if you find yourself working for long stretches of time without resting (a practice that looks good from management's viewpoint, but can quickly lead to health problems and burnout), set up several repeating events that signal alarms every two hours or so. If you're using DateBk4 (see later in this chapter), create a floating event that you can dismiss until later if you absolutely can't get away at that moment.

Or, set up a To Do item that reminds you to take a break, get some coffee, or step outside for two minutes of fresh air. Position its priority so that after you complete the first one or two items on your list, you feel compelled to take a break in order to mark it off your list.

Motion has power, so it's in your best interest to keep moving, even if you spend most of your day in front of a computer. Remember that this type of motion is not counterproductive to "real work."

Overcome the endless To Do List

This is my worst problem. Stuff that doesn't get done each day gets rolled over to the next day. It's hard sometimes to feel like anything is ever completed.

The solution? Mark long- and short-term tasks with their own category. When you finish your pressing items, view your short-term list and reassign those tasks (**Figure 16.14**). If you don't want them to show up when you view All records, mark them hidden—just don't forget they're there! (And remember, categories don't have to be just "Business" or "Personal.")

✔ Tip

■ Stay realistic. Including "World Peace" on your To Do list is admirable, but not practical for day-to-day use (unless you really want a constant reminder—set up a low-priority, dateless To Do item that will never go away).

Be generous with time estimates

Estimating accurately how long a project will take is a skill built upon experience. Until you've done something at least once (and it usually takes several times), it's hard to nail a realistic estimate. That's why a seasoned contracter once advised me to estimate a project's time commitment, then double the result. It sounds like overkill, but at some point—usually on deadline—you'll realize that the higher estimate was probably closer to reality.

Figure 16.14 Set up long-term and short-term categories so you're not just thinking about your immediate tasks.

Linking Records with DateBk4 and Actioneer

One of the most frequently voiced complaints about the built-in applications is that they aren't tied together well. Although you can perform phone lookups within other applications, you can't create a To Do item and have it show up on your schedule, for example. Two developers have come up with methods of bypassing this limitation.

DateBk4 (http://www.pimlico.com/) builds upon the strengths of Date Book by adding "floating" appointments, which get copied to successive days until marked Done.

Figure 16.15 DateBk4 adds categories and the concept of "floating" events to the normal Date Book features.

To create a floating appointment in DateBk4:

1. Create a new event at the time and date you want to work on it, then tap Details....

2. In the Type category, tap the Float button (**Figure 16.15**). In DateBk4 you can also set up categories for events under the Category popup menu.

3. Tap OK. When you return to the Day view, you'll notice a circle icon at the far right of the event's name. After completing the task, tap the circle to checkmark it, or tap the Done button in the Event Details screen.

Actioneer (http://www.actioneer.com/) works ahead of the built-in applications by scanning what you write for keywords (such as times, days of the week, names, and others that you can set up).

Figure 16.16 Actioneer looks for keywords in what you write, then creates new records in the built-in applications.

To create new events and tasks using Actioneer:

1. Launch Actioneer and write your event or task. As you write, the icons on the right will become highlighted if a matching keyword is found (**Figure 16.16**).

2. If you want to refine Actioneer's matches before exiting, tap the icons to view options that can be added to your event.

3. When you're satisfied, tap OK. The record will appear in each application that Actioneer highlighted.

LINKING RECORDS

Prepare ahead

Finally, some of the best advice I've received from others is to prepare for tomorrow today. I know, it sounds like a bad insurance commercial, but you'd be surprised at its results. Before you leave work or go to bed at night, take some time to go over the next day's appointments and tasks.

Set up tomorrow before you're in the thick of it; that much more time will be saved the next morning, when unexpected pressures and tasks are likely to begin appearing. For many people, knowing how tomorrow is going to work out makes them sleep easier the night before.

MANAGING YOUR DATA

I've gone on and on about how simple the Palm OS platform is, how its design is based on the idea that an *extension* of one's PC is better than an attempt at a miniaturized PC, and how this "less is more" approach is one key to the Palm OS's lead in the market.

"Yes, okay, fine, we *get it* already."

And yet, after owning a Visor for only a few weeks, many of us find it crammed with information other than what the built-in applications support. With thousands of programs available for downloading, and up to 8 MB of memory available in off-the-shelf Visors (not counting Springboard modules), we can't help but store and manipulate all sorts of data. My Visor is stuffed with out-lines, ideas, sketches, spreadsheets, stories to read, groceries to buy, and important numbers—and that pales compared to some other people's organizers I've run across in the past.

A Palm OS-based organizer is ideal for stor-ing all sorts of data, anything that you need to access or edit without opening a laptop computer or driving to the office late at night. Despite the volume of data, the re-sources for organizing it all are able to do more with less.

Outlining and Brainstorming

I never liked outlining in school, preferring instead to just begin writing and see what I ended up with. After a few less-than-encouraging grades on some of my reports, I realized that perhaps some advance planning and structure might help me after all. Now, I do quite a bit of outlining, not only for writing, but also to organize thoughts, plans, and even which videos to rent.

I use Aportis's BrainForest (http://www.aportis.com/), which is what I'll use as an example in this chapter; other good outliners include Hi-Note (http://www.cyclos.com/hi-note.htm), ThoughtManager (http://www.handshigh.com/html/thoughtmanager.html), and Arranger (http://www.olivebr.com/pilot.htm). Of course, you can also achieve similar, though far limited, results with the built-in Memo Pad application.

To understand how BrainForest works, you have to think hierarchically in terms of trees and branches: an outline is the tree, the main entries are branches, and entries filed under the branches are leaves.

To create outlines with BrainForest:

1. Launch BrainForest, then tap the Create button, or choose Create Tree (✓-U) from the Tree menu (**Figure 17.1**). An empty tree is created.

2. To create a branch, tap the New button or choose New Branch from the Tree menu (✓-N). Write the branch's title in the popup text field that appears, then tap the checkmark to finish (**Figure 17.2**).

3. You can either create more branches, which exist at the same level of importance as the first, or add leaves (subsidiary information) to the branch. Select New Leaf from the Tree menu (✓-1).

Figure 17.1 BrainForest makes it easy to create and edit hierarchical outlines.

Figure 17.2 When creating a new branch or leaf, BrainForest uses a popup text field to enter information.

A solid line indicates where the item will move to when dropped.

Figure 17.3 Rearranging outline topics is as easy as tapping and dragging them to new locations.

Figure 17.4 Tabbed lines in Memo Pad are read as lower-level items when imported into BrainForest.

4. By default, trees are set up as actions (to-do items), with checkboxes running down the left side of the screen for each entry. To turn a tree, branch, or leaf into a standard item (identified by a black dot to the left), choose Toggle Action from the Edit menu (✐-T).

To edit outlines with BrainForest:

1. At the main screen, select the outline you want and tap the Open button, or choose Open Tree from the Tree menu (✐-L).

2. Tap and drag items to reposition them within the tree; a horizontal line appears to indicate where the item will end up when you lift your stylus (**Figure 17.3**).

   To place an item under another item in the hierarchy (reducing its importance, as opposed to moving its position), drag and drop it onto the branch you wish to use as a parent item; the indicator line will disappear, and the parent will be highlighted before you drop it.

3. To rename a branch or leaf, double-tap its title to display the popup text field.

✔ Tips

■ If you're brainstorming and don't want to tangle with BrainForest's trees and branches, go ahead and write your ideas in the Memo Pad. Later, when you have more time, choose Import... from the Tree menu (make sure the plug-in "BF Text Plug.prc" has been installed) to bring your notes into BrainForest.

■ If you do write a note using the Memo Pad, add tab characters (·⌐) at the front of each line based on the level in the hierarchy the item will reside (**Figure 17.4**).

OUTLINING AND BRAINSTORMING

Making Lists

The first time I walked into the grocery store with a hastily scrawled list in one hand and my organizer in the other, I knew that one would have to go. Now, in addition to saving some paper, I have a shopping list that remembers everything I normally buy so I don't have to start from scratch every time.

Lists, of course, go beyond noting the things I need to pick up at the store. You can create reusable checklists of procedures, clothing to pack when you travel, music you want to buy...the list of lists is practically unending. For generating lists of all kinds, try List-Maker (http://www.synsolutions.com/); JShopper (http://www.land-j.com/) is an advanced list tool that's tailored for shopping, with support for 15 different stores, item lookups, and even the ability to track coupons.

For Palm OS purists, the To Do List application can also expand its usefulness to include other types of lists.

To create lists using the To Do List:

1. Open the To Do List.

2. Tap the category popup menu in the upper-right corner of the screen and choose Edit Categories....

3. Each built-in application can support up to 15 categories, but there's no rule saying that they have to all be related (**Figure 17.5**). Tap the New button and name your category (such as "Grocery store").

4. When you want to access your list, simply launch the To Do List and select that category from the popup menu. You may want to mark the Show Completed Items checkbox in the To Do Preferences screen (✓-R), so you can uncheck items when you need them again (**Figure 17.6**).

Figure 17.5 The To Do list can be used for other purposes in a pinch. Set up a new category representing your topic.

Figure 17.6 Turning on the Show Completed Items option lets you go back and unmark the items you've completed to "reset" the list.

MAKING LISTS

Figure 17.7 Priorities and due dates can be used to sort your lists.

Figure 17.8 Total Recall's Recording screen includes controls for setting bookmarks, erasing sections, and setting the volume.

Figure 17.9 Set voice alarms to remind you of specific appointments.

✔ Tips

- Attach notes to items that require more explanation. In a grocery store list, you could include specific brand names in the note.

- If you already use several categories, things might get confusing if you choose to display them all at once; mark the non-task records Private to hide them during everyday use.

- To reorder items in your list, assign priorities or set varying due dates to the records (**Figure 17.7**).

Digital Voice Recorders

I like the Palm OS, but here's a gripe: you can't (and shouldn't) jot down a quick note when you're driving or otherwise occupied. What's needed is some sort of voice recorder that you could store on your handheld and... okay, you knew this was coming. Now I have no gripe—two digital voice recorders are currently available that plug into the Visor's Springboard slot: the Targus Total Recall (http://www.targus.com/) and the my-Vox (http://www.my-vox.com/my-vox.htm) digital recording devices.

Each features a speaker in the module, can be voice activated, and includes headphone ports. The Total Recall (**Figure 17.8**) also comes with a clip-on battery pack to let you use the unit independently of the Visor, and can transfer audio messages to your PC.

✔ Tip

- The my-Vox can set alarms that play recordings instead of a typical system beep (**Figure 17.9**). It's much more effective to hear myself say "Wake up!" than to ignore yet another electronic chime.

Databases and Spreadsheets

It's always been the job of database and spreadsheet software to elevate computers above the "toy" stage into the realm of "serious business." The next time someone asks you if your Visor is some sort of handheld gaming device, show them how you can crunch data with one of these programs (*then* you can get back to that game of YahtC—see Chapter 20).

JFile, MobileDB, HanDBase, and FileMaker Mobile

For actual database functionality, turn to JFile (http://www.land-j.com/), MobileDB (http://www.mobilegeneration.com/), or HanDBase (http://www.ddhsoftware.com/). If you use FileMaker on your PC, FileMaker Mobile (http://www.filemaker.com/) can read and edit, but not create, FileMaker databases. There are a number of existing databases available to download, ranging from subway schedules to medical references.

To create a database:

1. Tap the New DB (JFile) or the New (MobileDB and HanDBase) button.

2. Write the name of the database, then enter the field names in the lines provided (**Figure 17.10**). Click Done.

3. Within your new database, tap the New button (MobileDB and HanDBase) or Add button (JFile) to create a new record.

4. Enter the field data for that record (**Figure 17.11**). Tapping New on this screen creates a new blank record.

5. Tap Done (or OK) to go back to the list of records, where you can sort the records, perform searches, or choose other options (**Figure 17.12**).

Figure 17.10 When creating a new database in JFile, enter the column headings in the New Database fields.

Figure 17.11 Once you're in a database (JFile shown here), you can enter your data next to the field titles you set up.

Figure 17.12 View, sort, and find the records from the database's main screen (HanDBase shown here).

DATABASES AND SPREADSHEETS

Figure 17.13 Quicksheet looks and acts like a desktop spreadsheet program.

Figure 17.14 TinySheet turns out to be not so tiny after all.

Figure 17.15 The SheetView component of Documents To Go views and edits Excel spreadsheets.

✔ **Tip**

■ You can also get a variety of programs that let you interface your handheld database with one on your PC. Check the Web sites of each application above for links.

Quicksheet, TinySheet, and Documents to Go

If you spend much of your time locked in Microsoft Excel's data cells, you'll be happy to know that Quicksheet (http://www.cesinc.com/), TinySheet (http://www.iambic.com/), and Documents To Go (http://www.dataviz.com/) put a true spreadsheet onto your handheld's small screen, complete with built-in functions, linking of named spreadsheets within workbooks, and a surprisingly easy method of maneuvering lots of data within a small space (**Figures 17.13**, **17.14**, and **17.15**).

All three spreadsheets include conduits that synchronize the data on your device with the data on your hard disk.

Printing from Your Visor

Remember all the hoopla about paperless offices? A Visor would seem to be the perfect antidote to mass paper consumption, but every now and again it would be handy to print something from your handheld. A few utilities will do just that: PrintBoy (http://www.bachmannsoftware.com/printboy.htm), TealPrint (http://www.tealpoint.com/), and PalmPrint (http://www.stevenscreek.com/palm/) enable you to connect to a variety of printers using either a special cable or, better yet, via infrared.

To print from your Visor:

1. Launch your printing utility (I'm using PrintBoy as an example), and select the type of document you wish to print, or choose which application to print from (**Figure 17.16**).

2. If the printer is equipped with an infrared port, aim your Visor at the printer and tap the Print button (**Figure 17.17**).

✔ Tips

- If your printer doesn't have a built-in infrared port, consider buying the InfraReady adapter, an IR adapter that plugs into a printer's serial port (http://www.bachmannsoftware.com/).

- Sometimes it's just easier to print out a portion of your schedule and share it with someone. If you're not near your PC, use one of these printing programs to output your appointments over a span of time (**Figure 17.18**).

Figure 17.16 Don't wait to HotSync before printing something. Most document types can be printed directly from your Visor.

Figure 17.17 Printing from the Memo Pad is as simple as reading a memo.

Figure 17.18 If you want to share a week's schedule, don't beam every event to someone else. Simply print the week's appointments.

TRAVELING
WITH YOUR VISOR

One of the reasons the laptop computer really took off was the demand from business travelers who needed to take their data with them. The Visor is no exception; I've heard of people who are now refusing to lug around a bulky laptop on trips when they can take a handheld instead.

But simply carrying your Visor doesn't make it any more unique of a tool—you probably used to carry a paper-based notebook, too. In addition to the bulk saved by storing information electronically, there are a number of advantages for travelers in terms of software and hardware: add-ons that will help you get to your location, figure out what to do while you're there, and then get you home again.

And who can resist the temptation of having a GPS (Global Positioning Satellite) signal receiver operating within their Visor? Finally, you get the chance to definitively say, "Here I am, world!"

City Time

In addition to Date Book+ (see Chapter 4), Handspring chose to differentiate the Visor from other Palm OS handhelds by including a free application called City Time. With it, you can check the current time anywhere in the world.

The four fields at the bottom of the screen provide popup menus to list favorite cities, while the main map displays the current areas of daytime and nighttime across the globe (**Figure 18.1**). To quickly check the time in a major city, you can also tap the screen directly to view a time label (**Figure 18.2**). Other features include:

◆ You can add new cities to the list by choosing Edit Cities from the Options menu, or writing ╱-E. Enter the time zone difference from the Greenwich Mean Time (such as "-8" for Seattle); the latitude and longitude coordinates if you know them (you can also tap the approximate location on a map); and the dates when Daylight Savings Time is active.

◆ City Time calculates the sunrise and sunset of any location. Choose Sun Rise/Set... from the Utilities Menu, or write ╱-S.

◆ If you're skipping through time zones during a trip, choose Change Location... from the Utilities Menu, or write ╱-L. When you tap the OK button, the Visor's system time will be changed to reflect the new local time.

✔ Tip

■ The city popup menus can be a chore to scroll through, especially if you live in a city like Seattle or Zurich that appears at the bottom of the list. After you tap the popup menu, write the first letter of the city you want in the Graffiti area to jump down to that listing (**Figure 18.3**).

Figure 18.1 Forget about calculating time zone differences in your head. It's all available on City Time's main screen.

Figure 18.2 Tapping a location on the map displays the current time in a city near your tap.

Figure 18.3 To quickly jump to a popup menu listing, tap the menu, then write the first letter of the city you want.

Figure 18.4 You may not have to rely on a wake up call to get up each morning while you're on the road.

Figure 18.5 Palm Zone Pro makes it easier to cross time zones without having to manually change settings.

Figure 18.6 TravelPal rolls a time tracking utility in with a trip log and currency converter.

The Well-Equipped World Traveler

If you do a lot of traveling, you're probably familiar with that odd, surreal sense when your body's clock is nowhere near the clocks in your new location. These utilities will help you gain some sense of equilibrium.

Travel Clock

Travel Clock (http://www.boswell.demon.co.uk/) keeps track of the current time, but also lets you specify an "away" location (perfect if you travel to the same location frequently). With two taps of the stylus, your handheld's clock can be adjusted to the current time (**Figure 18.4**).

Palm Zone Pro

Palm Zone Pro (http://www.geocities.com/SiliconValley/Campus/7631/software.html) lacks an alarm, but can automatically switch locations at pre-specified times (**Figure 18.5**).

TravelPal

For an extra boost of usefulness, install TravelPal, by the same developer (**Figure 18.6**). TravelPal includes the same time-tracking features as Palm Zone Pro, but adds a trip log and currency converter—perfect for those of us who sometimes have trouble counting our own currency, much less factoring in another country's exchange rate. Be sure to download the latest version of TravelPal's currency conversion database, which is updated regularly.

✔ Tip

■ When you travel, record your parking space, frequent flyer number, ticketless travel numbers, etc. in your organizer for easy access later.

Information that Travels with You

It's helpful to keep important travel-related information with you on your handheld. For drivers, Kar Kare (http://www.geocities.com/ResearchTriangle/6608/) tracks your mileage, fuel consumption, and maintenance dates and locations. You also can set it to remind you when the next service or check up is due (**Figure 18.7**).

If you're a heavy-duty frequent flyer, consider using a program such as AirMiles (http://www.handshigh.com/), which keeps your airline frequent flyer numbers close at hand (**Figure 18.8**). You can keep track of your flights for reference later (when you need to trump the guy at the hotel bar stool next to you who's bragging about how many miles he's flown so far).

Figure 18.7 Keep track of your gas fill-ups as well as any maintenance done on your car with Kar Kare.

Figure 18.8 The miles may go by in a haze, but you'll have something to show for them besides yet another in-flight magazine.

Figure 18.9 Specify your location using the popup menu at upper right, then select a type of location (in this case, a Cajun restaurant).

Figure 18.10 With a destination selected, tap the Map tab to get a sense of where you are in relation to the place.

Figure 18.11 Tapping the Go tab provides walking directions from your current location.

Navigating City Life

Although I enjoy traveling, I'm not a big fan of finding myself in an unfamiliar city with no idea where to go. Sure, I could pick up a telephone book or newspaper, but what I really want is the equivalent of a personal guide to the city.

So far, Vindigo (http://www.vindigo.com/) is the best product I've seen that feels most like being with a good friend who's lived in a city for years (without the bad puns and prying questions, of course!). It currently supports 20 cities worldwide, and updates its content when you HotSync your Visor the same way AvantGo does (see Chapter 11).

Other similar services include Lonely Planet's CitySync (http://www.conceptkitchen.com/) and the Zagat Restaurant Guide (http://www.landware.com/).

To find a destination in Vindigo:

1. Make sure your current location is set in the popup menu at the upper-right corner, then choose selection criteria in the left-hand column (**Figure 18.9**).

2. Tap the name of one of the destinations that appear in the main column to see more detail about the place and its location.

3. Tap the Review tab to read a commentary, or tap the Map tab to get an overview of where the destination is in relation to your location (**Figure 18.10**).

4. When you've decided where to go, tap the Go tab to view walking directions from your location (**Figure 18.11**).

✔ Tip

- Vindigo will work with a GPS receiver to pinpoint your current location.

NAVIGATING CITY LIFE

Finding Your Way with GPS

Let's take a step back for a moment and consider the realm of Cool Technology. As you may have guessed, I think Visors—and handhelds in general—are extremely cool and even futuristic sometimes. That said, I think GPS narrowly trumps palmtops in sheer geeky coolness.

The GPS (Global Positioning Satellite) system is a collection of satellites that can be used to pinpoint one's location to within inches. And although this capability was once the toy of the military, now anyone with a small receiver can do the same thing. Currently there are three GPS devices available that snap into the Visor's Springboard slot: Nexian's HandyGPS (http://www.nexian.com/), GeoDiscovery's Geode (http://www.geodiscovery.com/), and the Magellan GPS Companion (http://www.magellangps.com/).

With a GPS receiver, you can go back-country hiking with a better sense of security (though bring plenty of batteries), find a location on a downloadable map, or even use software like Vindigo (see previous page) to discover a new restaurant nearby.

Each Springboard module comes with its own software, but the general method of using them is quite similar. I'm using the HandyGPS module for this example.

GPS module basics

◆ When you insert the module, it must first locate the nearest satellites. When it does, a host of information is displayed, including latitude, longitude, altitude, and even speed if you're in motion (**Figure 18.12**).

◆ To see how many satellites are contributing to the Handy GPS module's calculations, select Satellite from the Preference menu or write ╱-S (**Figure 18.13**).

Figure 18.12 Find your place in the universe (okay, just Earth) with a GPS receiver.

Figure 18.13 You can see how many satellites are overhead, and their signal strengths (black squares mean better reception).

Figure 18.14 Once you've been found, you can zoom in and out of the map by tapping the plus and minus buttons.

Figure 18.15 A collection of lines and the odd street name can still be confusing. Use the pencil tool to customize your map and save it for later viewing.

◆ To add context to your location data, download a map of your area from the vendor's Web site. Switch to the mapping software. When the GPS module has located you, a pulsing circle appears. You can zoom in and out by tapping the plus and minus buttons at the bottom of the screen (**Figure 18.14**).

◆ In UbiGo, the HandyGPS mapping software, you can use the pencil tool to scribble a note on the map and save it for later viewing (**Figure 18.15**). Please write something more informative than my example.

◆ The GPS device's mapping software should also include methods of recording a trip, plus storing locations in order to build trip plans. Over time, it's not unusual to end up with a map that's dotted with a mass of flagged locations.

✔ Tips

■ The Springboard GPS receivers aren't very powerful, so try to keep as few obstacles as possible between you and the satellites. You can probably get by with setting the Visor on the dashboard of your car, but don't expect any coverage indoors. For this reason, too, don't be surprised if it takes several minutes for the module to first latch onto the satellites.

■ GPS technology is sophisticated, but don't rely 100 percent on it to guide you—especially when driving. A GPS satellite can't tell you if a road is closed, for example, and sometimes the distances (say, between you and the edge of that cliff there) might be off.

■ If you're planning a trip where getting lost or disoriented could be potentially dangerous, consider other dedicated devices with better power supplies.

FINDING YOUR WAY WITH GPS

MANAGING YOUR MONEY

I've often heard the expression "time is money," but rarely do I hear the phrase, "money is sure a lot like time." As sayings go it kind of stinks, I'll admit—yet in my experience, this nugget of wisdom has repeatedly proven itself true. As with time, you can burn through money without noticing it if you're not careful. Also like time (or rather, deadlines), bills have the uncanny ability to sneak up on you quickly.

Fortunately, I can use my handheld to keep track of my finances as well as to help me manage my time. Having that information at my disposal allows me to update my checkbook register when I'm away from my computer, minimizing the number of faded paper receipts that I'd normally have to organize.

Track Your Personal Finances

If your spending seems out of control, or you just want to get a better idea of where your money is going, track your usage for a week or a month—just as you tracked your time in Chapter 16.

The built-in Expense application is all set up to make it easy for you to track your money's trajectory from wallet to the outside world.

To track your cash flow with Expense:

1. To create a new record, tap New or begin writing either the expense amount or the first letter of the expense type in the Graffiti area.

2. With the record still highlighted, tap the Details button to enter the Vendor, City, and any other information you want to store (**Figure 19.1**).

3. At the end of the tracking period, perform a HotSync and then tap the Expense button in Palm Desktop for Windows. You'll be able to open the data in an Excel spreadsheet and get an overview of where your money went (**Figure 19.2**).

✔ Tip

■ I created a master list of the bills I pay each month, so that even if my income varies from month to month (one curse of freelancing), I know how much I need to pay. That list has made its way onto my handheld, first in the form of a Memo Pad entry, and lately as a spreadsheet.

Figure 19.1 The more information you add to expense items, the better you'll be able to track your money.

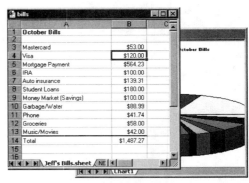

Figure 19.2 Gather your raw data into a program such as Excel to get an overview of your expenses.

Accounts

Name	Type	Balance
Jeff-Checking	Bank	501.06
NEC-Checking	Bank	991.55
Jeff-VISA-WF	Credit	-456.72

Balance Total:	1,035.89

(Edit...) (Register)

Figure 19.3 Pocket Quicken features the same straightforward interface as the desktop Quicken application.

PMT Transaction Record

Date: 6/19/2001
Repeat: None
Transfer to Cash
From Account Checking
Description: TAX
Check Num: 1138 ☐ Cleared
Amount: 450.87 ▼ $
Note: More money for The Man

(Done)(Cancel)(Nxt Check) 🡡

Figure 19.4 Personal Money Tracker is an all-in-one financial center residing on your handheld.

Pocket Quicken 2.0

As this book went to press, LandWare had announced Pocket Quicken 2.0, a significant release that improves nearly every aspect of the program. Alas, I wasn't able to incorporate Pocket Quicken 2.0 information into this chapter; look for an update at the Visor VQS Web site (http://www.peachpit.com/vqs/visor/), hopefully available by the time you read this.

Manage Your Financial Accounts

My checkbook used to serve only as a convenient place to store money-related papers such as ATM withdrawal receipts, upcoming bills, and more than a few overdraft notices. Then I bought a copy of Quicken (http://www.quicken.com/), which allowed me to see how and where I spent my cash.

A few financial applications have appeared for the Palm organizer during the last year or so. Pocket Quicken (http://www.landware.com/) so far is the only one that syncs directly with Quicken on the PC (**Figure 19.3**). QMate (http://www.wco.com/~sdakin/qmate.html), one of the first financial apps, can take data from the handheld to be imported into Quicken. And there are others as well that don't need a desktop program, such as Personal Money Tracker (find it at http://www.palmgear.com/) (**Figure 19.4**).

Getting started in Pocket Quicken

One of the great things about LandWare's Pocket Quicken is that all you need to do is install the desktop conduit and perform a HotSync operation. Your Quicken account names and balances are transferred to the handheld. Optionally, you can have your categories transferred as well.

✔ Tips

- A maximum of 15 accounts will be transferred. Unfortunately, if you have any inactive or hidden accounts in Quicken, those get sent over as well. However, you can delete an account from Pocket Quicken and still keep it in Quicken.

- You can add accounts on the handheld if you want, but they won't be created on the desktop after you HotSync.

To enter a transaction in Pocket Quicken:

1. Tap the New button and choose the type of transaction from the popup menu that appears: Payment, Deposit, or Transfer. The transaction looks like Quicken's check format (**Figure 19.5**).

2. Write the information in the fields provided, or tap the field titles to access more information like categories (**Figure 19.6**).

3. Pocket Quicken supports split transactions. Tap Split... to break out individual components (**Figure 19.7**).

4. Tap Done to apply the transaction, or Cancel to delete it.

✔ Tips

- Start writing the payee's name in the Graffiti area to create a new transaction.

- In the Transaction Categories screen, tap the shortcut letters at the bottom to take you to that block of categories. Tapping each one repeatedly cycles through the letters; for example, tapping mno once takes you to the top of the "m" list, but tapping it again jumps down to the "n" categories.

- Pocket Quicken also supports features like memorized, cleared, and voided transactions. Plus, if a payee isn't in your list of memorized transactions, you can look up a name from the Address Book.

Figure 19.5 Pocket Quicken's transaction screen looks almost like the checks buried at the bottom of your purse or briefcase, without the paper.

Figure 19.6 All of your Quicken categories transfer to the handheld.

Figure 19.7 Splitting transactions in Pocket Quicken makes it easier to identify your expenses when you run reports in Quicken.

MANAGE YOUR FINANCIAL ACCOUNTS

Figure 19.8 QMate accounts need to share the same names of related accounts in Quicken.

Figure 19.9 The New Transaction window roughly resembles a check, with options for marking the record's status.

Table 19.1

Number field codes		
SHORTCUT	CODE	DESCRIPTION
A	ATM	Automatic Teller Machine
C	CCARD	Credit Card
D	DEP	Deposit
E	EFT	Electronic Funds Transfer
K	—	Advances check number by one
P	PRINT	Printed check
S	SEND	
T	TXFR	Transfer
W	WITHD	Withdrawal
X	XMIT	Transmission

To set up accounts in QMate:

1. From the main Accounts window, tap the New button to create a new account. Make sure its name exactly matches the name of your corresponding Quicken account (**Figure 19.8**).

2. Choose an account type from the Type popup menu.

3. Enter the account's current balance in the Balance field. Tap OK to save the account's information.

To enter a transaction:

1. Once your account is set up, tap the Transactions button, or double-tap the account name to open it. The transaction is structured like a check (**Figure 19.9**).

2. Tap the Date, Payee, or Cat (category) button to view a list of memorized transactions; or, write the information in the fields provided. Tap OK to apply the transaction, or Cancel to get rid of it.

✔ Tips

■ To easily change the date in the New Transaction window, tap the date itself (not the Date button): tapping the year advances by a day, tapping the month falls back by a day.

■ The Number field can display more than just numbers. Write the letters in **Table 19.1** to bring up the action codes.

To transfer data to Quicken:

1. Perform a HotSync under Windows.

2. Run the QSync application, which creates a Quicken .qif data file for your accounts.

3. In Quicken, choose the account you want to update and choose Import... from the File menu.

MANAGE YOUR FINANCIAL ACCOUNTS

Manage Your Investments

I remember being in school and not caring one whit about stocks, bonds, or anything else related to investing. I didn't have great stashes of money to throw at the stock market, so why bother? Now, in our era of IPOs and millionaires sprouting like weeds, stock tracking is moving to the masses. (If your stock portfolio took a big hit during the downturn in the economy, as mine did, think of these utilities as mere entertainment.)

Several solutions exist to track one's investments on a Visor. Programs like Personal Stock Tracker (find it at http://www.palmgear.com/) enable you to enter your stocks and trades manually (**Figure 19.10**). For the more serious (or more fanatical) trader, a Visor connected to the Internet offers market information whenever you log on. Popular services such as E*Trade have created free Palm Query Applications (PQAs) that can tie into your accounts and make transactions (**Figure 19.11**). (See Chapter 11 for more information about PQAs.)

✔ Tip

■ If you do have a wireless Net connection and a Web browser on your Palm, you can access many online financial services just as you would on your computer. Not all browser software will work, however, as most financial Web sites use encrypted data and Web cookies to identify you while you're on their sites. Check the specs of the browser software.

Figure 19.10 Monitor your investments by entering your stocks and trades into Personal Stock Tracker.

Figure 19.11 Online users can get up-to-the minute information on how their favorite stocks are performing, including buying and selling stock.

GAMES & ENTERTAINMENT

You're a working professional with a lot to accomplish in a limited time. Since purchasing your Visor, you've discovered new ways to squeeze your workload into the tight confines of your daily schedule, and finally carved out the quality time you've been dreaming about for months.

And yet, while on the bus or train, standing in line at the grocery store, or waiting at the airport—transitional time that would be ripe for reviewing the latest project outline—you just don't have it in you to *work*. These are the moments when the Visor really shines, when you realize the full power of your investment. These are the times to play games.

I couldn't hope to cover all the games that are available for the Palm OS platform, but my conscience wouldn't allow me to write a book about these splendid devices without including a chapter about games and entertainment. The following programs are games I've become addicted to at one time or another, or are beguiling diversions that just deserve notice.

Stress Relievers

Vexed

There are games that try to squeeze the best 3D graphics performance out of their processors, but every once in a while a simple gem arrives and gets all of the attention. Vexed (http://spacetube.darktech.org/Projects/Vexed/) asks you to clear the screen of patterned tiles by making two or more touch and disappear. The 59 levels vary from easy to fiendishly obscure, and will occupy your thoughts as well as your time (**Figure 20.1**).

YahtChallenge

"Hmm," I thought, "a Yahtzee game... this should be entertaining for a few minutes." If I had only known then that YahtC (http://home1.pacific.net.sg/~kokmun/) would occupy all of my spare Visor time. Roll dice and come up with combinations to score the most points against a friend or the Visor (**Figure 20.2**).

PocketChess

This excellent chess program provides all the functions an average chess player needs, and takes up only 39K (**Figure 20.3**). And lest you think that the Visor's teeny processor can't provide enough challenge, just try to play on level eight. PocketChess (http://www.tinyware.com/) sometimes kills me—I mean, um, friends of mine—on level one!

PocketChess Deluxe (http://www.pocket-express.com/) is available as a Springboard module and includes full color support with customizable color schemes, a game database, the capability to import and export games, and a Windows companion program.

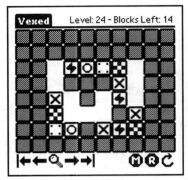

Figure 20.1 Vexed seems easy enough, though you might not think that when you've run your batteries down trying to get past its 59 levels.

Figure 20.2 A typical screen (note the score) from YahtChallenge, an addictive Yahtzee-type dice game.

Figure 20.3 PocketChess packs a well-designed chess engine into 39K.

Figure 20.4 The most-often used Windows program is on the Palm OS!

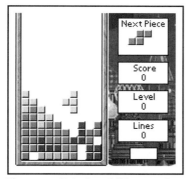

Figure 20.5 Spinning, shifting, rotating, interlocking... the obsession known as Tetris will make your Visor's batteries run dry.

Figure 20.6 SimCity brings the megalo-maniacal power of running a city to your Visor.

Klondike and FreeCell

No consumer electronic device should exist without a solitaire game installed. These two variations, the traditional Klondike and the more nefarious FreeCell (both at http://www.electronhut.com/pilot/), can occupy your hours without the need for table space to set up real cards (**Figure 20.4**).

Tetris

Cultural anthropologists are going to stumble upon Tetris one day, and either wonder at how backward our society was or marvel at how fast the human mind could move shapes into place in order to get rid of horizontal rows (http://www.pocketexpress.com/). I'd ponder this some more, but I really must clear a few more rows... just one or two... really, I can stop when I want to... (**Figure 20.5**).

SimCity Classic

You're the city mayor, responsible for promoting growth, prosperity, and above all the adulation of your citizens. SimCity Classic (http://www.ateliersoftware.com/palm/) is just like the original hallmark game on the Mac or PC (**Figure 20.6**), complete with fires, earthquakes, hurricanes, and the dreaded monster attacks.

DopeWars

Are you a budding entrepeneur, looking for the high life? Does the thrill of making deals pump through your veins? Then perhaps you need to try your hand at DopeWars (http://www.pdaguy.com/dopewars/), a game geared toward making as much money as possible within a given timeframe. If you're uncomfortable with the DopeWars theme, install Taipan (http://mdbowen.ne.mediaone.net/taipan/) instead and trade across the high seas of the Orient.

Notable Diversions

Zap!2000 and Zap!2016

Zoom through space blasting everything in sight in Zap!2000 (http://www.astraware.com/). The game play is fast, the graphics are crisp, and the color version, Zap!2016, takes advantage of the thousands of colors of the Visor Prism screen (**Figure 20.7**).

To really appreciate the game (and others), then get serious about your recreation and buy the GameFace (find it at http://www.handspring.com/), a snap-on device that adds a joystick and two buttons to your Visor (**Figure 20.8**).

Tricorder II

More than a few people have noticed that the Visor is about the same size and shape as a Star Trek tricorder, an all-in-one device with the power to scan and analyze nearly anything. Jeff Jetton (http://www.jeffjetton.com/) took that one step further by developing the software for this fictional device. When you're finished scanning the household pets for baryon particle build-up, be sure to peruse the program's Read Me file, certainly one of the best I've read in years. Now you're ready for that away mission, Ensign... sorry, what was your name?

Tiger Woods PGA Tour Golf

A celebrity endorsement of a game on the Palm OS? These days, anything can happen. Electronic Arts ported this impressive golf game to the Palm OS (**Figure 20.9**), complete with grayscale graphics and a roster of golf pros to keep you at the top of your game (http://www.easports.ea.com/games/tigerpalm/main.html). The game is also available as a Springboard module (http://www.handspring.com/products/sbmodules/twgolfdetails.jhtml).

Figure 20.7 One of the best uses of color, Zap!2016 on the Visor Prism is beautiful and action-packed.

Figure 20.8 A joystick on your Visor? Well... sure, why not?

Figure 20.9 Hit the links from anywhere, even if it's raining outside.

BASIC TROUBLESHOOTING

A

My handheld is one of the most trustworthy electronic devices I've ever owned, but that doesn't mean it doesn't act up on occasion. Often the cause of problems and error messages is a conflict among the installed applications (some system extensions can be picky neighbors with other programs' code; see Chapter 8). Occasionally the problem is hardware-related, ranging from the components of the device itself, to upgrade cards, to batteries. Knowing how to deal with possible problems will go a long way toward reducing that first moment of panic when something isn't working.

If the problem requires you to send it back to the manufacturer, the situation is actually rather good. Although I've never needed to send a Visor back to Handspring (knock on wood), my original PalmPilot Personal developed a black smudge on the screen, so Palm sent a padded shipping container marked with the correct postage. After doing a complete backup of my data, I sent it off, then was amazed when it returned three days later—including the shipping time. Your mileage may vary, as they say, but in general the companies understand the value of keeping their customers happy.

Back Up Your Data

When you perform a HotSync, the data on your handheld gets copied to your user directory on your PC or Macintosh—or rather, most of it gets copied. The data from third-party applications may get backed up at HotSync, but the applications themselves sometimes don't, depending on which version of the Palm OS you're running (versions prior to Palm OS 3.3 can be problematic in this respect). In the event of a hard reset, where all data on the device is lost (see next section), it's great to be able to restore everything to the state it was in before the reset. To ensure that you're getting a full backup, I recommend two essential utilities: BackupBuddy (http://www.bluenomad.com/) and, for Macintosh users only, Palm Buddy (http://perso.wanadoo.fr/fpillet/).

Both programs allow you to back up and restore your full data, as well as perform incremental backups (**Figure A.1**). If you have to do a complete restoration of your data, BackupBuddy users simply do a HotSync. Palm Buddy owners drag the data from their backup folder in the Finder to the active Palm Buddy window (**Figure A.2**).

Figure A.1 BackupBuddy backs up all of your handheld files—even those stored in ROM—during HotSync.

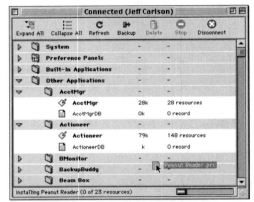

Figure A.2 Restore your programs and databases after a crash by dragging them from the Mac OS Finder to Palm Buddy's directory window.

Figure A.3 The reset pin in the Visor's stylus slides into the reset hole and presses the button inside.

Figure A.4 The Visor's stylus includes a reset pin and a small screwdriver.

Resetting Your Handheld

Like turning your desktop computer off and on, a Visor occasionally needs to be reset (though infrequently). Three methods of resetting the device are available.

A *soft reset* is like rebooting a computer, initializing its internal system files and libraries. All of your data will remain intact.

If something is giving you errors as your device starts up from a soft reset (such as a system update patch, for example), try doing a *warm reset*. This is analagous to booting Windows in Safe Mode or starting a Mac with extensions turned off.

A *hard reset* is the action of last resort, erasing all of your data and taking the handheld back to its original state. Be sure you have a recent backup of your information.

To perform a soft reset:

Insert the straight end of the stylus's reset pin into the reset hole on the back of the device (**Figures A.3** and **A.4**).

To perform a warm reset:

1. Hold down the plastic Scroll Up button on the front of the device case.

2. Insert the reset pin into the reset hole on the back of the device, then release the button. The screen should flash, then restart normally.

To perform a hard reset:

1. Hold down the power button.

2. With the power button still held down, insert the reset pin into the reset hole on the back of the device, then release the power button.

3. A confirmation message appears on the screen. Press the Scroll Up button to erase the memory, then restore your data.

Restoring applications after a hard reset

For the most part, performing a HotSync operation after a hard reset should reinstall your data files and any applications that were loaded on your handheld. However, a glitch in system versions prior to Palm OS 3.3 would sometimes cause applications you had deleted from the handheld to be reinstalled. This was because deleted programs still hung out in your User folder, but the handheld knew they should be ignored. Palm OS 3.3 improved the way it treats backed-up files, so now doing a HotSync operation resets the device to the state of the last HotSync.

To determine which version of Palm OS you are running, go to the Applications screen and choose Info from the App menu or write ╱-I. Tap the Version button at the bottom of the screen (**Figure A.5**).

Palm OS version

Figure A.5 The Info screen displays the version numbers of your applications as well as the Palm OS.

Contacting Handheld Technical Support

Handspring, Inc. support

◆ Web site: http://www.handspring.com/support/

◆ Technical Support (716-871-6448).

◆ CustomerCare Center (888-565-9393) to coordinate repairs or replacements.

Palm, Inc. support

◆ Web site: http://www.palm.com/support/

◆ Technical Support (847-262-7256) can answer your software questions.

RESETTING YOUR HANDHELD

HotSync Troubleshooting

If you have any troubles at all, they're likely to be related to HotSync. Although in practice HotSync is a simple process, it relies on several factors that control the communication with your computer.

Common HotSync fixes

◆ In Palm Desktop, check that your settings in the HotSync Setup screen are correct.

◆ Under Windows, exit HotSync Manager, then launch it again. On a Macintosh, make sure Local HotSync is enabled; if it is already on, disable it manually, wait a few seconds, then re-enable it.

◆ Verify that the HotSync cable or cradle is plugged into the correct port on your computer.

◆ Reduce the port speed in the Setup screen.

◆ Disable any software that might be sharing the communication ports. Fax software is often the culprit, because it's always monitoring for incoming faxes.

◆ Under the Mac OS, turn off AppleTalk by opening the Chooser and clicking the AppleTalk Inactive button.

◆ If you're using a USB hub, try plugging the HotSync cradle directly into the USB connection on the computer.

To set Macintosh memory allocation:

1. Try increasing the memory allocated to the Conduit Manager application. On your hard disk, open the Palm folder and click on the Conduit Manager.

2. Choose Memory from the Get Info submenu under the File menu.

3. Increase the number in the Preferred Size field, then close the Get Info window.

Windows COM port conflicts

If the previous suggestions don't produce a successful HotSync, your COM ports may be misconfigured or confused. COM ports are the physical ports used to hook up devices such as modems and mice to the back of your computer. Some machines also use COM ports for internal devices.

To work together, these ports communicate with the computer's processor over Interrupt Request (IRQ) channels. Often, one IRQ channel is shared by two COM ports, which means they can both be vying for attention (COM 1 and COM 3 usually share an IRQ, while COM 2 and COM 4 share another IRQ). If you have the option of doing so, move your HotSync cable to a different COM port. If not, and if you're skilled in complex computer configuration, try reassigning the port settings.

Keep in mind that tinkering with IRQ settings has the potential to cause conflicts where none existed before. Make changes one at a time; if they don't fix the problem, undo the change and reboot your computer before making any more changes.

To modify Windows COM settings:

1. Double-click the System icon from the Windows Control Panels.

2. Click the Device Manager tab, then click the plus sign next to Ports (COM & LPT).

3. Double-click the Communications Port you want to change.

4. Click the Resources tab. If the Use automatic settings checkbox is on, click to unmark it.

5. Choose an alternate configuration from the Settings based on popup menu.

6. When finished, click OK, then restart your computer.

Macintosh HotSync problems with certain models

Owners of computers based on the "Tanzania" motherboard design (Power Macintosh G3s, 5400, 6400, 4400, PowerBook 3400, and clones from Motorola, Umax, APS, and Power Computing) have had more than their share of HotSync problems. Fortunately, there are two possible solutions to try.

To reverse HotSync steps:

1. Open the HotSync control panel.

2. Turn HotSync monitoring off.

3. Put your Visor in its cradle and press the HotSync button to start synchronizing.

4. After the Visor has begun its portion of the HotSync process, turn HotSync monitoring back on.

Install Serial DMA

Some people have reported success with this fix, but it doesn't seem to be a cure-all. Download and install Apple's Serial DMA v2.1 extension (`ftp://ftp.info.apple.com/ Apple_Support_ Area/Apple_Software_ Updates/US/Macintosh/Networking-Communications/ Other_N-C/SerialDMA/`). Note that this does not apply to the Power-Book 3400. Also note that on more recent Mac models, Serial DMA can actually be the culprit of errors. If you have it installed, try removing it and HotSync again.

Time out errors

If you have a slower (older) computer, or you're synchronizing a lot of data, you may receive a message that the handheld timed out while transferring the information. To get around this, try activating the "developer's backdoor" feature, which disables the set amount of time the Visor will wait to receive data.

To activate the Developer's Backdoor:

1. On the Visor, go to HotSync by selecting it from the Applications screen (don't press the HotSync button on the cradle).

2. Hold down the up and down scroll buttons on the front of the case.

3. With the buttons still pressed, tap the upper-right corner of the screen. You'll see the message DLServer Wait Forever is ON in the DEVELOPER'S BACKDOOR dialog box that appears. Tap OK and perform a HotSync again. The feature will be disabled after the HotSync, or if you power off your handheld.

GRAFFITI REFERENCE

Normal and alternate characters

Letter	Graffiti		Letter	Graffiti
A	∧		N	N ∿ ∼
B	B B 3		O	O O
C	C <		P	P P P
D	D Q ℓ		Q	Ơ U
E	Ɛ ≶ ℰ		R	R R ℟
F	Γ ⌐		S	S ∫ ƅ
G	G 6		T	⅂
H	h		U	U
I	∣		V	V V
J	J ⌐		W	W
K	∝		X	X ∞
L	L ∠		Y	¥ ⅄ r
M	m m		Z	Z

Graffiti numbers and special strokes

Letter	Graffiti		Letter	Graffiti
1	∣		8	8 8 ⅄
2	2 ≳		9	9
3	3		0	O O
4	∟ C <		backspace	→
5	5 ƅ S		return	∕
6	6		shift	∣
7	⅂ ⊃		space	—

Graffiti navigation strokes

Command	Graffiti	Command	Graffiti
cursor right	→	next field	∤
cursor left	←	shortcut	ℓ
previous field	∤	command	∕

Graffiti punctuation (with alternates)

Symbol	Graffiti	Symbol	Graffiti
.	• •	+	•
,	• ╱	=	• Z
'	• '	|	•
?	• ? ⌐	<	• <
!	• |	>	• >
-	• —	\	• \
(	• (	{	• ε
)	•)	}	• 3
/	• ╱	[	• ε
$	• S	]	• 3
@	• O	~	• N ~
#	• Ⴖ h	`	• \
%	• ୪	;	• ╱
^	• ∧	:	• |
&	• ୪	"	• N
*	• ୪	tab	• ⌐
_	• —		

Graffiti symbols/extended characters

Symbol	Graffiti	Symbol	Graffiti
•	\ •	×	\ ╱
TM	\ m	÷	\ ୪
®	\ R	=	\ Z
©	\ C	¢	\ C
'	\ ⌐	¥	\ ୪
,	\ ⌐	£	\ L
"	\ N	¿	\ L
"	\ Ⴖ	i	\ |
§	\ S	ß	\ B
·	\ O	µ	\ m
+	\ ∝	f	\ S
−	\ —	ø	\ O

Graffiti accent characters

Symbol	Graffiti	Symbol	Graffiti
à	∧ \	è	ε \
á	∧ ╱	é	ε ╱
â	∧ ∧	ê	ε ∧
ä	∧ ୪	ü	U ୪
å	∧ O	ç	C
ñ	N N	æ	ε

RESOURCES

Essential Information

Handspring Visor
Visual QuickStart Guide Web site
http://www.peachpit.com/vqs/visor/

Handspring, Inc.
http://www.handspring.com/

Palm, Inc.
http://www.palm.com/

Calvin's PalmPilot FAQ
http://www.palmgear.com/faq/

Software Libraries

Palm Gear HQ
http://www.palmgear.com/

PDA.Tucows.com
http://pda.tucows.com/palm/

EuroCool
http://www.eurocool.com/

Handango
http://www.handango.com/

Palm Boulevard
http://www.palmblvd.com/

Magazines/News

VisorCentral
http://www.visorcentral.com/

VisorVillage
http://www.visorvillage.com/

PalmPower Magazine
http://www.palmpower.com/

Handheld Computing Magazine
http://www.hhcmag.com/

The Piloteer
http://www.pmn.co.uk/

PalmStation
http://www.palmstation.com/

Palm Boulevard
http://www.palmblvd.com/

Palm Infocenter
http://www.palminfocenter.com/

Smaller.com
http://www.smaller.com/

Electronic Texts

MemoWare
http://www.memoware.com/

Peanut Press
http://www.peanutpress.com/

Healthy PalmPilot (health care information)
http://www.healthypalmpilot.com/

Online Originals
http://www.onlineoriginals.com/

Fictionwise
http://www.fictionwise.com/

Mailing Lists

PalmPilot list at Ultraviolet.org
pilot-pda-subscribe@freeside.ultraviolet.org
http://www.ultraviolet.org/pilot.html

PalmPilot Power Boards (click the PowerBoards link at the bottom of the page)
http://www.palmpower.com/

Usenet Newsgroups

alt.comp.sys.handhelds.pilot

comp.sys.handhelds.pilot

RESOURCES

INDEX

copying files
to Springboard expansion modules, 46
synchronizing compared to copying, 54
cordless phones, 184
See also VisorPhone
countries, foreign
adding to Currency popup menu, 169
Formats preferences, 35
covers, 15
cradle. *See* HotSync cradle
Create Eudora Pro Message AppleScript, 134
creating passwords, 48
credit card information, storing, 237
Cross Digital Writer, 15
CryptoPad, 235, 236
@ctiveLink modem, 194
Culligan, Ed, 4
currency settings, 169
Current Privacy setting, 126
current time, displaying, 78
custom calculator views, 162, 163
custom categories, 125, 148
custom currencies, 169
custom field labels, 122
customer service phone numbers, 302
customizing application buttons, 34, 180

D

Daily calendar window, 152
data
backing up, 74, 300
encrypting, 234, 235, 236
filtering, 98, 133, 153, 203–204
organizing, 273–279
overwriting, 67
resetting Visors, 301–302
restoring backed up data, 300
restoring lost data, 67, 74
sharing with other applications, 131, 150, 151,
170–171
See also synchronizing data
data security. *See* security
data speed
Connection preferences, 37
Modem preferences, 38
database files, sending via email, 209
databases, 278
Date Book
Agenda view, 81
alarm settings, 76, 87
archiving events, 86, 95
beaming events, 94, 100
creating events, 83–84, 85, 88, 107

Day view, 77–78
deleting events, 86
editing events, 86, 104, 107
jumping to dates, 82
linking records between applications, 271
marking events private, 93
Month view, 80
notes, attaching to events, 90–91, 108–109
Palm Desktop (Macintosh), 106–109
Palm Desktop (Windows), 104–105
"penciling in" events, 85
phone lookups, 92, 105
preferences, 76
printing appointments, 105
purging events, 95
records, attaching to events, 107
repeating events, 80, 88–89, 107
reporting time spent, 265
security settings, 93
tracking time, 262–263
Week view, 79, 84
See also Date Book+; DateBk4; time
management
Date Book+
activating, 96
creating events, 100
duplicating events, 100
floating events, 101
journal entries, 101
List view, 98
preferences, 99
receiving beamed data, 94, 100
restoring archived events, 102
templates, 102
Week View with Text view, 97
Year view, 97
See also Date Book; DateBk4
DateBk4
color-coding events, 85
features, 103
floating appointments, 271
See also Date Book; Date Book+
dates
current date, setting, 32
display format, setting, 35
due dates of tasks, 138, 142
event dates, changing, 86
full-screen clock, 180
jumping to, 82
See also events
Day view, 77–78, 104
deactivating hacks, 175
default calculator views, restoring, 163
DejaNews, 224

INDEX

viewing, 245
See also images
pictures. *See* images; photographs
Pimlico Software, 103
PIMs
  importing data from, 129
  primitive, 111
  third-party, 58
planning. *See* Date Book
plastic application buttons
  customizing, 34
  overview, 7
  turning on Visor, 8
Platinum (Visor)
  batteries, 11, 12
  description, 5
players, MP3, 249–250
Plonk utility, 142
plus-sign icon, HackMaster (⊞), 175
Pocket Quicken
  creating transactions, 292
  transferring accounts, 291
PocketChess, 296
PocketMirror, 58
POP accounts
  POP setup, 206–207
  retrieving messages, 208
popup menus, tapping, 20
PopUp Names, 136
port, infrared, 8
Portable Document Format (PDF) files, 260
ports
  AppleTalk and serial ports, 57
  enabling HotSync port monitoring, 56–57
  infrared port, 8
  serial port security flaw, 232
power button, 6
Power Computing clones, troubleshooting
    HotSync, 304
Power Macintosh, troubleshooting HotSync, 304
PowerBooks, troubleshooting HotSync, 304
PowerPoint presentations, 247–248
PQAs, 217–220
PRC files, 42, 209
preferences
  Blazer, 216
  Buttons, 34
  Connection, 37, 59
  Date Book, 76
  Date Book+, 99
  To Do List, 138
  Formats, 35
  General, 32–33
  hacks, 175

Modem, 38
Network, 39–40
Owner, 35
ShortCuts, 36
VisorPhone, 191
preferred phone number, specifying, 113
preparing next day's tasks, 272
presentations, 247–248
Presenter-to-Go, 247–248
printing appointments, 105
printing records, 130, 150
prioritizing tasks, 141, 267, 270
Prism (Visor)
  batteries, 11, 12
  description, 5
  screen, 6
privacy
  Current Privacy setting, 126
  encrypting records, 235–236
  marking records as private, 93, 126, 141, 145
  Palm Desktop security, 233, 234
  SafeHack, 178, 229
  Security application, 228
  TealLock, 231–232
  See also private records
private records
  contacts, 126
  events, 93
  exporting, 71
  forgotten passwords, 48
  hiding automatically, 49
  memos, 145
  overview, 228
  Security application, 48
  tasks, 141
  See also privacy
profiles, HotSync, 72
programs. *See* applications
protectors, screen, 14
punctuation, 27
punctuation, Graffiti strokes, 27
Punctuation Shift mode, 27
purging deleted messages, 202
purging events, 95
purging records, 144

Q

QED, 256
QMate, 291, 293
QSync, 293
Query DNS setting, 40
question mark (?) as wildcard character, 177
question-mark icon, HackMaster (?), 175

INDEX

INDEX